SOUNDS
of **VACATION**

SOUNDS
of VACATION

JOCELYNE GUILBAULT AND
TIMOTHY ROMMEN, EDITORS

Political Economies of Caribbean Tourism

Duke University Press · Durham and London · 2019

Designed by Courtney Leigh Baker and typeset in
Whitman and Avenir by Tseng Information Systems, Inc.

Library of Congress Cataloging-in-Publication Data
Names: Guilbault, Jocelyne, editor. | Rommen, Timothy, editor.
Title: Sounds of vacation : political economies of Caribbean
tourism / Jocelyne Guilbault and Timothy Rommen, editors.
Description: Durham : Duke University Press, 2019. | Includes
bibliographical references and index.
Identifiers: LCCN 2018055385 (print) | LCCN 2019014499 (ebook)
ISBN 9781478005315 (ebook)
ISBN 9781478004288 (hardcover)
ISBN 9781478004882 (pbk.)
Subjects: LCSH: Music and tourism—Caribbean Area. | Music—
Social aspects—Caribbean Area. | Music—Economic aspects—
Caribbean Area. | Tourism—Political aspects—Caribbean Area.
Classification: LCC ML3917.C38 (ebook) | LCC ML3917.C38 s68
2019 (print) | DDC 306.4/842409729—dc23
LC record available at https://lccn.loc.gov/2018055385

COVER ART: Courtesy LiuNian/E+/Getty Images.

Contents

Acknowledgments

This book emerged in a series of conversations between Jocelyne Guilbault and Timothy Rommen in which we remarked on how Caribbean tourism has now become the main source of income for musicians throughout the entire region. And yet, even after working for many years in the region, we acknowledged how little we know about the cultural politics and the economies that drive not only the hotels' financial investments and their entertainment management strategies, but also the artistic choices musicians make in these spaces. We also recognized how sound (the surf, bird song) plays a crucial role in tourism promotion and how, paradoxically, little attention has been paid to the ways in which sound in touristic resorts has been commoditized. We then began to envision an edited collection that would address these concerns, drawing on new inquiries by experienced researchers throughout the region. The resulting volume explores both the range of theoretical issues previously unaddressed as well as new perspectives on specific Caribbean sites and settings. It is our hope that this work will open a new series of conversations at the juncture of music and sound studies and tourism studies.

We are very grateful to the Institute of International Studies, the Townsend Center for the Humanities, and the Department of Music at the University of California, Berkeley, for their generous support of a symposium that afforded us the opportunity to gather all of the contributors to this volume and continue developing our ideas. Our warmest thanks go to Ken Wissoker at Duke University Press, who believed in this project. We are also grateful to Susan Albury for shepherding the book through the production process, and to David Heath for judicious and meticulous copy editing. The external reviewers of our manuscript deserve special thanks for their helpful suggestions and encouragement. The book reflects the care and energy that went into their reviews and we are most grateful. Finally, we wish to thank all of our interlocutors throughout the Caribbean for their generosity, their insights, and their willingness to think with us about the Sounds of Vacation.

Prologue

STEVEN FELD

In her reflective Afterword to *Sun, Sea, and Sound* (Rommen and Neely 2014), Jocelyne Guilbault poses two provocative questions:

> What would it mean to take music and tourism studies not simply as an additional area of focus at the end of the day, but as the critical starting point, as the first chapter one must write to begin examining twentieth-century Caribbean musical histories of encounters? What would happen if the twentieth-century "tourist other" and the historicized and already-complex character of the "Caribbean local" were described as co-present and co-producers of contemporary musical practices? (314)

Her answer to both: "Tourists and tourism would then be consistently woven into the analysis of the colonial and the postcolonial, the local and the global, the national and the transnational, and the very idea of tradition and the past into the present" (314).

This book picks up right there. Seizing on the ubiquitous ways sound and music inform tourists' experience, editors Guilbault and Rommen's substantial theoretical introduction takes tourism management and performance as a direct springboard for reexamining Caribbean histories of sonic and musical encounters. And, as if this springboard were not springy enough, something else is very much added to the mix: the silences and noises within and beyond "the music" and the musicians who labor to produce it in and for tourism's central Caribbean institutional nexus, the all-inclusive hotels. Exploring the distinctive forms of these popular beach resorts with one-stop, package-priced hotel, food/drink, and entertainment options, five probing studies follow, written by Caribbeanists with experience studying populations that are complex products of multiple movements across island geographies: Timothy Rommen writing about the Bahamas, Jerome Camal about Guadeloupe, Susan Harewood about Barbados, Francio Guadeloupe and Jordi Halfman about Sint Maarten, and Jocelyne Guilbault about Saint Lucia.

Guilbault and Rommen's framing, like the essays that follow, takes no prisoners when it comes to deconstructing dismissive commonplaces about tourism and tourists as an inauthentic or spurious subject, including assumptions about tourist music as "bad" music, bad in both musical form and content, and bad for local integrity. What is critically at stake, as Guilbault puts it in the opening to her Saint Lucia chapter, is "to investigate the complexity of management's and musicians' agency in a site that is often dominated by too much attitude . . . and too little empirical research."

To study tourism not with a sledgehammer but with ethnographic, historical, and critical subtlety—by deeply listening to it—the introduction proposes, and the case studies that follow specifically deliver on, a political economy approach, an approach to revealing, in Jerome Camal's words, just how "labor structures and their histories are audible." Colonialism and slavery provide an opening frame to examine histories of labor and its appropriation and exploitation. Labor as wealth and resource reorganization in turn specifically underlie stories of how race, gender, class, and identity build and then stack the structures of action and agency in favor of rulers against the majority of subjectivities. In other words, it is impossible to separate the history of tourism from the history of slavery and colonization, the history of gaze, the history of reproduction of power relations of tourists and touristed. And thus, it is equally impossible to dismiss the centrality of tourism to the very substance of Caribbean history, a history as sonically alive and musically vibrant as the complexities that have routed its makers and listeners through space and time.

That the tourism industry is central to large and increasing percentages of GDP in most of the islands means that tourism is critical for musical employment. For many Caribbean musicians, all-inclusive hotels are the main source of regular work in an industrial music economy where steady income opportunity is precarious and where musicians cannot count on recording revenues, royalties, or union scale and protections. Political Economy 101 again: musicians are ever and always workers as much as they are creative artists. They labor relationally not just to live audiences of local and visiting listeners, but to managers and to corporate management invested in regimes of music and sound control, understood as integral to the industrialized hospitality business. From a management standpoint, music and sound are supply necessities as critical as ample and enticing food and drink, or beautiful ambiance and weather. Sounds on the ears are thus as critical as sands on the toes in the making of a sensuous experiential zone for vacationers. Music and sound, then, must be located within a management ecology of strategically located and owned property, employable resources across entertainment and service sectors, locally available skill assets, and market competition driven and made predictable by consumer desires.

In what follows we get multiple instances of the intertwined anxieties and complexities of taking seriously tourist and management subjectivities through what Guadeloupe and Halfman call "listening without prejudice." This experience of sound is multisensual, always an environmental betweenness of specialized sound and image, often compounded by feel, taste, smell, and surrounding acoustic ambiances and architectures that are deliberately and carefully crafted and managed. What does it mean to engage such a zone of experience mindful both of a necessary openness and a critically informed suspicion? What does it mean to engage such a zone fully mindful that, in Jerome Camal's words, "the camera—rather than the sound recorder—remains the quintessential tourist accessory" (not to mention the quintessential ethnographic accessory). What does it mean to engage contestation as central to audibility in both the colonial and postcolonial, to juxtapose the takedown of an "imperial gaze" and an "imperial audition"?

It might not have taken four months of sitting in all-inclusive hotel lobbies for Francio Guadeloupe to grasp the colonial-global reality that for Sint Maarten: "France actually borders the Netherlands in the Caribbean Sea." But surely such a distinctive way of hearing the conjunctions of (post)-colonial sonic geographies yielded a very grounded reasoning for asking how and why "all-inclusive modes of vacationing create the forts of the twenty-first century." In other words, it is listening to, and recording, sound as emplaced subjectivity that yields a rich sense of how a multiplicity of overlapping languages, voices, and accents—French, Dutch, Spanish, English, Creole, Caribbean—echoes a larger, multiply hybrid, sonic and musical ecology, in all ways and at all times porous but unequal, local but cosmopolitan, raced and placed, bounded and unbounded in space and time. What better medium than sound to inform a researcher's desire "to undo the certitudes and identities of today," as Guadeloupe and Halfman put it?

Susan Harewood has another powerful answer to the "undoing" in that question: to listen for noise, the unwanted sounds in the background that get in the way of the pristine, the beautiful, the utopian, the island getaway. And doing so in Barbados, she hears a thunderous noise indeed: the silence where "sonic walls replace militarized walls." Listening to the central clock chime a repertoire of Westminster quarters, reveille, Bunessan, the national anthem, Christmas carols, and popular songs, she hears "disturbing noises of persistent coloniality." Asking how much hearing "heritage" entails a complicated resounding, a relistening to the "noisy viciousness of imperialism," she reveals how the Barbados clock chime is a machine for alternating noises and silences that sound "routes of Caribbean diaspora" in the ambient background to the sonic erasures, overdubs, and reroutings of the ambient and musical interior of the local all-inclusive hotels.

Another way "to undo the certitudes and identities of today" is offered by Timothy Rommen's take on why "the musical 'it' that the Bahamas is selling to tourists" is difficult to identify. Tracing how "cosmopolitan set lists" replaced the more popular and singular sound of 1970s calypso, Rommen moves from local tourism administrative history to conversations with musicians Funky D (born 1958) and Alia Coley (born 1974). Those conversations reveal how globally informed and locally infused listening biographies proliferate expansively. Generational and gendered, they insist on their emplacements while sounding exponentially "at home" to multiplying layers of visitors, from near and far.

Equally engaged with cosmopolitics, Jerome Camal's research on an all-inclusive hotel in Guadeloupe started distinctly, with a denial of research access. This resulted, quite anxiously, in Camal's decision to visit as a paying tourist and to write through the reflexive and self-questioning voice of auto-ethnography. Sensing multiple ways that all the relational forms he experienced were raced and classed structurations of power, Camal invokes sociologist Henri Lefebvre's approach to the social production of space, specifically his "rhythmanalysis" of the repetitions, alternations, and cyclics of everyday life, to reveal how "rhythms . . . are also productive and symptomatic of social hierarchies." Through this analytic lens, Camal analyzes the "all-inclusive as a repeating machine, which is itself the repetition, or more precisely a remix, of the plantation machine." His concerns with consonance and dissonance, arrhythmia and polyrhythmia, echo other anxieties, as well as counterproposals, about how the tourism system parallels, emerges from, mimics, and diverges from the plantation system.

Jocelyne Guilbault's Saint Lucia chapter draws on many of these political economic issues of labor and power, particularly adding a more detailed socioeconomic analysis of the gendered spaces and subjectivities of labor. Her sustained emphasis on placing "in conversation the managers' and musicians' predicaments" juxtaposes the differing outlooks, and differing registers of work necessities, ethics, and pragmatics in specific subjective accounts.

Taken as conjunctions "that reveal the mediating forces of history, politics, and economics," Guilbault comes full circle to infuse the analysis of labor with its affective dimension, analyzing how musicians working in all-inclusive hotels don't just perform songs but rather labor in the fields of hospitality enhancement, working to provide "affective ambience" and "experiences that are memorable." Here we come to understand one of the many ways that political economy expands into the terrain of managing and commodifying pleasure. The musicians who perform for tourists, and the managers who select, employ, and pay them, are thus entangled in an economy where musical entertainment and hospitality skills extend far beyond the immediacies of musical performance for hire.

All that said, it's time to explore the distinctive audacity of my appreciation for this book. I mean, why does someone who has never visited or studied the Caribbean islands and has no expertise in tourism studies get to have the first words here? By what stretch of the imagination does an anthropologist of sound experienced in faraway Papua New Guinea and Ghana get to introduce, to larger scholarly communities in anthropology, ethnomusicology, and sound studies, a work on the political economy of music and sound in the Caribbean?

One way to answer is to explain how reading these pages deeply helped me reflect critically on my own experiences of sonic tourism. No, I've never set foot in the Caribbean, but I occasionally visit via the hundred or so Caribbean LPS, cassettes, and CDS in my music collection. Scanning them anew, and scrutinizing their content and the authority of their production, notes, and representations, I'm thinking about the construction of Caribbean "music" and the exclusion of noises and silences, the presentation of "authentic" hybrid creole cultures and the representation of tourism. Then I ask, having just read this book, why and how do these widely circulating mediations erase or mute the very world historical complexities these essays reveal to be so poignant? What does it take to (re)listen and hear the noises, silences, aporias, the colonial violence and postcolonial conjunctions and disjunctions so consistently revealed in this book's way of resituating the very subject of Caribbean music as its political economy of sound?

Then I pull an LP from the Caribbean section of my shelves. It is the Esso Steel Band's *On Top*, recorded in Bermuda in 1969. The liner notes speak of the band's "new and exciting music to entertain the thousands who come to Bermuda" and how it "will serve both as an introduction and a lasting memento of their visit to this tropic paradise." I put on side 2. The covers start with the Paul Mauriat easy-listening French hit "L'amour est bleu," then proceed to Otis Redding's "Sitting on the Dock of the Bay," then Mozart's *Eine kleine Nachtmusik*, then Francis Lai's theme song for the 1966 Claude Lelouch Academy Award–winning best foreign film *A Man and a Woman*, then conclude with "Mr. Walker," a well-known calypso hit by the Mighty Sparrow.

Curious about this wildly diverse repertoire and a novice to all things Caribbean, I did a quick internet search for the name listed on the LP as the band leader, Rudolph Commissiong. The first item that came up under his name was a May 21, 2016, article that he wrote, "Steel Pan Man's Forty Years of Music" for Bermuda's *Royal Gazette* newspaper. The autobiographical piece tells of the musical journey that took him from hotel music work in Trinidad to Bermuda in the 1950s, details of the band's Esso sponsorship and numerous Caribbean, Canadian, and U.S. tours, his advocacy and action work against racial segregation in Bermuda, and his thirty-plus-year career in hotels and lounges, including eight hit albums. Add to that his musical relocation to Maui for seven years to work in the top hotels there, and, finally, a life in retirement on Cape Cod, Massachusetts.

All of a sudden, I'm stunned by how much more I've just listened to the kind of historical and contemporary soundtrack revealed by this book, a soundtrack featuring musicians laboring in the circumstances, circuits, and circulatory politics chronicled by each author here. There's the colonial and postcolonial story of oil and steelpan music, the discrepant and vernacular cosmopolitanism of a repertoire filled with the silences and noises, the inclusions and exclusions, the routes and roots of Caribbean labor and laborers in a political and affective economy of sound. All of a sudden, as an outsider to Caribbean studies, I really get it about why tourism is the real "critical starting point" to the region's postcolonial history of music and sound.

There's a second reason why my appreciation of this book runs deep. As someone long associated with advocacy for the fused study of sound across species and technologies, languages, musics, and environmental ambiences, and specifically for the study of acoustemology (acoustic epistemology—sound as a way of knowing), I've tended to crankiness about much of the new "sound studies." Why? First, because I find it a market-rationalized attempt to round up, commodify, and manage diffuse ideas into products with a more singular identity. Next, because I find that it totalizes the object "sound," and then presumes an imagined coherence to that object that one is supposed to know in advance. And finally, because I find most of the work to be sound technology studies, and most of that to be Western in focus. So if I refuse "sound studies," it is because I think that studying dynamic interactions of species and materials is a vital way to listen to histories of listening.

That's a way of saying that I want studies of sound that embrace relating and relationality across environments, histories, species, and materialities: more "sound agency studies," more "sound *actant* studies," more "sound plural ontology studies," more "sound relationality studies," more "sound companion species studies," more "sound difference studies." Of course, that means more empirically informed and critically engaged political/affective economy studies of precisely the sort you hold in your hands, studies that both substantially increase historical and cultural knowledge, and that resist forms of ideological text reading where answers are known in advance of questions. So read on. I think you'll hear what I've heard: how the multi-tracked, amplified, and always noisy polyphonies and polyrhythms of "listening without prejudice" is the real future of sound studies.

INTRODUCTION · THE POLITICAL ECONOMY OF MUSIC AND SOUND

Case Studies in the Caribbean Tourism Industry

JOCELYNE GUILBAULT AND TIMOTHY ROMMEN

Why does the tourist site and class remain an inauthentic, unauthorized, or otherwise spurious subject? Is it because the term *vacation*, in the West in particular, has become a taboo topic, increasingly viewed as a questionable and deficient use of time in regard to a range of moral and economic issues? Is vacation simply deemed a luxury in a research landscape dominated by work? Is vacation the "gap" made all the more glaring in the frenzied neo-liberal ecumene?[1] Perhaps the overwhelming focus on the visual and material aspects of tourism has silenced the importance of the political economy of music and sound in sites of leisure? Or (might this last possibility be the main reason?), is it because musics played for tourists on vacation have typically been regarded as "bad" music — as sanitized, commoditized, lacking authenticity, and devoid of originality?

This volume responds to these questions, and has two aims. The first is to emphasize the need to examine all the ways in which economics and politics (read capitalism and power) are intertwined and interpenetrated across social scale and musical production. The second is to propose a new perspective on the tourism industry by linking political economy with the notion of hospitality by and through music and sound. Focusing on how music and sound are managed, performed, and offered as part of the commodities essential to touristic resorts makes it possible to argue, following novelist Earl Lovelace (1998, 56), that to speak about Caribbean aesthetics is to speak about Caribbean politics. And to speak about politics in the tourism industry, we need to add, is to speak about calculations, judgments, and aspirations that are not solely cultural, but also economic.

"In the classic, holistic anthropology of the founding fathers and mothers," James Ferguson (1988, 488) reports, "economy and culture were inevitably connected." As he explains, "Whether economic institutions or practices were seen as 'total social facts' (Mauss), as parts of an interdependent, 'functioning whole' (Malinowski), or as aspects of a total 'culture pattern' (Benedict, Kroeber), their analysis was inseparable from the analysis of the larger culture whole" (1988, 488). Even though "economic anthropology" in the United States was seemingly dropped in the 1960s and 1970s in favor of a focus on culture, since the 1980s cultural analysts have recognized that they cannot ignore political economy any more than economic anthropologists can ignore the fact that culture matters (Ferguson 1988, 491).

The pioneers of ethnomusicology were not generally concerned with the interrelations of musical practices and economy—referring here to the relative scale of the social network and the materialities involved in the production, distribution, and consumption of musical goods and services. The great majority of ethnomusicologists focused exclusively on musical forms and then on practices. Concerns about aesthetic, religious, social, moral, and political values—political values here usually understood in relation to colonial power, the nation-state, or particular community formations—were developed later. By the 1960s and 1970s the connections between music and economy were the main concerns of popular music studies and cultural studies. Even though a few ethnomusicologists and anthropologists did address not only the politics but also the economy of the musical practices they were studying (cf. Charles Keil, A. J. Racy, H. S. Becker, David Coplan, Veit Erlmann, Roger Wallis and Krister Malm, Peter Manuel), by the 1960s political economy did not have much currency as a term, nor did it provide the analytical framework for the vast majority of music studies in these academic disciplines until the mid-1980s.

To paraphrase David N. Balaam and Michael A. Veseth's definition,[2] political economy in this volume examines the social, political, and economic pressures and interests that affect music labor and the commoditization of music and sound. It explores how these pressures influence the political process, taking into account a range of social priorities, the local, national, and regional competition in the Caribbean tourism industry, development and promotional strategies, and philosophical perspectives. As Balaam and Veseth explain, political economy significantly differs from the mathematical, putatively "objective" analytical framework of economics. Its broad perspective provides us with a deeper understanding of the many aspects informing music labor and the commoditization of music and sound that cannot be assessed simply in economic terms.

Interestingly, Jacques Attali (1985), neither a musician nor a sociologist, but a prominent economist, is arguably the first to have prominently foregrounded a preoccupation with the political economy of music by provocatively calling his book *Noise: The Political Economy of Music*.[3] This book was important not so much because of what it said, but because of what it overlooked and silenced. It provided a universal history of the relation of music to politics and economics in four unilinear phases that he calls sacrificing, representing, repeating, and composing.[4] The problem is that Attali's teleological scheme overlooked history and materiality such as colonialism and slavery. It silenced insurgent voices and ignored agency. It conflated nation-states' politics and economic agendas. It universalized the definition of value.

Arjun Appadurai's exciting Introduction to *The Social Life of Things*, published one year after Attali's book, did much to reinvigorate the notion of political economy by looking at what he refers to as "the social lives of things" to address commoditization as process. By considering commoditization as process, he (re)inserted time, space, power, agency, and the relative degree of investment in things by various people with varying interests. His emphasis on the social lives of things implies that things' relation to commoditization is neither fixed nor static but goes through different phases, in and out of commoditization, during their social lives. Their "candidacy," to use Appadurai's term, to be a commodity varies according to what he calls "regimes of value" (1986, 15). This notion of "regimes of value" is here understood as calling attention to the different worlds an object becomes associated with and the contrasting ways objects become valued (desired) at different times and for different reasons. Appadurai thus speaks of the commodity potential of all things to be part of a form of exchange. This notion of the "commodity potential of all things" is useful in the context of the commoditization of music and sound in tourism.[5]

Significantly, Appadurai adds, the notion of "regimes of value" does not imply that every act of commodity exchange presupposes a complete cultural sharing of assumptions, but rather that the degree of value coherence may be highly variable from situation to situation, and from commodity to commodity" (1986, 15). When music is in the commodity phase, it is able to circulate across cultural boundaries precisely because it does not require all parties to share in equal measure the value standards promoted in the commodity (music) exchange. Two important publications, both tellingly on world music (also called "world beat"), marked this latter point about regimes of value in music studies. In his 1988 "Notes on World Beat," Steven Feld drew on this understanding of regimes of value and commodities' circulation outlined by Appadurai and also by Charles Keil to think about "world music" and music globalization as "sonic touristry" — a trend that brought political economy perspectives to the 1980s–90s story of interpenetrations of pop and world music makers and styles.[6] Nine years later, Timothy D. Taylor, in his book entitled *Global Pop: World Music, World Markets* (1997) foregrounded this new focus on political economy (at least for many musicologists and ethnomusicologists), astutely exploring music commodities and musical exchange from around the globe to recognize the persistent workings of Western hegemony through and also against the dizzying variety of local appropriations and alterations of styles and musical identities.

But in his introduction to *The Empire of Things*, Fred Myers (2001, 6) significantly furthers Appadurai's notion of regimes of value by looking at how such regimes simultaneously exist and compete with each other. They are not all regimes of value governed by economics. They are, rather, also informed by political, religious, class, gender, nationalist, activist, and many other concerns and desires. They are "regimes" in the sense that they consolidate certain kinds of values, incessantly in need of reinforcement and reification.

Appadurai's notion of "regimes of value" and its elaboration by Myers are most useful here to explore the political economy of music and sound in the context of human encounters in touristic sites. By definition, such encounters bring into contact overlapping and contrasting regimes of value about music and sound. Myers's (2001, 29) insistence that "art is not just another example of material culture" helps emphasize how the specificities of certain commodities such as music play a significant role in both the particular "cultures of circulation" (Lee and LiPuma 2002) and specific regimes of value in which these commodities become embedded.[7] Accordingly, what needs to be examined is the labor, rationales, and motivations that go into producing, out of specific things like music and sound, commodities for specific spaces and places. This volume explores what goes on in the commoditization of music and sound in touristic sites and how such commoditization is intimately linked to particular notions of *hospitality* entailing both regimes of value and governing regimes.[8]

The meaning and practice of hospitality through music and sound in touristic sites cannot be taken as evidence.[9] The notion of hospitality is not only culturally defined, but also historically, politically, economically, and materially informed. It is, furthermore, influenced by who is involved in these human encounters, that is, by the types of visitors and the personnel—in our case, the entertainment staff and the musicians—hired to work at the hotel. In that sense, as Guilbault suggests in her chapter in this volume, the political economy of music and sound directly implicates the *political economy* of hospitality—as is demonstrated in our case studies, discussed further below.

In the tourism industry, Guilbault further remarks, hospitality means "commercial hospitality."[10] In contrast to private hospitality, where welcoming behavior and caring acts by individuals toward other individuals are performed for free in a private setting such as the home, commercial hospitality provides guests with lodging, food, and entertainment for profit. In the context of the Caribbean, however, this latter definition is not so simple, for it cannot be isolated from history. Commercial hospitality cannot but be understood as inextricably linked to the experience of colonialism, slavery, and the colonial legacies that endure to this day.[11] It is indeed hard to use the term *political economy* in the Caribbean tourism industry without foregrounding specifically the historical relationship of human labor—the labor of the slaves and of the colonized marshaled by the colonizers to reproduce the structure of wealth abroad and poverty at home. Appropriation of materials, exploitation of laboring bodies, and regimes of colonial enforcement functioned politically to normalize and expand imperial wealth and local subjugation. In this connection, our exploration of the political economy of hospitality builds from the body of work addressing the politics of race, ethnicity, and class by Caribbeanists C. L. R. James, Eric Williams, Aimé Césaire, Gordon K. Lewis, Frantz Fanon, Edouard Glissant, Stuart Hall, Sylvia Wynter, Antonio Benítez-Rojo, Kamau Brathwaite, Sidney W. Mintz, Mervyn C Alleyne, Roger Abrahams, Percy C. Hintzen, Selwyn Ryan, Hilbourne A. Watson, Belinda Edmondson, Anton Allahar, Obika Gray, Jamaica Kincaid, Brian Meeks, Hilary McD. Beckles, Anthony Bogues, Kevin A. Yelvington, Mimi Sheller, and Deborah Thomas.

In the context of the "Caribbean postcolonial," as Shalini Puri (2004) calls it, it is also impossible to study the political economy of hospitality through music and sound without foregrounding how music is linked to the specter of race. As Ronald Radano and Philip V. Bohlman, the editors of *Music and the Racial Imagination*, write, "The imagination of race not only informs perceptions of musical practice but is at once constituted within and projected into the social through sound" (Radano and Bohlman 2000, 5). The discursive impact of linking music with race, and more specifically with blackness, has not only produced understandings of black music as a "figure of liberation," but has also generated a "highly problematic romance of race" (Keil and Feld 1994, cited in Radano and Bohlman 2000, 32). Such conceptions have conveniently overlooked the impact that race has had on the business side of the music industry and on the material world of musicians, as is eloquently addressed in R&B *Rhythm and Business: The Political Economy of Black Music*, edited by Norman Kelley (2002).[12]

This volume cannot but also be in conversation with existing scholarship that reminds us that the linking of music with race never stops there. Discourses about music in the Caribbean indeed loudly point to how race interacts and intersects with gender, class, and ethnicity—themes that are addressed in this volume and that are informed by the foundational work of Rhoda Reddock, Patricia Mohammed, Carole Boyce Davies, Carolyn Cooper, and Linden Lewis.

Ronald Radano and Tejumola Olaniyan's (2016) call to hear and critique the *Audible Empire*, the capitalist global expansion by means of colonial and neocolonial politics of ordering and disciplining through sound, is echoed in the essays included in this book. In the context of the Caribbean, the volume turns on how empires (in the plural), past and present, continue to be audible in the way some musics and sounds are valued and others are not, and in the way that "peace and quiet" takes on the quality of exclusivity. As Radano and Olaniyan remark, "Since the ground of resistance is veritably impure—it must of necessity work within the terrain it is resisting against—only the hard *work* of conscious counteridentification and misidentification can harvest the possibilities of a susceptible hegemony" (2016, 18). Our case studies address not only the work of counteridentification and misidentification, but also the local ambivalences toward, as well as the embrace of, what has become putatively, after centuries of empires' audibility, "normative aesthetics."

Sounds of Vacation in the Caribbean tourism industry expands the purview of sound studies whose "epistemic center," according to Jonathan Sterne (2015, 73), is still "the West." Exploring a distinctive and long-standing non-Western site of vacation, these essays examine the political economy of musics and sounds performed and listened to in spaces that are arguably central to global tourism and most emblematic of "vacation": the Caribbean islands. Following Sterne's call to broaden the sites and issues addressed by sound studies, this book takes a different focus and approach to the mainstream literature in sound studies, exemplified by these three main publications: Bull and Back's *The Auditory Culture Reader* (2003), Pinch and Bijsterveld's *The Oxford Handbook of Sound Studies* (2012), and Sterne's *The Sound Studies Reader* (2012). Instead, this book aligns with the broader and more explicitly anthropological focus for the field enunciated in *Keywords in Sound* (Novak and Sakakeeny 2015), following a long line of calls in the last ten to fifteen years for a less Western, less technology-centered, more agency- and practice-oriented approach to sound studies.[13] In this vein, what *Sounds of Vacation* seeks to do is not to provide an exhaustive survey of Caribbean touristic sites. The aim, rather, is to bring together cultural theorization and empirical studies linking the political economy of music and sound with tourism. Our focus on lived experience, touristic musical cultures, human and nonhuman sounding ecologies, and ubiquitous musics[14] in Caribbean resorts marks an important step in this direction.

Critical theoretical and ethnographic studies of tourism are well known.[15] While music is beginning to receive attention in tourist studies (see the 2014 special issue of the journal *Tourist Studies* on "Music and Tourism" with Brett Lashua et al.), in contrast with our project, few publications address the phenomenology of sound in and at tourist sites.[16] *Sounds of Vacation* empirically explores the histories, management, and experience of sound- and music-making designed for touristic encounters. It examines the cultures of listening to both musics and sounds, whether ambient, mechanical, animal, or human. These sounds and their auditions, we argue, powerfully interact to inhabit, emerge through, and shape the Caribbean tourism industry.

Our project also differs from the recent publication *Sun, Sea, and Sound: Music and Tourism in the Circum-Caribbean* (Rommen and Neely 2014), which presents widely divergent case studies ranging from mass tourism, ecotourism, and cruise ship tourism, to festival tourism, expatriate tourism, sex tourism, and heritage tourism, in order to illustrate the many vectors of tourism that find their way into the Caribbean. We are, instead, interested in a more focused study of so-called all-inclusive hotels (the all-inclusive hotels, also called all-inclusive resorts, refer to prepaid vacation plans that include lodging, a minimum of three meals a day, soft and alcoholic drinks, sport facilities, free entertainment, and other services in the same price). In her chapter in this volume, Susan Harewood reports how in the Caribbean the all-inclusive hotels were developed in Jamaica out of a need to be able to market the hotels in spite of the political and economic upheaval the country was facing.[17] The Jamaican concept of all-inclusive hotels was literally conceived as a way to shield the tourists—and, she adds, "for the tourists to shield themselves"—from the country's problems. The goal was to delink the touristic site as much as possible from the rest of the country, to the point of making the touristic site an "island" within the country-island. While the concept of the all-inclusive hotels overlaps with that of the cruise ships, it also differs from it in significant ways. In contrast to the cruise ships, where the personnel typically hail from many different countries, the great majority of the all-inclusive hotel personnel in the English-speaking islands are nationals of the islands where the hotels are located.[18] Hence, even though they hardly ever venture outside of the hotels' comfort zones, the visitors in these hotels are nonetheless still in contact with the members of a local culture, associated with distinct linguistic accents, dominant religious traditions, normative values, and more.

The reader may still wonder, why choose all-inclusive hotels to study the political economy of music and sound? We chose to conduct our research in all-inclusive hotels because they are the dominant institutions and thus the dominant sites of encounter in the Caribbean tourism industry. The all-inclusive hotel is a site where not only questions of what is local and what is not are negotiated, but also questions of what musics and sounds can be bought and sold are asked and answered. It is also a site that allows us to observe the collaboration (or lack thereof) between corporations (or private ownership) and state governments, and thereby to understand who is responsible for selling, for example, the Bahamas. The all-inclusive hotels also represent a focal point to address the entertainment staff and musicians as workers and the role they play in the political economy of music and sound, and the political economy of hospitality in these sites.

Our goal is not to compare relative degrees of difference or similarity between all-inclusive resorts. We did not ask the contributors to this volume to investigate a specific list of elements expected to play a significant role in the selection or availability of the all-inclusive resorts' music and sounds. Our studies follow a humanistic tradition. They are empirical and interpretive. They reveal the contrasts between the all-inclusive resorts examined here, and bring out the salient mediations that produce difference even when things look similar. Coming from different academic perspectives, and with different research interests, experiences, and convictions, the contributors each highlight and explore various facets of the political economy of music and sound that inform their selected sites. Our hope is to provide an *aggregate knowledge* and a better understanding of the various economies and politics that are at play in the management, performance, and consumption of music and sound in Caribbean all-inclusive resorts. This volume sets out to investigate how key concepts and concerns central to sound studies and tourism studies have been articulated in the Caribbean region. It also seeks to identify the new questions that empirically based case studies on the political economy of music and sound in touristic sites raise for both the tourism industry and sound studies.

The long-held disregard for the sounds of vacation has engendered numerous myths and scholarly silences about both the sound environments and musical performances in/at Caribbean hotels. Misconceptions about the status of the musician still abound. Often, they are assumed to be amateurs, possessing only basic musicianship, not good enough to be "real" professionals — not highly skilled and/or formally trained performers. The long-standing disregard for the sounds of vacation has also led scholars to overlook the power of programmed music broadcast through loudspeakers on tourist compounds. It has, furthermore, fostered a regrettable inattention to the ways that natural and built environments, the materiality of sound-producing sources, participate in the construction and perception of hotels as fully social sites.

And yet all of these musics and sounds are, in fact, central to the rhythms vacation takes, whether in the physical loosening up of walking styles, through the affective encounters between tourists and workers and among tourists themselves (including musicians, amateur and professional, who also vacation and take in local music and sounds and scenes), or through the sensibility one develops toward the environment. All of these sources, actors, and agents inform in myriad ways how workers and tourists experience life in these hotels, what they value, and who they are and are becoming. In this book, we view live performances, programmed musics, and all contiguous sounds and sound sources across technologies, species, and environmental presences as contributing significantly to an understanding of sound as a way of knowing and making place, and as a means of locating and heightening the social experience of being on vacation.

Exploring how music and sound help promote vacation sites, attract tourists, create employment, and drive revenues is crucial in a region whose GDP thoroughly depends on tourism.[19] To give only a few examples:

In 2018, Index Mundi reports that in the Bahamas, "Tourism accounts for approximately 75–80 percent of the GDP and directly or indirectly employs half of the archipelago's labor force." "Tourism is Saint Lucia's main source of jobs and income — accounting for 65 percent of GDP — and the island's main source of foreign exchange earnings."[20] In "Travel & Tourism Economic Impact 2018 Caribbean," the World/Travel and Tourism Council indicates that "the direct contribution of Travel & Tourism to GDP [for the region] was USD 17.9bn (4.8 percent of total GDP) in 2017, and is forecast to rise by 3.2 percent in 2018." The report adds: "In 2017 Travel & Tourism directly supported 758,000 jobs (4.3 percent of total employment). This is expected to rise by 2.8 percent in 2018 and rise by 2.2 percent pa to 965,000 jobs (5.1 percent of total employment) in 2028."[21] It should be emphasized that these numbers only account for the employment *directly* generated by travel and tourism.

The overall contribution of travel and tourism is even more impressive. "In 2017," we are told, "the total contribution of Travel & Tourism to employment, including jobs indirectly supported by the industry, was 13.8 percent of the total employment (2,434,000 jobs). This is expected to rise by 2.8 percent in 2018 to 2,502,000 jobs."[22] The money generated in foreign exports (money spent by foreign visitors) in the Caribbean was $31.8 billion (19.8 percent of total exports) in 2017. "This is forecast to grow by 3.7 percent in 2018."[23] Significantly, despite the growing number of people living below the poverty line worldwide and the challenges of 2016 (including acts of terrorism and massive migration), according to the World Tourism Organization (UNWTO), "international tourist arrivals grew by a remarkable 7 percent in 2017 to reach a total of 1,322 million, according to the latest UNWTO World Tourism Barometer [January 15, 2018]. . . . This is well above the sustained and consistent trend of 4 percent or higher growth since 2010 and represents the strongest results in seven years."[24] In the Caribbean, "Leisure travel spending (inbound and domestic) generated 89.1 percent of direct Travel & Tourism GDP in 2017 (USD39.3bn) compared with 10.9 percent for business travel spending (USD4.8bn)."[25]

There is no question that tourism constitutes an outsized portion of the Caribbean economy and that music and ambient sounds play a crucial role in the political economy of vacation spaces.[26] This political economy takes in the role of labor, work ethics, aesthetics, and the dynamics of the encounter, and it is these postcolonial conjunctures and the regimes of value that they index and mobilize that are explored by this book.

Our empirical studies of all-inclusive hotels include five cases presented by researchers with long-term ethnographic and historical experience in the Caribbean. These chapters focus on all-inclusive resorts based in different islands, including the Bahamas (Rommen), Guadeloupe (Camal), Barbados (Harewood), Sint Maarten (Guadeloupe and Halfman), and Saint Lucia (Guilbault). The methodologies used in these studies vary according to the authors' research backgrounds in anthropology, ethnomusicology, and communication studies. The use of ethnographic tools, textual analysis, reflective and reflexive writing, ideological reading, as well as sociological, historical, and empirical approaches lead to different kinds of knowledge and different points of emphasis. Just as there is no standard narrative about the management, the workers, the musicians, and the tourists in all-inclusive resorts, in an interpretive project such as ours, expectations and appreciations of difference come with different emphases.

The following pages foreground the main themes that have emerged from our case studies.

The Politics of Inclusivity

In her chapter in this volume, Harewood points out that the logic driving all-inclusive hotels is often predicated on isolating/insulating tourists from the "sounds, tastes, smells, or feel" of local politics, histories, and economics. As Sheller puts it, the all-inclusive hotel "has long served as a way of creating spatial/temporal enclaves that carved out tourist territories and performances largely cut off from the surrounding locality, and from local inhabitants" (Sheller 2009, 1395). These spatial/temporal enclaves offer travelers the convenience of a one-price-for-everything model, actively commodifying experiences of and desires for inclusivity in the process.

And yet, all-inclusive hotels should never be confused with all-access, for the real economics of selling this model are predicated on its opposite — on curating exclusivity. It is not enough to market the conveniences of an all-inclusive resort without also reminding guests that their access to its pleasures is highly privileged. All-inclusive hotels do not adhere to a shared philosophy regarding local access to their grounds or to the entertainment they provide. Some all-inclusive hotels give access to locals, but only to those who can afford the high cost of the services offered. The extent to which guests are encouraged to venture beyond hotel grounds is also highly variable. As this volume illustrates, there exists within the all-inclusive model a wide range of approaches and possibilities for curating inclusivity and managing exclusivity.

Jerome Camal, for instance, examines the exclusivity of place generated in and through strategies that serve effectively to isolate tourists from easy access to the rest of Guadeloupe. Timothy Rommen, in contrast, explores the issues that arise when an all-inclusive hotel such as SuperClubs Breezes in Nassau, Bahamas, allows (even encourages) local residents to buy time at the resort (day and night passes are available). What kinds of challenges does entertaining both local visitors and tourists pose for the musicians performing at the hotel? How does the hotel profit from offering entertainment to both locals and tourists?

Francio Guadeloupe and Jordi Halfman address perhaps the most open model of access represented in this volume, exploring the Great Bay Beach Resort in Philipsburg, Sint Maarten, where full access to the resort is granted to local residents. Anyone may dine at the restaurant or rent a room. No day or night passes are required here—rather, local individuals are treated fully as clients just as are the tourists. They further examine the social and musical implications of one of the most radical ideas at play in Sint Maarten: that the entire island is commercially marketed as all-inclusive. Tourists visiting the Great Bay Beach Resort have thus secured accommodations and entertainment in the resort itself, but the entire island is presented as available to them and curated as an extension of the resort. Guadeloupe and Halfman ask: What socialization of the local population or pedagogical project has rendered this formula possible? To what extent is the framing of the island as an extension of the resort enhancing or undermining the market for the all-inclusive hotels in Sint Maarten?

The politics of inclusivity also impacts directly on scholarship in all-inclusive hotels, for questions of access accompany not only the research questions one can ask, but also directly structure the potential outcomes of empirical research in these spaces. No generalizations can be made about securing access for fieldwork at commercial enterprises such as all-inclusive hotels because permissions depend greatly on the protocols of individual institutions. As Greg Urban and Kyung-Nan Koh (2013, 139) note, "academically based ethnographic research inside corporations has grown only modestly since the 1980s . . . the questions of access to corporate inner workings pose both practical and ethical challenges."

The chapters included in this volume reflect well the wide range of challenges (both practical and ethical) and possibilities resulting from working out in individual contexts these complex questions of access. In Saint Lucia, Jocelyne Guilbault was given permission to do on-site interviews with both management and musicians and to observe all of the activities including music. Although she was not a paying guest, this sanctioned access enabled her to address the management's notion of hospitality and the politics of musical aesthetics and labor for the management, the musicians, and the entertainment personnel. Like Guilbault, and building on his previous work on tourism in the Bahamas, Rommen was also granted broad access to the all-inclusive hotel in which he conducted research. He was also able to work with musicians with whom he already had long-established relationships. Although he did not stay at the resort, he was able to interview management, musicians, and staff on-site, and to participate in the daily and nightly musical and entertainment offerings throughout the hotel.

Harewood, returning home to Barbados, worked mainly off-site, for example, to interview the musician who regularly works at the boutique hotel where she conducted her research. She focused primarily on the sounds and silences of colonial history around the periphery of the hotel, especially as they played out at the UNESCO World Heritage Site located next to the all-inclusive. Her study led her to address the "quiet" of the hotel, where tourists are insulated (both sonically and politically) in relation to what she refers to as "the noises of violent colonial history"—noises that barely reach the tourists' ears.

Francio Guadeloupe, in addition to working at the University of Sint Maarten, is a member of the Sint Maarten Hospitality and Trade Association. Since in this context he works closely with the general manager of the establishment where he conducted his collaborative study (with Halfman), the question of access did not pose a problem. However, perhaps because of his close relationship with the general manager and due to his desire to avoid any potential conflicts of interest, he chose not to examine the inner workings of the corporation, instead conducting his study mainly in the lobby of the resort. His close attention to the sounds and faces that came his way turned into a field of investigation of its own, a critical examination as "a local" of his imaginaries of Others through sound. Thus, connections with management can at once present challenges as well as opportunities.

But permission to do research was not granted to all of us. In Guadeloupe, Camal was told that his research was of no interest to the administration (which in this case is part of a corporation), but that he was welcome to come as a paying guest and observe. While it was impossible for him as a researcher/tourist to fully experience the complexities of the structure of the all-inclusive corporation in Guadeloupe where he did his research, Camal was struck by the culture of the administration (by the inner workings and particular values of this social group) made visible through the embodied division of labor. This theme is central to his chapter.

The politics of inclusivity, then, is a major analytical node through which to understand all-inclusive hotels' infrastructure, entertainment activities, and aesthetic choices. It further reveals how the politics of access impact the poetics of the authors' writings, enabling certain paths of inquiry while foreclosing others.

Colonial Specters

When Radano and Bohlman wrote that "a specter lurks in the house of music and it goes by the name of race" (2000, 1), they were not thinking of all-inclusive hotels in the Caribbean. But they could easily have turned their attention to that context, for any inquiry into the political economy of all-inclusive hotels cannot fail to confront this specter. In the Caribbean, this plays out along paths charted by colonial histories, and it affects everything from labor conditions to modes of production and tourist expectations. From a political economy perspective, under the colonial regime, slaves' and ex-slaves' music-making and dancing until the early twentieth century offered free spectacles to colonial elites and visitors alike. In no publication of the time was it presented as a bonus. Rather, without having to say it, it was understood as part of the colonial elite's (and tourists') entitlement.[27] These mediations set the stage for a particular kind of listening to and engagement with the Caribbean.

While they can't be said to have determined in the last instance foreigners' experience of Caribbean sounds, these mediations can hardly be dissociated from the ways they have helped constitute the production, consumption, and circulation of these sounds in the contemporary moment. During the twentieth century and into the twenty-first, Caribbean sounds (not to mention bodies, flora, fauna, beaches, and reefs) have continued to be presented as readily available for consumption by those able to travel to the region or afford entry into its touristic spaces.[28] The all-inclusive hotel in the Caribbean, far from being immune to such colonial specters, in fact reproduces many of the conditions and logics that have animated these dynamics in the region.

The chapters that follow encounter and confront these colonial and racial specters and illustrate how such specters powerfully shape the experiential and material realities that characterize all-inclusive hotels. However, as our case studies show, colonial specters are not experienced to the same degree or in the same way in every all-inclusive hotel. Harewood, for instance, explores the deliberate silencing of colonial histories in Barbados, illustrating how "colonial and postcolonial narratives produce a sound environment that converts some of the more disturbing noises of history into the more muted tones of Heritage." She is interested in what happens when, just outside the all-inclusive hotel she studies, a UNESCO World Heritage Site transforms grounds and sounds that once marked colonial power over local populations—that once marked freedom for some and slavery for others—into the more benign frame of national heritage. She questions what is at stake in translating the violence of colonial histories into a contemporary story about "little England." In the process, she illustrates how all-inclusive guests benefit from (and draw comfort from) the peace, quiet, and gentility that are, in fact, legacies of colonial domination, but which are narrated (and sounded) instead as part and parcel of a quaint local identity.

Camal understands the entire structure of the all-inclusive hotel as an example of how the plantation continues to operate as a model of power and control, and sees listening as a mode through which to "apprehend what would rather remain hidden: alienating labor practices and the long history of colonialism that informs them in the Caribbean." Throughout his chapter, he is alert to the rhythms of the resort. He listens for the "traces of their antecedents on the plantation but also for what they reveal about a contemporary labor regime intended to extract capital from the production of 'happiness.'" His analysis explores how the ideological and organizational structures of the plantation, translated into the context of the all-inclusive hotel, can help shed light on the power dynamics that continue to animate touristic encounters in the contemporary Caribbean.

Guadeloupe and Halfman, by contrast, acknowledge the historical dynamics of colonial specters and then address what it might mean to begin to undo the contemporary relations upon which such specters rely for their power. Working in Sint Maarten, they ask a series of questions designed to engage both tourists and locals in this island space of encounter, problematizing the nature of both categories in the process. They do this by positing Sint Maarten itself as an "unfinished project," electing to maintain a future open to new possibilities beyond those already charted by colonial histories. Ultimately, they ask what it would look and sound like to work toward resolving the colonial and racial specters that haunt touristic spaces like Sint Maarten.

Mediations and Expectations

We recognize that what makes a given music particularly apt at promoting a vacation site or for creating aesthetic pleasure does not reside in the music alone, but, as sociologist Antoine Hennion (2003, 2) argues, "in all the details of the gestures, bodies, habits, materials, spaces, languages, and institutions which it inhabits." Hennion goes on to point out that "mediations [be it an instrument, a particular stage, or media discourse, to name only a few] are neither mere carriers of the work, nor substitutes which dissolve its reality; they are the art itself" (3). To think about mediation this way does not take anything away from the creativity of the musicians (7) but reveals, instead, the things, discourses, consumers, and technology that are integral to the process of music's emergence, recognition, and appreciation. Put another way, it acknowledges how "[musical] taste, pleasure and meaning are contingent, conjunctural and hence transient; and they result from specific yet varying combinations of particular intermediaries, considered not as the neutral channels through which pre-determined social relations operate, but as productive entities which have effectivities of their own" (Hennion 2002, 3).

To be clear, the political economy of music and sound is not fixed. The musical pleasures, meanings, and expectations generated in and through the sounds of vacation are constantly changing, shifting in response to new technologies available at the time; the political party in power and its own politics of representation at a given moment (which can influence what is played at vacation sites); the regional and global musics that happen to be dominating the airwaves during a particular decade; the seasons (Christmas, carnival, summer); the weather (rain, storm, or sunshine) and its effects on ambient sounds; the hotel management's own musical tastes and the distinct skills of the musicians hired to play in that hotel that particular year; and so on. The mediations that are integral to the sounds of vacation also exert a cumulative effect on the ways these sounds are experienced. The memory of a film soundtrack shot in the Caribbean featuring the mellow yet vibrant tones of the steelpan in and of itself preforms, as it were, the expectation, the reception, the musical pleasure, and the meaning of the steelpan sounds heard some time later while on vacation. Based on such a "mediation perspective," the affective marketing and place-making of Caribbean sites as desirable vacation destinations through sound must thus be situated historically. Each author asks what historical mediations have continued to participate in shaping the expectations and imaginaries of a great majority of tourists regarding the Caribbean, its peoples, musical expressions, and sonic ecology?

The previous section has already introduced the legacies of mediation—the specters of coloniality—that continue to inform contemporary practice and tourist expectations in the region. From the outset, Caribbean music is raced and cannot be dissociated from the history of slavery. Up to the turn of the twentieth century, its description, almost exclusively articulated by colonial elites and missionaries, sutured local sounds and rhythms to black bodies, loudness, and exuberant sexuality. The growth of tourism in the twentieth century, moreover, was predicated on the expectations and imaginaries that such written representations (and later recordings and radio broadcasts) conjured among potential vacationers. The anticolonial, nationalist movements of the 1950s, and the postcolonial, nation-building efforts of newly elected governments throughout the region also deeply mediated how each country officially presented itself sonically—the idea being that it was not sufficient to be independent politically, but that one had to demonstrate cultural independence as well. The common practice, discussed by Guilbault and Rommen, of programming at least one night of local musical traditions each week in touristic sites such as hotels is an example of this rhetoric in action.

However, while such soundings were (and to some extent, continue to be) deemed crucial to distinguishing one island from others, they could not be the only ones performed. In fact, traditional music, or even the most well-known popular music from any given island, could hardly ever be the only music that musicians perform in hotel sites. Musicians, as much as elected officials and business people, made it very clear to the authors of this volume: they never want to be viewed as "premodern," as defined exclusively by back-in-time music or simply through the popular musics created locally. The delicate balance to achieve politically and culturally as much for the tourist industry as for the region and the world at large, then, is to be able to demonstrate local knowledge and pride while also exhibiting a cosmopolitan outlook and affinity. Anthropologist Aisha Khan addresses the kinds of challenges that this poses most eloquently in a passage that is worth quoting at length here:

> In the Caribbean we see a pull between two kinds of epistemological (and political) projects: the region as symbolizing the defiance of lodging culture in place due to its essential qualities of fluidity and hybridity, and the region as symbolizing the affirmation of lodging culture in place due to its history of being denied "ruins" — i.e., cultural heritage and traditions. Caribbean cultural thought reflects both of these projects of self-making, the struggle to locate culture and interpret authenticity in the face of so-called "mimicked" cultural reproduction and "artificial" rather than "organic" cultural genesis. The Caribbean exemplifies the wisdom of theoretically dislodging culture from place, and authenticity from natural origins while at the same time interrogating the meaning of "natural," the significance of "culture," and the ability to claim and redefine them. The Caribbean reminds us that decoupling "culture" from "place" and presenting these as consisting of performative flows without clear limits (as much as contemporary cultural theory does), requires a sense of ownership of one's history and possession of culture. Perhaps the key is that we have to feel stable to be able to valorize instability. (Khan 2013, 621–22)

How this delicate balance/instability through sound is managed and mediated in all-inclusive hotels is what the authors of this volume seek to address. And analyzing the day-to-day challenges of achieving such a balance in the contemporary moment requires both a sense of past mediations and an engagement with the current possibilities and expectations attendant to the political economy of sound and music in the region.

The Political Economy of Hospitality

As mentioned earlier, the political economy of all-inclusive hotels directly implicates the political economy of hospitality, which to a great extent is defined by entertainment. The substantial budget devoted to entertainment personnel (including musicians) raises a crucial question: *Who is it that the all-inclusive hotels are entertaining?* From the perspective of Caribbean governments, this question has a fairly straightforward answer: those individuals who travel to and stay at an all-inclusive hotel are categorized as tourists.[29] And yet, as our case studies show, hotels generally go out of their way to refer to these individuals as "guests" or "club members," and specifically *not* as tourists. Why? The politics of naming, we believe, is at the heart of how all-inclusive hotels arrive at a sense of not only who they are entertaining, but also the type of hospitality—entertainment—they set out to provide. Referring to the travelers as "guests" or "club members" hints at the fact that hotel administrators view their paying clientele not as "tourists," but as vacation seekers (vacationers) who have chosen as ideal the all-inclusive resort.

Thus, Harewood, echoing Claudio Minca's (2010) powerful reminder, reflects on how "the island has been constructed in the European archive as this ideal space of re-creation." She adds, "The tourist industry has consistently made use of this ideal and it has been especially important to enclavic tourist properties like all-inclusive hotels." The all-inclusive hotel is conceived by vacationers and promoted by the administration as "away from the hurly-burly of 'modern' life and labor" and as a space of leisure, as a "fun property," to use Rommen's wording.

So, for the management of the hotel, the staff, and the musicians, the implications of thinking about the travelers as vacationers are numerous. In his essay, Camal describes a large sign in the hotel lobby that reads: "The goal in life is to be happy. The place to be happy is here. The time to be happy is now." As he explains, "the staff is there to turn this into a reality for every person who comes to stay at the resort." Through different sources of information (managers, musicians, staff, locals), different sonic experiences, and historical records, the authors in this volume inquire about the strategies the hotel management deploys to reach out to vacationers. The creation of an island of leisure and pleasure within a physical island can indeed only exist at the expense of erasing the insurgent and noisy sounds of that locale's past. But how does the hotel management create these distinct "islands" within island countries? How does sonic experience shape soothing, energizing, and pleasurable feelings of vacation? How do sound walls separate the inside of the all-inclusive from the outside? Moving out of the "peace and quiet" of the hotel and into the surrounding neighborhood and back again, Harewood asks, "What historical narratives are emphasized and what narratives are muted in the production of 'tourist island'?"

To heighten the feeling of vacation and hyperreality, the acoustic evidence of some of the most labor-intensive activity in the all-inclusive hotels are deliberately masked. For example, sounds of kitchen work are typically muted to the vacationers' ears. As Camal observes, the result is that "many tourists—complicit in the practice—would sooner remain blind [deaf?] to the work that their leisure demands." Additionally, the labor performed by entertainment staff and musicians, like that of the other employees, can go unnoticed, foregrounding for many of them the specter of colonialism, "blurring the lines between service and servitude." But, as Camal indicates, not everyone employed at the all-inclusive hotels views their work this way. Guilbault's and Rommen's ethnographies indeed show that for many of the interviewed musicians, their main concern is more about the opportunity and revenue their work provides than its vexed symbolism.

If the primary goal of hospitality at all-inclusive hotels is to procure satisfaction and enjoyment, the primary effect is to foster affective relations between personnel and vacationers. It is to create, as Guilbault puts it, "experiences that are memorable, emotional, and interactive." To this end, she explores the entertainment infrastructure that is put into place to provide music for the ear and for the body. Bearing in mind hotel management's concern to please, she further asks: What policies and politics govern the hiring of musicians? To what extent is aural architecture a preoccupation in hotel design and renovation plans to foster hospitality?[30]

For the staff and the musicians, then, entertainment is profoundly connected to the issue of employment. Each author in this volume thus provides detailed descriptions of how all-inclusive hotel performers work to "tune in" to the vacationers and, to paraphrase Guadeloupe and Halfman, to privilege antiphonic techniques to boost modes of social and affective engagement. Moreover, the satisfaction and enjoyment (or lack thereof) that vacationers attribute to these sonic performances translates into renewal or suspension of workers' employment. What is made clear, then, is how hospitality is measured in terms of the vacationers' relative degree of "happiness," and how this "happiness" is understood and monetized by management. In business terms, the production of happiness then becomes key to whether or not the vacationers will want to come back.

Curating Sounds

As the case studies in this volume attest, there is no question that musicians are beholden to the tastes and desires of their vacationer audiences, and that they are also keenly aware of the expectations placed on them by hotel management (good reviews, no complaints, happy guests, etc.). In fact, it is worth asking whether it is a priority for the hotel management to feature the "local" (food, music, traditions, style, language, etc.) in such a configuration of entertainment. If so, is the programming a way of marketing a nation-state's distinctiveness merely through decor, sounds, and overall atmosphere? The case studies in this volume illustrate divergent answers to these questions about the local, national, and international, but they all point to the efforts all-inclusive hotels deploy to cater for their visitors' various notions of vacation, as shaped by a globalized industry. In effect, business is curation, and curation is business.

That music and sound in all-inclusive hotels would be carefully curated should come as no surprise. Drawing on Ochoa Gautier's concept of aurality, Camal recalls the colonial efforts "both to make sense of the world through the acoustic but also to control the sonic environment." As he argues, "The myths that first came to life on the plantation continue to inform which sounds should be included, even foregrounded, on the resort and which should be eliminated. Some tropical sounds remain wondrous (the rushing of waterfalls, the gentle rolling of waves) while others still prove incommensurable (the shrilling of nighttime tree frogs — or are they crickets?) or threatening (the buzzing of mosquitoes)."

Like Harewood, Camal remarks, "The 'listening ear' shaped by colonialism and exoticism recasts roots reggae, steelpan, calypso, or zouk (all musical styles that have, at some point, carried an anticolonialist or anti-imperialist message) as evidence of the inherent warmth, happiness, and laid-back personalities of Caribbean people."

Influenced by the colonial history in the islands, in all-inclusive hotels, Guilbault writes, "there is a tacit management theory that understands hearing and listening as controllable or partially controllable through the staging of tourist space and the music programming by the staff." She reports how the entertainment management establishes the do's and the don'ts in relation to the selection of music. Lyrics perceived as containing "profanity" and the sounds of musics such as dancehall or reggaeton that could potentially disturb or annoy the vacationers are avoided. As she puts it, "Entertainment managers thus define through their musical selections the geo-moral space of the Sandals resort in terms of political economy." The goal, adds Harewood, is "to maintain what Minca calls the 'harmonious' interior of the all-inclusive island within the island."

Soundscape curation by all-inclusive hotels does not only pertain to environmental sounds and the music performed or diffused through the resorts' speakers. It also extends to speech accents. Guadeloupe and Half-man underscore how in promoting the whole island of Sint Maarten as an all-inclusive, Sint Maarteners of all social stations had to be "inducted into a cosmopolitan ethic friendly to the machinations of capital" and engage tourists on a daily basis as "a pleasant matter of fact." Their anecdote about the virtuosic ability of Sint Maarteners to switch accents to make visitors at ease is telling of how accents convert into assets and commodities in the all-inclusive context (extended here to the whole island). As they indicate, Sint Maartener children's ability to imitate foreigners' accents and their tendency to associate these accents with specific countries, ethnicities, and/or races show how stereotypes can emerge as much from the locals about the tourists as from the tourists about the locals.

The curation of business and the business of curation is also located in the empirical analysis of musical performance presented in this volume. Close attention is paid to how musicians use musical genre and style to express their identifications with their own nation-states and also with other places, histories, and futures. Rommen, Harewood, and Guilbault address how the strategies employed by all-inclusive hotel musicians are carefully calibrated not only to achieve both commercial and personal success, but also to signal their creative agency. After attending to the actual musical and political labor that the all-inclusive hotel musicians perform, these authors revisit the long-held assumption that local musicians would rather only play local music. Far more complex than a simple attribution to the imagined "evil" demands of the generic tourism industry, Rommen, Harewood, and Guilbault turn to the musicians' biographies to grasp what informs their musical tastes and affinities.

And this leads to what this book's authors find to be one of the strikingly common characteristics of the entertainment staff and musicians in the all-inclusive hotels: they are all seasoned travelers. The implications of this are significant. As Guilbault remarks, "The history of encounters in and through sound in a touristic site such as Sandals Halcyon [in Saint Lucia] must [thus] be viewed as encounters among cosmopolitans whose experiences may differ on numerous points and yet overlap in others. The entertainment staff and musicians can not only imagine but also relate to many of their guests' musical habitus and preferences." As employees of the all-inclusive hotels, they use this knowledge to reach out to tourists and to calibrate their performance of familiar sounds with new sonic experiences for them. In a similar vein, Guadeloupe and Halfman asked themselves what would be unfamiliar to Sint Maarteners (read the local musicians). Their answer: not much. "As most Sint Maarteners have access to more than fifty American TV channels in real time, and the middle class travel regularly to the United States, they can easily make the tourists feel at home. Genuine relations between tourists and Sint Maarteners are possible."

Questions of authenticity, tied as they are to notions of identity and grounded in locality, are thus complicated by the all-inclusive hotel musicians' intertwined local and international experiences, their multiple senses of belonging, and their globally local outlook. These musicians render moot the question of whether they are performing (or failing to perform) authentic, local music for hotel guests. Nonetheless, Rommen reports, the question for many islanders remains: What is considered local and what is global in cosmopolitan Nassau? What counts as Bahamian music in the contemporary moment? "The all-inclusive hotel," he suggests, "has now become the context within which the current shapes and future possibilities of what constitutes Bahamian music are being negotiated."

Labor Politics

Musicians playing at all-inclusive hotels need to be addressed not only as artists, but also as workers — as participants in the political economy of all-inclusive hotels. All of the authors in this volume explore critically what sustained attention to several factors can reveal about labor politics within these touristic spaces. These factors include hiring practices, the precarity of insecure or seasonal labor, the often negative perceptions of hotel musicians as a category of entertainer, the role (or, more often, the lack thereof) of musicians' unions, the expectations of management and audiences alike, and the demands that all of these factors place on musicians (and staff).

The political status of the island on which an all-inclusive hotel is located, for instance, determines employment visa requirements and thus significantly impacts hiring policies. Whereas in a French overseas department such as Guadeloupe, an all-inclusive resort can recruit workers from different parts of Europe without visas, the independent English-speaking islands have such strict employment visa requirements that most employees working in the resorts are locals. To assess how all-inclusive hotels have developed their approach to staffing, Guilbault and Rommen situate contemporary labor politics in relation to the long history of the service industry in the Caribbean, and by doing so trace the dramatic changes that have accompanied the rise of all-inclusive hotels in the region.

Guilbault, for instance, learns from musician Ronald Hinkson that in years past, Saint Lucian hotels viewed musical entertainment as a source of revenue. This had concrete effects on musicians' ability to negotiate contracts, fee structures, labor conditions, and so on. But, with the advent of the all-inclusive hotel, music entertainment came to be regarded as "an expense, and accordingly is simply assessed as one of the 'services' the hotel provides." Guilbault thus explores what effects this transformation from partner in profit to contractor on a budget line continues to have on Saint Lucian musicians.

Rommen, too, traces the history of labor politics, illustrating how Bahamian musicians were, in the past, supported by a powerful musicians' union that assisted them with everything from contract negotiations to job placement and working conditions. Today, the union has largely lost the influence it once wielded, but perhaps more significantly, the all-inclusive hotel Rommen explores operates as a completely nonunion employer. What, he asks, does this mean for those who labor in such spaces, and how do musicians, in particular, manage the expectations of both audiences and their employers in such an environment?

Generating answers to such questions about the labor politics of all-inclusive hotels involves careful consideration of both the relative agency of the entertainment staff and musicians and attention to their material and "immaterial" labor. Here we are drawing on Michael Hardt and Antonio Negri's definition of immaterial labor as entailing both a "manipulation of symbols" and a "manipulation of affect" (2005, 111).[31] Camal, for example, analyzes the structure of material and immaterial labor at Club Poseidon, pointing out that long workdays filled with specific physical tasks and highly routinized daily schedules are coupled with the emotionally taxing labor of consistently encouraging and cajoling hotel guests (club members) to participate in the fun atmosphere for which the hotel is known.

Musicians, too, are constantly engaged in both material and immaterial labor. Harewood, Rommen, and Guilbault examine the challenges and stakes attendant to everything from procuring equipment to laboring on stage, and also the ways in which the immaterial labor of these musicians often becomes a barometer of success or failure in all-inclusive hotels. As Rommen points out, reviews on tripadvisor.com and other travel sites become a powerful index of musicians' effectiveness — a form of performance review that is taken very seriously by management. The particular demands placed on musicians and staff in all-inclusive hotels, however, also leave traces on musicians and staff alike. Camal, for instance, reports that fatigue, boredom, and alienation among staff members is often the cost associated with doing their jobs — the human cost of producing the energy, excitement, and belonging that guests at Club Poseidon have paid to experience.

But schedules, routines, and expectations also offer opportunities for individual agency, and Rommen, Harewood, and Guilbault all explore how musicians' choices shape their experiences of their specific labor regimes and their relationships to their own product. Rommen, for instance, points out that some musicians are willing to perform music they do not personally enjoy in order to negotiate between the expectations of audiences and management, whereas others find musical pathways to ensure that they are, themselves, always deriving pleasure from their performances. Harewood reports similar considerations in relation to musicians who choose to perform classic Caribbean hits for tourists in Barbados. Guilbault makes similar observations but also underscores the gendered realities of labor politics, exploring how a female saxophonist navigates professional life in the hotels of Saint Lucia.

The labor politics in all-inclusive hotels, then, provides windows onto the political economy of sound and music in these institutions. Attending to *what* work and *which* expectations help enliven these spaces from day to day affords all of the authors insights into how the complex relations and affects that are produced by musicians and staff continuously affirm the value of the all-inclusive for vacationers.

The Commodification of Experience

The commodification of experience in the all-inclusive hotels is grounded in the ubiquitous commoditization process central to globalization (Brown 2003). As Guilbault reports, "Business scholar S. Maitel summarizes the contemporary orientation in marketing by this motto: 'Don't sell commodities, sell experience.'" As she points out, however, "What Maitel does not mention is how the selling of experience does not mean by default only 'new' experience." The all-inclusive hotels indeed convert into commodities daily or weekly activities that are part of the vacationers' routine at home.

Listening to music diffused on speakers throughout the resort—a most common practice in public places at the vacationers' "home"—is part of commodity exchange at the resort. The hotels provide this commodity and sell it to vacationers who buy it as part of their vacation package.

Commodification aims to make experience reproducible, malleable, and salable. Take, for example, the "themed nights" discussed in Rommen's, Camal's, and Guilbault's essays. The weekly music programming that is offered as part of the vacationers' experience intersects with what is bought and what is sold. It is a musical experience that is monetized by the hotel. Similar to other commodities, the weekly music programming is reproducible from one week to the next for another group of vacationers. It is also malleable in the sense that it changes according to season, and in doing so can acquire an even greater value for the vacationers as well as for the hotel.

By including in December an evening of Christmas music, for example, the hotel boosts the "emotional economies"[32] of hospitality, the heightened emotions generated by the various hotel activities (musical and nonmusical) that simultaneously become constitutive of the hotel's "goods" and are sold to the vacationers.

The musicians' creative agency is also shaped and forged in the commercial arena of the vacation site. Rommen, Harewood, and Guilbault present instances of performing a familiar tune with a Caribbean inflection or performing a Caribbean tune with a twist of jazz. Knowing what tune to play to entice vacationers onto the dance floor indicates how musicians create musical meaning and, in doing so, consolidate musical value for both vacationers and hotel management.

Vacationers' participation in musical activities is also commodified at the all-inclusive hotels. Guadeloupe and Halfman, for example, reveal how participation becomes part of an "experience economy" (a notion from B. J. Pine and J. H Gilmore's work, explored in Guilbault's essay). "Leroy . . . made sure to constantly interpellate the tourists and the regular workers of the hotel, as an audience that was simultaneously part of his band. He gave them a sense that they were the ones entertaining themselves. His movement throughout the hotel had purpose, strategically sharing the microphone with specific tourists, or inviting them to dance and gain an audience while also being part of the audience."

An all-inclusive hotel audience enjoying itself here becomes what

Smythe (1977) calls a "commodity audience" for other vacationers. Harewood productively uses this concept to explain both how this commodity audience is produced and how it becomes inextricably part of the commodification of experience.[33] In effect, the enjoyment of some audience members becomes the drawing card for others—a commodity that curates the experience of other vacationers. This commodity audience acquires yet another use value for the hotel management by becoming a selling point in promotional photographs—look at how these vacationers enjoy themselves—to attract other visitors. In addition, Harewood explains, the commodity audience becomes the product on which the hotel musician's work depends and out of which the hotel's commercial success is built.

All of the strategies used to heighten the vacation experience intersect with the commodities that all-inclusive hotels offer. Space in the resort is staged. Shows take place in different places around the property to offer a unique sonic experience of music mixed with different environmental sounds (see Guilbault). Architecture and landscaping are used to produce the "peace and quiet" that some vacationers are looking for, while the sounds of the violent colonial history of the heritage site nearby are muted to reinforce the vacationers' feeling of innocence (see Harewood). The hotels make use of sound technologies to enable music to be projected at different levels of intensity—loudly near the bar to energize the audience and quietly near the bedrooms (see Guadeloupe and Halfman). All of these strategies and many others turn experience—listening to environmental sounds, dancing to music played by a live band, exercising to the sound of music in the gym, musicians' performances—into commodities, into vacation products that are bought and sold in all-inclusive hotels. It is in this sense that music and sound are consistently central to the political economy of vacation in the all-inclusive Caribbean hotels.

Taken as a whole, this book speaks about political economy, but not in relation to the top-down level, the national organization of the tourist industry as mediated by ministries or tourist boards, nor in relation to the corporatization of tourist resorts that are linked to the travel industry. We do not principally examine the political economy of the sounds of vacation in all-inclusive hotels at the national, regional, or global level. In this volume, we instead address the political economy at the site of vacationers' presence, activities, and visitations, and at the site of the labor force that makes the tourists' experience of vacation memorable and pleasurable. We seek to make audible the silences and the erasures of the past, and to account for the cosmopolitan experience, knowledge, and work of the management, the musicians, and the entertainment personnel in these touristic sites.

NOTES

1. Malcolm Crick (1989, 311) goes further, asking, "Is it that academic personalities find it difficult to take as a serious area of research a phenomenon so bound with leisure and hedonism?" See also Botterill (2001, 209).

2. From "Political Economy" in *Encyclopedia Britannica*.

3. It should be noted, however, that Attali was not the first author to be preoccupied with questions related to the political economy of music. As Maynard Solomon indicates, "The earliest emphasis of the Frankfurt School was on political economy" (1979, 371). On the other side of the Atlantic, Marxist musicologists also paid attention to the inextricable interrelations between individuals, states, markets, and society. To give only one example, Sidney Finkelstein (1947, 1960), through his Marxist lens, discusses how material production shapes not only musical thinking and its products, but also the composers' philosophy about the market and their involvement with both patronage and music publishing. In the 1970s, sociologists like Simon Frith in *The Sociology of Rock* (1978), and Steve Chapple and Reebee Garofalo in *Rock 'n' Roll Is Here to Pay* (1977) have also argued that the history of music such as rock can only be understood by addressing the interrelationship between politics, markets, and cultural values. Since Attali, other authors, such as Jann Pasler (2008), have emphasized "political economy" as the focal point of their studies by using the term in the titles of their publications. Save for a few exceptions (for example, Hellier-Tinoco 2011), music studies addressing tourism still rarely engage political economy as the main point of inquiry.

4. As Denis Constant-Martin (1993) remarks, the prophetic quality of music, often mentioned in reference to Attali's book, should not be viewed as an isolated case, but as part of what Georges Balandier calls the "social detectors" [*révélateurs sociaux*] that enable one, in spite of apparent continuities, to detect changing trends (Guilbault's translation).

5. See, however, the limits of Appadurai's notion of value in Graeber (2001, 30–33).

6. Two points of clarification: The expression *sonic touristry* comes from Feld in an informal conversation with Guilbault. In "Notes on World Beat," Feld (1988) refers to Charles Keil's *Urban Blues* to address regimes of value and the circulation of commodities.

7. In the context of the Caribbean, musical genres are fraught with precisely the complications and nuances suggested by Myers. The cultures of circulation addressed by Lee and LiPuma are, moreover, particularly sharply delineated in all-inclusive resorts. This is the case because Caribbean musical genres tend to circulate as markers of particular communities and are often understood as bearing the sonic signatures of

deep-seated and long-standing rivalries—rivalries that may matter little to the tourists wishing to hear "island music" but which matter urgently to local populations and local musicians. Any analysis of these cultures of circulation must then account for the fact that local musicians and service workers cultivate very different relationships to Caribbean genres than do the tourists they entertain and must therefore negotiate carefully between local and regional concerns and histories in the process of performing for their largely transnational audiences.

8. In 2012, Matei Candea and Giovanni da Col coedited a special issue of the *Journal of the Royal Anthropological Institute* entitled "The Return to Hospitality: Strangers, Guests, and Ambiguous Encounters." They remark how in contrast to disciplines such as classics or history, anthropological discussions of hospitality have until recently been limited to analyses of "tourism as imperialist formation . . . or of the constitutive economic role of visitors in relation to the domestic sphere" (2012, S3). But, they add, the publications devoted to hospitality by prominent continental philosophers such as Jacques Derrida (1999a, 1999b, 2000) created a surge of interest in the subject. Anthropological discussions of hospitality are not new. As the authors put it, "they are both everywhere and (nearly) nowhere." Hospitality has been typically mentioned as a passing reference to Marcel Mauss's notion of gift or acknowledged as what makes possible ethnographers' fieldwork. However, until recently, scant attention has been given to hospitality as a theoretically important concept in the discipline. The same could be said about ethnomusicological studies.

9. See Scott's insightful remarks on the "Evidence of Experience" (1991).

10. See King (1995) on the subject.

11. As King reminds us, "The antecedent of commercial hospitality is the behavior of the courtier toward his sovereign or lord" (1995, 219).

12. This book's intellectual project is visually reinforced in its cover art, which exhibits right in the middle a dollar sign painted in black against a backdrop fleshed out by the revealingly selected red, green, and yellow colors—the colors of the Rastafarian activist movement.

13. See, for example, Erlmann (2004), Feld and Brenneis (2004), Keeling and Kun (2011), Samuels et al. (2010), and recently summarized in Feld (2012) and elaborated in Meintjes (2017).

14. Quiñones et al. (2013).

15. On tourism in general, see for instance Gibson and Connell (2005), Krüger and Trandafoiu (2013), MacCannell (2013), Rojek and Urry (1997), Urry and Larsen (2011), and Yelvington, Simms, and Murray (2012). On Caribbean tourism in particular, see Baver and Deutsch Lynch (2006), Cohen (2010), Daye, Chamber, and Roberts (2008), Gregory (2007), Padilla (2007), Sheller (2003), and Siegel and Righter (2011).

16. Notable exceptions include Cooley (2005), Hellier-Tinoco (2011), Kaul (2009), and the special issue on "Music, Travel, and Tourism" of the journal *The World of Music* (Baumann and Fujie 1999).

17. As J. J. Issa and C. Jayawardena (2003, 167) explain, "The concept [of all-inclusive hotels] was first introduced in holiday camps in Britain during the 1930s. Club Med is credited for popularizing the concept globally in the 1950s." As they indicate, however,

"the credit for introducing a luxury version of the all-inclusive concept goes to a Jamaican hotelier. . . . In defining the concept of all-inclusives, one cannot ignore the significant role Jamaica has played."

18. As noted in this volume, Guadeloupe as an overseas French department marks an exception to this general hiring policy.

19. In a study titled "Beyond Tourism: The Future of the Service Industry in the Caribbean," Erikson and Lawrence (2008, 5) assert that "the Caribbean is the most tourism-intensive region in the world and tourism is the leading source of foreign exchange for most Caribbean nations."

20. From *Index Mundi*, "The Economic Profile of 2018," indexmundi.com, accessed on March 9, 2018.

21. From the "Travel & Tourism Economic Impact 2018 Caribbean" report of the World/Travel and Tourism Council, https://www.wttc.org/research/economic-research/economic-impact-analysis/regional-reports/#undefined, accessed on March 28, 2018.

22. From the "Travel & Tourism Economic Impact 2017 Caribbean" report of the World/Travel and Tourism Council.

23. From the "Travel & Tourism Economic Impact 2018 Caribbean" report of the World/Travel and Tourism Council.

24. World Tourism Organization (unwto), http://media.unwto.org/press-release/2018-01-15/2017-international-tourism-results-highest-seven-years, accessed on March 28, 2018.

25. From the "Travel & Tourism Economic Impact 2017 Caribbean" report of the World/Travel and Tourism Council. If Thomas Cook and Son travel firm was the most impressive economic organization to emerge in nineteenth-century Britain, Scott Lash and John Urry suggest, "there is some justification for suggesting that twentieth-century [and we could add, twenty-first-century] organized capitalism might be better described as "Cookism'" rather than "Fordism" (1999, 261).

26. As Barbara Kirshenblatt-Gimblett (2006, 163) aptly remarks, while culture is "an externality in economic theories of markets (the idea that markets operate according to their own logic and can be accounted for without reference to culture), economics is not an externality in theories of culture." In a hopeful footnote, she indicates that "some cultural economists are trying to address this issue" (2006, 197n5). The economics of music and sound-making in touristic sites, however, remain to this day largely unaccounted for.

27. For an elaboration on this subject, see Radano (2016).

28. For a more sustained meditation on these ideas, see Mimi Sheller's *Consuming the Caribbean: From Arawaks to Zombies* (2003).

29. That the "tourist" is a complicated and vexed topic is already amply demonstrated by the consistent and sustained engagement with this idea in mobility and leisure studies. An entire discipline called tourism studies has developed around the activities of such actors, and offers additional evidence of the intellectual resources committed to understanding tourists' practices. One of the clear findings emerging from these literatures is that there is no unifying or stabilizing definition of the tourist.

Rather, just as there are many forms of tourism, those individuals referred to as tourists are profoundly variegated (by class, ethnicity, motivations for travel, etc.). This is, by now, a virtual truism—a truism confirmed throughout the essays in this volume.

30. See Blesser and Salter (2007).

31. While we recognize that Hardt and Negri's overall argument for immaterial labor has received ample critique (see Camfield 2006, Gill and Pratt 2008, Graeber 2008, and Wright 2005 for excellent examples), our purpose is to name and thus highlight the profound importance of symbolic and affective labor within the overall labor politics of all-inclusive hotels throughout the Caribbean. Our use of the term here is thus a heuristic claim.

32. We owe the expression *emotional economies* to Candea and da Col (2012, S12).

33. Smythe (1977, 3) explains his concept of commodity audience as follows: "I submit that the materialist answer to the question—What is the commodity form of mass-produced, advertiser-supported communications under monopoly capitalism?—is audiences and readerships (hereafter referred to for simplicity as audiences). The material reality under monopoly capitalism is that all non-sleeping time of most of the population is work time. This work time is devoted to the production of commodities-in-general (both where people get paid for their work and as members of audiences)."

1 · IT SOUNDS BETTER IN THE BAHAMAS

Musicians, Management, and Markets
in Nassau's All-Inclusive Hotels

TIMOTHY ROMMEN

This chapter explores the day-to-day interactions of musicians with their tourist audiences in the context of all-inclusive hotels in the Bahamas, paying particular attention to notions of craft, to genre expectations, to agency, and to encounter. In so doing, I explore the ambivalences, joys, and frustrations musicians experience in negotiating their positions within all-inclusive hotels (both as employees and as performers). I also illustrate how these day-to-day performances and encounters are inextricably entangled in and vital to the (often competing) concerns of all-inclusive hotels, local institutions, and the government itself. A series of questions are raised in the process: What is considered local and what is global in cosmopolitan Nassau? What does it mean to be Bahamian in the context of an all-inclusive hotel? And, perhaps most pressingly, what counts as Bahamian music in touristic encounters characterized by shared cosmopolitanisms?[1]

In one sense, these inquiries trace along well-worn paths, for attempts to define, understand, and qualify the local or the national in this manner are inevitably bound up in questions of identity. Identitarian projects of this sort accompanied the Caribbean through the mid- and late twentieth-century independence movements and have continued to shape the region's postcolonial life as nations (and communities within them) work to reframe local histories through appeals to roots and heritage. Music scholars working in the Caribbean have been particularly attuned to these identitarian discourses. This is the case not least because these discourses have offered productive insights into the ways that musical practices have been mobilized to think about the challenges and possibilities of nationalism (Austerlitz 1997; Berrian 2000; Dudley 2007; Guilbault 1993; Largey

2006; Miller 2008; Moore 1997; Rommen 2011), representation and recognition (Bilby 2008; Greene 2017; Rommen 2007a, 2007b), race and class (Cooper 2004; Guadeloupe 2009; Manuel 2000; Pacini Hernandez 1995; Ramnarine 2001), and gender (Cooper 1995; Guilbault 2007; Hutchinson 2016; Pacini Hernandez 1995), to name only some of the most common paths of inquiry.[2]

The questions raised by this chapter's case studies, however, are not only about identity. They also concern the issue of branding—the need to define and capitalize on a signature sound in all-inclusive hotels. The history of tourism in the Caribbean, especially in those destinations aiming to develop a mass tourism appeal, is marked with efforts to connect or even to equate (sonic) national identity with branding efforts. But, as this chapter illustrates, recent developments have shifted the scale and focus of such efforts: in the context of the all-inclusive hotels in the Bahamas, at least, branding no longer necessarily concerns developing or supporting a national sound to attract visitors to the island, but requires, instead, a sound-as-commodity that sells the globalized, corporate space of the all-inclusive hotel as an island within the island.[3] And this shift away from representing the nation (historically a major component of Bahamian musicians' performances) and toward branding the corporation (increasingly the primary focus of musicians) means that the all-inclusive hotel has become a particularly important musical site in the contemporary Bahamas.

Just what a signature or branded sound might entail for an all-inclusive hotel, however, remains an open question. On the one hand, the global connections fostered in the all-inclusive hotel create the possibility for shared cosmopolitanisms, and musicians, as I illustrate below, are keen to engage in and celebrate such sonic solidarities. On the other hand, these global connections and their musical consequences create *frictions* (to use Anna Tsing's term)—frictions engendered by moving beyond local specificities and thereby deemphasizing established sonic identities historically attached to a national sound while simultaneously working to present visitors with *some* version of the Bahamas. Tsing writes: "How does one do an ethnography of global connections? . . . My answer has been to focus on zones of awkward engagement, where words [and sound] mean something different across a divide even as people agree to speak. These zones of cultural friction are transient, they arise out of encounters and interactions. They reappear in new places with changing events" (Tsing 2005, xi). I analyze the all-inclusive hotel as such a zone of cultural friction and understand the musical encounters that animate this space as a continuation of the long history of attempts to negotiate both global connections and local specificities within a tourist destination. I also understand the all-inclusive hotel as a site in which such musical negotiations are displaced from the sphere of the nation to the purview of the corporation.[4]

In exploring these ideas and questions, I focus on the music of Funky D and Alia Coley, two musicians who have spent the majority of their careers performing for audiences in all-inclusive hotels. I focus, in particular, on their employment by SuperClubs Breezes Resort and Spa, Bahamas, which has, since 1995, been one of the premier all-inclusive hotels in Nassau. Their experiences in this context lead me to suggest that all-inclusive hotels like Breezes — not the Ministry of Tourism or local institutions such as the Musicians and Entertainers Union — have now become the primary context within which the current shapes and future possibilities of what constitutes Bahamian music are being negotiated.

In order to set the context for considering these musical labors, touristic encounters, and shared cosmopolitanisms, however, it is necessary briefly to trace the history of the political economy of music within the tourism industry in the Bahamas.

Music and Tourism in the Bahamas

What is the earthly paradise for our visitors? Two weeks without rain and a mahogany tan, and, at sunset, local troubadours in straw hats and floral shirts beating "Yellow Bird" and "Banana Boat Song" to death.

—Derek Walcott (1992)

Tourism is a sort of chemotherapy. You have cancer and it's the only possible cure, but it might kill you before the cancer does.

—Juan Antonio Blanco quoted in McGeary and Booth (1993)

"It's better in the Bahamas!" This slogan has defined the marketing efforts of the Bahamas Ministry of Tourism since 1976. But what might this "it" entail when explored in relation to music, dance, and cultural productions? It is no exaggeration to claim that musicians were instrumental in shaping the tourism product that spurred the rapid growth in the industry during the second half of the twentieth century — that the sounds of vacation supported, confirmed, and animated the spaces of tourist desire. Fire dancers, limbo dancers, musicians, and junkanoo groups were all enlisted to showcase the sounds of the Bahamas to the world, whether abroad at conventions or at home in hotels and nightclubs. Their performances, moreover, also offered sights (costumes, dancing) and explored themes that satisfied the expectations (desires) with which tourists arrived in the Bahamas. A brief exploration of the deep connections between music and entertainment and the growth of tourism is instructive here, especially since these ties have, for a variety of reasons, been rather dramatically reconfigured since the 1970s.[5]

1949–1967: Stafford Sands, the Development Board, and the Ministry of Tourism

In 1949, when Stafford Sands was installed as president of the Bahamas Development Board, the Bahamas hosted a fledgling, seasonal industry playing out in segregated hotels—an industry that attracted a mere 32,018 visitors that year. During the subsequent decade, however, Sands directed the Development Board aggressively to pursue a strategy designed to brand the Bahamas as a mass tourism destination.[6] Initial results were encouraging—indeed, by 1959, the Development Board recorded 264,758 visitor arrivals.[7] The entire infrastructure of the Bahamas was shifted toward the needs of the tourism industry, and the increasingly heavy advertising and promotional expenditures by the Development Board were easily justified by the many new jobs and construction projects the growing industry was creating in its wake. In 1952, the institutional and legal landscape was also shifted toward supporting the growing industry. The Bahamas Hotel Association was founded in order to "jointly promote their properties and to help the Development Board market The Bahamas as a destination" (Cleare 2007, 114).[8] The first Hotels Encouragement Act was passed in 1954 in order to assist in attracting new projects (provisions included customs duty refunds for construction materials and various tax breaks and incentives).[9] The Bahamas Tour Operators and Sightseeing Association was founded in 1957 and became a major partner with the Development Board, helping to set fair rates and create a consistent product.[10]

Most significantly, in response to a resolution to ban segregation in the Bahamas, proposed in the House of Assembly in 1956, the formerly segregated hotels opened their doors to all, prompting other businesses throughout the Bahamas to follow suit in the months that followed.[11] In spite of these shifts, however, racial discrimination remained entrenched and widespread throughout the industry. The overall results of these efforts and changes were nevertheless impressive—by the end of the decade, tourism accounted for almost 25 percent of government revenue (up from about 19 percent in 1950).

Musicians and entertainers, for their part, became an indispensable component of the marketing strategy promulgated by Sands during those years. The 1950s found Bahamian entertainers performing their roles as "picturesque natives" at the segregated hotels (until 1956) and in the dozens of Bahamian-owned, integrated clubs in the section of Nassau called Over-the-Hill. They performed for tourists and locals alike, ever aware of the expectations of their clientele, and they were marketed in predictably exoticized fashion.[12] The jacket copy included on souvenir albums also regularly reinforced these ideas.[13] And yet, even as musicians and entertainers were cast into racialized, renaturalized, and stereotyped roles, the rapid growth of the industry created a lot of work. Peanuts Taylor, one of the great entertainers of the time, recalls: "I worked three jobs: I worked at Buena Vista from 7 to 10, I worked at the Imperial Hotel Garden with George [Symonette] from 10 o'clock until 2 o'clock, and then I went and worked with Paul Meeres Jr. over at the Paul Meeres until 5 o'clock in the morning. So work was not a problem for musicians and entertainers in this country back in those days."[14]

Musicians, moreover, worked in conjunction with floor shows featuring fire dancers such as Naomi Taylor in exotic costume, limbo dancers like Pepe exhibiting their flexibility, and junkanoo groups that invited audience participation and dance. The synergy between the marketing strategy of the Development Board and the set of branded entertainment options available to tourist during the 1950s was, in many respects, ideal. Musicians and entertainers, in a very real sense, confirmed and validated as true all of the advertising materials tourists had been exposed to prior to arriving in Nassau—confirming in the physical processes and experiences of actual tourism the tourist imagination so carefully cultivated in and through various media (Crouch, Jackson, and Thompson 2005, 2).

The 1960s saw even more rapid growth in the tourism sector than had the 1950s. The figures are dramatic. In 1960, 341,977 visitors arrived and, by 1967, that number increased to 822,317. Equally dramatic is the fact that some 7,000 hotel beds were added between 1960 and 1969.[15] Part of this rapid growth was due to the expansion from a seasonal to a year-round industry—an expansion first explored in the late 1950s and then firmly established during the 1960s. Another boon for the industry was the fact that the Bahamas saw a new influx of tourists in the years following the Cuban Revolution. These years were marked by continued hotel construction, the development of Paradise Island as a resort area, and the introduction of casinos. Significant changes, both politically and socially, marked the decade as well. In 1964, the Bahamas achieved internal self-government, occasioning the birth of the Ministry of Tourism under the Promotion of Tourism Act (passed in 1963, enacted in 1964). And in 1967 the Bahamas elected, for the first time, a black majority government, sweeping the old-guard minority government (mostly white and called the Bay Street Boys) out of power.

The 1960s found musicians thriving in Nassau. Dozens of nightclubs and hotel clubs made Nassau a premier entertainment destination, and veterans of these years recall them with excitement (and with no small amount of nostalgia).[16] And yet, as I have written elsewhere, although hotel clubs were doing well, the late 1960s also spelled the beginning of the end for most of the Over-the-Hill nightclubs.[17] Even as musicians were finding their way to the hotels and continuing to meet tourist demand, the Over-the-Hill nightclubs were coming under ever greater financial pressure, losing both their entertainers and their clientele.[18] Importantly, this situation also created a significant interruption to the path toward professionalization that most musicians and entertainers had relied upon. Whereas Over-the-Hill had provided a range of venues suitable for working up from amateur to fully professionalized skills, such a training ground was effectively eliminated as the Over-the-Hill scene suffered and, by the early 1970s, died.[19] The absence of training, or even of a clear pathway to becoming a professional, discouraged many younger Bahamians from pursuing careers in music during these years. This became a major issue (a crisis, even) in the late 1980s and early 1990s and, as the case studies of Funky D and Alia will illustrate, the situation has not been adequately addressed in the intervening years.[20] The growth in the tourism industry of the 1950s and 1960s was driven to a significant extent by the deep and mutually beneficial connection between tourism officials, hoteliers, and Bahamian musicians and entertainers. This close working relationship, however, was to be severely tested in the 1970s.

1967–1979: Majority Rule, Bahamianization,
and Independence

Clement Maynard was appointed to the Ministry of Tourism in 1969, and he served as minister until 1979, overseeing a decade of change and growth in the industry. Between 1967 and 1972, no fewer than ten new hotels were opened in the Nassau area (adding some 2,300 rooms to Nassau's capacity), and several existing properties were renovated and expanded.[21] The million-visitor threshold was surpassed in 1968, and by 1969 tourism accounted for 70 percent of the Bahamas' gross national product and 60 percent of government revenue (Cleare 2007, 173). In 1970, the government passed the Hotels Act 1970, by virtue of which hotels were subject to mandatory inspections and licensing, and which also created a hotel guest tax. The Bahamas was, by any metric, now a mass tourism destination, and the government initiated a Bahamianization policy with the aim of installing as many Bahamians as possible in the tourism industry (both at home and in sales and marketing services abroad).

The Bahamas achieved independence in 1973, creating a moment of great optimism, but, even so, real economics were difficult. In 1974, the government acquired three large hotels (the Hyatt Emerald Beach, the Balmoral, and the Sonesta Beach Hotel) and established the Hotel Corporation of the Bahamas to manage the properties. But management proved difficult in the extreme. As Michael Craton notes,

> The Corporation found that its deepening involvement in the ownership of hotels and the implementation of its Bahamianization policy in general ensured that it continued to be a net financial loser. It was caught in fact in a classic dilemma. Eager both to expand the tourist industry and to reap its profits for the benefit of Bahamians, it found that the only hotels easy to acquire were those least profitable, while at the same time it was forced to make expensive concessions in order to keep foreign owners happy and to attract further investment. (Craton 2002, 231)

This experience in the hotel sector, however, was only a small component of an already very complicated and difficult financial landscape. As the new nation began to establish itself (in the midst of a worldwide economic downturn), major initiatives were targeted at developing international banking, the casino industry, and aviation—all of which presented significant challenges to the new and relatively inexperienced government. Budgetary issues were paramount in the years immediately preceding and following independence, and the financial climate directly and dramatically affected how the government approached the question of arts and culture. A brief example illustrates this point well. A concerted effort to create and then invest in a permanent center for arts, crafts, and music—called Jumbey Village—was put forward as a means of supporting a venture for and by Bahamians from which tourists could also benefit (Rommen 2011). The idea, sponsored by member of Parliament and musician Edmund Moxey, had the further benefit of being located in Over-the-Hill, right in the heart of the community that was feeling the economic effects of the recently decimated nightclub scene. It would have brought local and tourist dollars back to this area of Nassau. And yet Jumbey Village represented a long-term investment that could not be easily converted into a vacation slogan or immediately monetized through tourist packages. It would have taken time to develop, care to do right, and commitment to maintain.

In the end, the government chose to invest in a promotion that would guarantee tourist dollars and also showcase Bahamian arts and culture, but would do so expressly as a tourist attraction. It was not, then, a decision that had the long-term interests of Bahamian entertainers or of Bahamian arts and culture in mind; it was, rather, a choice motivated by the promise of an immediate influx of capital. And, as it turns out, this promotion, inaugurated in 1971 and called Goombay Summer, was a massive success. Billed as a summer-long festival, Goombay Summer involved closing Bay Street for one day a week in order to offer a street parade and local entertainment, and afforded tourists opportunities to encounter Bahamian musicians and entertainers as well as locals (who also enjoyed the events) in a festive, outdoor party atmosphere. Other attractions connected to Goombay Summer included folklore, art, and fashion shows at various hotels, and all of this was attractively packaged to meet tourists' presumed vacation desires. Running for thirteen weeks each summer for twenty consecutive years, Goombay Summer became the longest-running and, arguably, the most successful promotion ever sponsored by the Ministry of Tourism. The festival became a good source of extra income for some musicians and entertainers, but could never support musicians' needs by itself. More importantly, it was a short-term solution that did nothing to address the underlying concerns of those worried about the health of Bahamian arts and culture — a concern that became more pronounced (and discussed) in the wake of independence.[22]

Another shift that took place starting in the 1960s and then became a staple of entertainment throughout the 1970s was the fact that tourists no longer considered calypso the soundtrack to their vacations. This regional connection was replaced by other possibilities in that many musicians turned to the *Billboard* charts in order to create cutting-edge set lists with which to entertain their audiences. Although there were exceptions to this strategy, the traditional sounds of Goombay, rake-n-scrape, and junkanoo were increasingly relegated to the margins of performances during these years.[23] Funk, R&B, soul, and pop became the staples of entertainment, and Bahamians increasingly shifted away from featuring local sounds and forms of artistic expression — a turn of events that was lamented by the small but vocal group of activists attempting to draw attention to this issue at the local level but which felt entirely comfortable for Bahamian musicians who had, like their tourist clientele, grown up listening to U.S. radio (Miami-based stations, in this case). And this musical dynamic, predicated on privileging shared cosmopolitanisms, has remained a hallmark of entertainment in Bahamian touristic sites into the contemporary moment.

With the exception of Goombay Summer, then, the Bahamas were, at the close of the 1970s, being marketed as a destination, but not as a place with truly distinctive arts and cultural possibilities. Tourism and local music had been separated from each other in practice, if not in rhetoric. Musicians were offering audiences the sounds they desired, and doing it very well, but the policy environment was devoid of a clear sense of how the Bahamas should sound, taste, and move, and how to ensure that Bahamians' long-term interests were being served. As Cleare points out, "the results of marketing research revealed an absence of a cultural identity for The Bahamas. The Islands for years had been the preferred destination for sun, sand, and sea, but the people and the culture played little role in the marketing of the destination" (2007, 211). Gone were the days of the 1950s and early 1960s, when musicians and entertainers and their local soundtracks had been understood as central to creating the Bahamas as a tourist destination. The political economy of the 1970s, combined with the shift toward more mainstream entertainment options, revealed a growing divide between tourism priorities and the desires of arts and culture advocates. Musicians and entertainers were, for better or worse, living with this friction, hearing both sides of the local debate but beholden to the expectations of their audiences and employers.

1980–2015: The Decline of Live Music

"My government done fuck me. Print that! The government ain't worth shit since Stafford Sands."[24] This comment by Ronnie Butler, one of the Bahamas' most distinguished entertainers, is echoed by Ray Munnings, who points out that, "once the government changed to a predominantly black government, that's when really the music died."[25] Nicolette Bethel, a major figure in theater arts, former director of culture, and a lecturer at the College of the Bahamas, agrees: "For a generation and a half—the entire time since Independence—our national policies have been shaped by a group of men and a handful of women whose actions and behavior cumulatively suggest that they would rather erase Bahamian culture than invest in it. Our cultural industries are in effective decline."[26] These statements offer a small window into how many musicians and artists (mostly belonging to the generation that came of age before or around independence) feel about the ability of their elected officials to protect their livelihoods. The Musicians and Entertainers Union, too, has lost credibility during the last two decades, becoming a mere shell of its former self, in terms of both membership and political influence.[27]

Even as musicians and entertainers progressively lost faith in their government and in their own union, however, the industry continued to grow. In 1989, 3,398,311 tourists arrived in the Bahamas and the nation now boasted more than 13,000 hotel beds.[28] But the news was not all good, for the dramatic growth in the industry came disproportionately from cruise arrivals and not from stay-over vacationers. Visitors arriving by air in 1980 had made up 62 percent of all arrivals. By 1991, however, that number had dropped to 39 percent. This meant, among other things, that hotels were not experiencing the growth they had enjoyed during the previous three decades. It also meant that the very institutions that employed musicians and entertainers were tightening their budgets in response to these developments in the industry. Accordingly, by the 1990s, only a handful of bands were still regularly playing in the hotels, most prominent among them the Baha Men, the VIP Band, Snapshot, and the Soulful Groovers. The hotels were now beginning to employ individual vocalists, small ensembles, or DJs instead of hiring bands. To make matters worse, customer satisfaction dropped steadily throughout the 1980s and, by 1992, many tourists no longer agreed that "It's Better in the Bahamas."

In 1992, the Free National Movement (FNM) defeated the Progressive Liberal Party (PLP) and, for the first time in twenty-five years, the government was run by someone other than Lynden Pindling (Hubert Ingraham became the new prime minister). The urgency of the situation was not lost on the new government, and efforts to solve both the slowing hotel market and the growing dissatisfaction with the Bahamian tourism product were set in motion. Between 1992 and 2002, the Hotel Corporation divested itself of all but two of the many properties it had, under PLP policy, purchased during the 1970s and 80s.[29] It was during this period that the financial and policy climate within the Bahamas—shifting toward a much less hands-on approach to the hotel industry—became favorable for SuperClubs Breezes and Sandals, which purchased existing properties, renovated them, and turned them into first-rate all-inclusive resorts. The 1990s was also the decade during which perhaps the most iconic hotel in the Bahamas—Atlantis—was built. Breezes, Sandals, and Atlantis promised an all-inclusive experience to their clients and, as a result, their own branding became as significant in attracting visitors as were the efforts of the Ministry of Tourism to sell the Bahamas. In fact, it is worth pointing out that, over the course of the last two decades, these big resorts have essentially operated as free agents within the Bahamas. Breezes, in particular, remains a nonunion employer and accepts no guidance from the government about how to handle its entertainment or advertising. Although Atlantis is a unionized employer, this resort, too, operates with great autonomy in the Bahamas. These changes in the tourism industry during the 1990s offer clear evidence of the extent to which money buys laws—of how successful entrepreneurship is intimately linked to the politics of concessions. Had the Bahamas been in a better position to negotiate during these years, the concessions would likely not have been nearly so sweeping or consequential.

By 2000, the Bahamas saw 4,203,834 visitors arrive, and growth in the sector has continued. In 2017, the total number of visitors reached 6,136,159. However, Robert Sands, articulating the perspective of the Bahamas Hotel and Tourism Association (BHTA) on this issue, notes that, "While entertainment still exists, it does not exist at the same quantity that existed in years gone by. . . . I think both entertainers and hotels maybe have to accept joint responsibility for this. . . . But I do believe there is a place for having some form of local entertainment in hotels going forward, and we just have to find the right mix, balance that both parties can mutually benefit" (BHTA 2012).

The deepening divide between the tourism industry and arts and culture activists first opened in the 1960s, and has been nourished since then by the financial and political realities of independence and a rapidly changing tourism market, contributing to an atmosphere in which clarity about what the Bahamian "it" might be has remained stubbornly out of reach. Sophia Rolle, writing about Bahamian tourism initiatives in the past decade, points out that one of the findings of the Destination Segmentation Report for the Bahamas in 2009 was that "operators and stakeholders could not agree on what elements should be termed 'authentically Bahamian'" (2015, 172). Ronald Simms, musician, radio host, and entertainment entrepreneur, agrees, framing the issue as a lack of commitment to educational and cultural policy.[30]

Putting aside for the moment whether such progress toward articulating arts and culture priorities is possible or even desirable, the Ministry of Tourism today has virtually no ability to influence whether or how tourists will experience "it" while visiting the Bahamas. This is the case in part because there is virtually no live music on offer outside of hotels.[31] The live music performed in the hotels, moreover, is almost entirely disconnected from (cultural) policy and labor concerns (due to the lack of an effective musicians' union and the presence of nonunion hotels). The hotels in which visitors experience their Bahamian vacations all have their own branding to worry about and their own commitments to clientele, and this is especially the case at the all-inclusive resorts such as Sandals and Breezes. What role, then, do musicians play in these contexts? What creative constraints do they face? How do they make decisions about repertory and style? Perhaps most significantly, does the tourism industry remain a sector within which local arts and culture should (or even can) be promoted, or do such efforts represent an anachronism within the current globalized and cosmopolitan scene? In order to begin answering these questions and illustrating these frictions, I turn now to a closer examination of Breezes as a site within which Funky D and Alia Coley have consistently entertained audiences of (mostly) tourists throughout their careers.

SuperClubs Breezes

One of the questions that I ask on an ongoing basis is, where is the Bahamian experience in the Bahamas?

—*Ronald Simms (interview, 2016)*

We are the only hotel that has a resident band in Nassau . . . that performs six nights a week.

—*Carlton McPhee (interview, 2016)*

"Turn around and tell someone you love them!" Funky D is down on the main floor, walking through the crowd of (mostly) seated guests, exhorting his audience to get ready for a night of fun and dancing, and determined to break as many of them out of the potentially disengaged role of "listener" as he can. He wants "participants" and he knows how to transform the room into a warm and engaging space. His group, called the Summer Breeze Band, consisting of a drummer, bass guitarist, guitarist, and a keyboard player (most days there are two keyboardists), is on the stage, tuned up and ready to go. He is using a wireless microphone and just spent the last few minutes before the show tweaking the equalization so that it won't create feedback when he walks out in front of the main speakers. The raised bandstand is located at one end of the room, and a large bar is located at the other end. Funky D walks the entire length of the room, hugging, speaking to, and generally acquainting himself with members of his audience, most of whom are sitting at tables arranged in the open floor space between the stage and the bar in Breezes' main hall. It is around 8:30 on Friday night, and the room is about half full. The band begins to perform a standard reggae tune (Bob Marley's "One Love") as an instrumental backdrop for this opening exchange between Funky D and the assembled crowd, and more people begin to wander over from other parts of the main floor even as he engages the room.

This works because the main floor of Breezes resort uses an open floor plan. When facing the stage, an audience member has the bar behind her, the pool area and beach to her right, the lobby to the left, and a gaming area, complete with pool and ping-pong tables, just behind her to the left. All of this open space is designed to create a sense of connection between the various areas of the main floor and to foster a flow of people from activity to activity. Sound travels freely through the entire area. Perhaps the best illustration of this is the recording of my recent interview with Breezes' entertainment manger, Carlton McPhee, which was held on the main floor. The background is full of the sounds of ping-pong, people laughing and talking at the bar, visitors checking in or out, the crack of shots at the pool tables, and groups of people heading back to their rooms or out to the pool. According to Carlton, this is absolutely intentional. "We are a fun property. So the Breezes line is not about rooms, it's not about glitz and glamour. It's about coming in and having a great time, having great activities, having great music, and people just having fun. And that is the vibe that we build. That is our branding."[32] So, when Funky D starts his set, people can experience it while finishing a game of pool, can choose to find a seat closer to the action, or can enjoy it as they relax by the bar. Leisure and fun by design.

This section considers Breezes as a place of leisure and employment, as an institution within the tourism industry in the Bahamas, and as a management regime for and curator of music and sound—in short, as a site within which the political economy of music in the Bahamas continues concretely to take shape. Carlton's role at Breezes affords him a direct hand in each of these areas of activity and programming. He has been part of the Bahamian music and entertainment industry for over two decades, working first at the Lowe's Harbor Cove Hotel and then at Compass Point Studio and Hotel before joining Breezes as entertainment manager in 1999. One of his goals as entertainment manager has been to promote local artists. As he describes it,

> I always look for young people, up and coming young people, to perform. And quite a number of our current people who are quite hot now, like Puzzle [Preston Wallace], started out here. And he still performs here, actually, on Wednesday nights. Julien Believe, who just performed for Ms. World in China, he has a hit song out that's really hot in the Caribbean right now, and Julien's first time on the stage was here at Breezes. So I always try to encourage new people, I try to encourage locals, so I don't bring in a lot of international acts. . . . We push really, really, really hard to keep it Bahamian, to employ as many locals as we can to keep it moving. (Carlton McPhee, interview with the author, February 19, 2016)

This emphasis on local talent and entertainers sets Breezes apart from its competitors in the Bahamian market. Explaining the difference between Breezes' approach to entertainment and that of Sandals, Carlton points out that much of this has to do with corporate policy and practice.

Most of Sandals properties they have the Jamaicans who they bring in from Jamaica to head their departments. So of course, they gravitate more to their culture . . . but here [at Breezes], it has always been a Bahamian, for the twenty years. I've been here fifteen, and prior to me there were two more Bahamians that were the entertainment managers. A Jamaican came in to set up the department but they turned it over to a Bahamian to run. And that plays a major part on who knows the music . . . who knows the people on island. . . . The owners here, the Issa family, really, really, invest in our Bahamian artists. (Carlton McPhee, interview with the author, February 19, 2016)[33]

In addition to all of the daytime activities available to guests, Carlton manages three discrete spaces within which music is the principal attraction—the main stage, a piano bar, and a disco. The daily programing in these spaces (live music in the first two, a DJ in the disco) is designed to overlap such that guests have more than one choice for entertainment for a good portion of each evening. As such, the main stage program runs from 8:30 to midnight, the piano bar is active from 9:30 to 1 AM, and the disco gets started at midnight and runs until 2 AM. The piano bar and the disco are both located on the lower level, tucked away from the open spaces that characterize the main floor, and provide a more intimate setting for their guests. Carlton has complete autonomy over personnel decisions and focuses on variety, rotating artists in and out of the program on a regular basis. Most artists entertain for a year or so and are then rotated off for a while before being brought back into the mix (a few are kept on much longer due to their popularity). He explained that "the reason why I go through a lot of entertainers a lot and switch them up and bring them in and turn them around and all that stuff is because our repeat clientele is so high that sometimes you need to try to offer different people to get a different vibe."[34] Indeed, repeat visitors—a loyal clientele—is one of the hallmarks of Breezes Bahamas.

Although Carlton is responsible for who he inserts into his entertainment plans from day to day, the corporation itself has a very clear and branded approach to the overall guest experience at their resorts, including an emphasis on themes for most days. This allows the company to set expectations among its repeat clientele that Tuesdays at Breezes are, for instance, always "Pajama Tuesdays," and that Thursdays at the resort are

Table 1.1. Entertainment Themes and Performers at Breezes

Monday	Pajama Tuesday	Oldies Wednesday	Toga Thursday	Friday	Super Saturday	Sumo Sunday
	Funky D	Funky D	Funky D	Funky D	Funky D	Funky D
Karaoke	Guest and Staff Talent Show	Oldies Cabaret Show	Island Spice Show	Mr. Unique (magician)	Trixie (fire dancer)	Game Trivia
The Illusionist			Anishka Lewis or Sonovia Pierre	Entertainment Staff Dancers	Action Jackson (limbo dancer)	
Karaoke				Alia Coley	Colours Junkanoo rush	
	Funky D	Funky D	Funky D	Funky D	Funky D	Funky D

themed as "Toga Thursdays." Regardless of where a Breezes property is actually located, guests who have stayed at a Breezes resort in the past will know that their "Super Saturday" will feature all things local (food, music, art, etc.). With the exception of Mondays, when the main floor stage hosts an illusionist and a karaoke singalong (it's Funky D's night off), each evening's entertainment follows a basic plan. Funky D and the Summer Breeze Band play an opening set for about an hour. Funky D then takes a break and a variety show takes over. Each night, this variety show, which lasts between sixty and ninety minutes, includes a range of performers connected to the night's theme and backed by tracked accompaniment or the Summer Breeze Band (depending on the performers). Funky D follows this variety show with a second set, wrapping up the show at midnight (see table 1.1).

The cornerstone of Breezes' entertainment offerings, then, is the presence of Funky D and the Summer Breeze Band, and this has been the case since 1995. This long tenure is, in itself, a remarkable achievement, but in the wake of decades of decline in the live music scene, Breezes is now not only the resort with the longest-tenured live band, but also the only hotel in Nassau that still employs a resident band six nights a week. What used to be a commonplace feature of the tourist experience in the Bahamas has, in the course of the last two decades (and for the reasons detailed above), become a novelty—a novelty that, according to Carlton, attracts quite a following. "The only thing that is consistent with us is Funky D. . . . They [our guests] love it. . . . Funky and the Summer Breeze Band have a repeat clientele that's crazy. Yeah, people just come back. People now know that he goes on vacation the first two weeks of September, so you have people that will not plan their vacation during that time that he's not here."[35]

In addition to first-time guests and repeat visitors, Breezes also caters to local businesses and individuals. Carlton notes that

> We get a lot of local business in the evening. Breezes do a lot of business with companies that bring people in on passes when they want an outing. What will happen is we would have a bank who wants to do employee recognition. And they'll say we'll bring fifty-five employees in. So then they would purchase passes, they'll bring them in and they'll come in for dinner and then they'll add the shows and any entertainment that we have for the evening they can participate in. (Carlton McPhee, interview with the author, February 19, 2016)

It is worth pausing here to consider the complicated dynamics of this kind of access for purchase. The real economics of selling an all-inclusive model are predicated on producing its opposite—on exclusivity.[36] As such, even though access to beachfront areas is a constitutional right throughout much of the Caribbean, for instance, resorts often cordon off their properties with fencing, gates, hedges, and security guards. This makes local presence in resort spaces at best complicated and at worst impossible (a theme frequently raised by local critics of the industry). The tensions accumulated in and through the gated/exclusive nature of all-inclusive resorts are thus best understood as one of the hidden costs of exclusivity (costs paid, in this case, not by hotel guests but by the local population). The rather moderate policy outlined by Carlton, too, remains focused on the economics of exclusivity, even as it is anchored in the register of class. In this management strategy, locals (or businesses) may purchase entry into the exclusive experiences offered at the hotel, but the price of entry ensures that only a certain type of (likely professional) local will be able to afford this luxury.[37] The exclusivity of the resort space, then, reinforces class distinctions while also creating the impetus for further class divisions within local communities.[38] This, too, is a dynamic that musicians need to understand as they perform in these spaces.

On any given night, then, the entertainers at Breezes are encountering audiences composed of locals and tourists and charged with providing the brand of fun that distinguishes Breezes from its competition. Management does not dictate what to wear, what to play, or even how to approach their contributions to the evening's entertainment. They are judged solely by whether they succeed in getting positive responses from their audience. As such, Carlton is pleased when he sees comments on tripadvisor.com about how much fun a particular performance was. He is concerned when he sees that an artist is not producing such results. The bottom-line metric, then, is calculated based on tourist satisfaction. In other words, it's not (only) about how technically good or aesthetically beautiful a given performance is, but rather about how much positive buzz the performer generates among guests.

As laudable as the emphasis on hiring local musicians and entertainers is, the framework for performance (the conditions under which these locals labor) does not necessarily guarantee that guests at Breezes will hear a lot of Bahamian music. Quite the contrary, the imperative to satisfy guests is more than likely to result in tourists hearing music they are already familiar with and are delighted to hear in a new context — contributing to celebrations of shared cosmopolitanisms — than in hearing a new Bahamian tune. This is a complex matter and I will return to it below when discussing the careers of Funky D and Alia Coley, but suffice it to say at this point that, in the absence of an articulated cultural policy, and in the empty spaces formerly occupied by a now weak and dysfunctional musicians' union, musicians are crafting their performances to secure a paycheck from the immediate management regime of the hotel they depend on for their livelihoods. Even if they wanted to perform Bahamian music (and, as we'll see, it is not clear what this might mean or include), the logic of playing for tourists with the primary goal of satisfaction in mind dictates a pragmatic approach to craft and repertory. And even as Carlton attempts to program local entertainment, he, too, is confronted with a significant dilemma as to how to define the range of what constitutes "Bahamian" entertainment — and this largely because of the mainstream forms of entertainment that have become staples of the local music and entertainment landscape. A good example of this dilemma is the programing offered on "Super Saturdays."

Saturdays are local nights throughout the Breezes chain, and in the Bahamas this means a variety show focused on entertainment historically considered particularly Bahamian. As such (and as illustrated in table 1.1) Funky D is joined by a fire dancer, a limbo dancer, and a junkanoo rush. This is an interesting collection of entertainments to offer guests — entertainments that, with the exception of the junkanoo rush, represent more an act of nostalgia and exoticism than an address to contemporary trends in Bahamian music and entertainment. Fire dancing and limbo dancing were prime entertainments during the so-called golden age of Bahamian tourism (the 1950s and 1960s). However, even though there are plenty of excellent dancers in the Bahamas, few are learning how to limbo or fire dance in the contemporary moment. Today's dancers in the Bahamas are, instead, developing their craft while listening to hip-hop, dancehall, and soca — genres of dance that would not work on "local" night at Breezes as currently conceived. Local night at Breezes, then, illustrates in its very programming the extent to which local musical and dance practices have transformed during the last several decades.

During our conversation, Carlton acknowledged this reality and admitted that he would (perhaps even at the risk of losing some autonomy) like to see more direction from the government on the issue of how to think about Bahamian arts and culture. But — and I repeat here the crucial distinction — while Breezes hires local musicians and entertainers, maintains a resident band, and offers a Bahamian show, none of these efforts necessarily mean that tourists are experiencing a soundtrack consisting of local genres or encountering Bahamian cultural productions that have contemporary currency in the Bahamas. Importantly, the extent to which this state of affairs is read as positive, neutral, or negative depends heavily on the generational and vocational subject position of the individuals making such determinations. Older musicians who remember the 1960s, cultural activists, and hotel managers of a certain generation, see in this trajectory a narrative of loss. Younger musicians, tourism officials, and younger hotel staff connect this trajectory to the clearly cosmopolitan stance of the Bahamas with respect to both local tastes and tourist expectations.

Funky D and Alia Coley

You don't always play what you like, you know. Sometimes I don't like it, but you know, the audience likes it.

—*Funky D (interview, 2016)*

Some songs are popular, but for me, I don't want to sing them. . . .
I really have to be feeling a song. It has to work for me too.

—*Alia Coley (interview, 2016)*

Funky D (David Ferguson) was born in Nassau on June 1, 1958. He went through primary school and high school without thinking much about music, with the exception of his participation in choir and the occasional solo at church. He went to the College of the Bahamas, studying science, and then secured a job with the attorney general's office upon graduation, where he worked for ten years. It was during the years immediately following college that Funky D became interested in music. He recalls, "I didn't grow up on Bahamian music, really because, as you know, a lot of pop music was being played on the radio in the 1970s." But he had a good voice and was an excellent dancer. As he recalls, in the late 1970s,

> I joined a dance group called the Backstabbers. They had a talent competition at one of the clubs in the Bahamas called the Backside. We won the competition. The Backside was a disco band club and the Frontside was a native show, the King and Knight's show [one of the last surviving nightclubs on Bay Street]. Because we won we were given a chance to appear in the Frontside . . . and we told them that we were not only a dance group but we sang, like the Temptations and the O'Jays—we modeled ourselves on them. And eventually we played all the spots in Nassau. . . . There was an exchange between the Bahamian and the United States musicians out of Atlantic City. And I went with my group . . . but unfortunately we couldn't be billed as the Backstabbers because there was another group in the States with that name, so we changed our name to the Nassau Movement. So Fred [Ferguson] and them would go as High Voltage and then we would go as the Nassau Movement. (Funky D, interview with the author, February 20, 2016)

When the exchange program was completed, the band returned, fully professional and ready to bring their shows back to the clubs in New Providence, but the Backstabbers experienced the effects of the contraction of the scene described earlier. According to Funky D, "When we came back to Nassau, there was nothing for us to do. When we were in Nassau before we played at Ronnie's Rebel Room and there were a lot of venues for us. Eventually all that stop. So we came back and we had nothing to do because we were a show group, not a dance band. We did shows! Those venues were gone. Cat and Fiddle, Ronnie's Rebel Room, the Drum Beat . . . all of these places had died out so we had to disband in the mid-1980s."[39] Funky D continued with his day job and, in 1985, took a job at the Bank of Montreal (now the Bank of the Bahamas), where he then worked for thirty years until his retirement in 2015. Having a steady salary and a good job meant that Funky D had options. He could perform for free or for much less than musicians who relied on music as a full-time profession, for instance. He was also able much more easily to procure equipment and secure loans when needed.

Shortly after he accepted the banking job, Funky D found his way to an experience that launched him into a very different relationship to Bahamian music and to performance.

> One night I stepped into a small club called the Family Island Lounge. . . . The Summer Breeze Band, the band I play with now, they were playing there at the time . . . and that's where I really got introduced to Bahamian music. . . . So I went in for a talent show and I went up and sang . . . the leader of the band came up to me and said, man you know you've got a good sound, man, would you like to join the band? And he already had a lead singer so [it was complicated] . . . he said, I can't pay you right now . . . eventually we'll have to get rid of the lead singer. So I worked there for two years for free! So eventually I became the singer of the band and we played there between 1987–89. . . . I was introduced to Bahamian music because the manager of the club, Mr. Rudy Grant, he insisted we play 95 percent Bahamian music. We worked seven nights a week, and it was packed every night, mostly Bahamians because this was *way* over the hill. And I was amazed at how people reacted to Bahamian music. . . . Goombay music, Ronnie Butler, Eddie Minnis, we played all them guys. . . . Eventually the leader of the band left and the band disbanded. So then, again, I was in limbo again. That was in 1989. (Funky D, interview with the author, February 20, 2016)

The next step for Funky D—the step that transformed him into a hotel musician—was to make the decision to become a solo artist. And in 1991, he took on his stage name (Funky D), recorded an album of songs with the help of Fred Ferguson, K.B., and a few other Bahamian songwriters, and decided to restart the Summer Breeze Band, this time as its leader. The band promptly won an open audition to play at the Radisson Hotel in Nassau. Funky D hasn't been without a hotel gig in the twenty-seven years since (a remarkable feat under any circumstances, and worth dwelling on for a moment). It was during this period in the early to mid-1990s that Funky D began to learn his trade as a hotel musician and to develop his approach to playing (primarily) for tourists. By the time he and his band were hired on at Breezes in 1995, he had a considerable skill set and a truly massive repertory of songs to draw from while entertaining guests. He recalls that his contracts both at the Radisson and at Breezes were very open, making no explicit demands regarding musical style, dress code, or staging. "I've never signed a contract where people tell you what to play. But you know what you're *expected* to play. Breezes didn't stipulate it either . . . just standard stuff."[40]

But the question of expectations presses on musicians like Funky D from two directions—from the tourists and locals who make up his audiences from night to night, and from the management at Breezes. Funky D has much to say about how this works and (at times) doesn't work. He has no illusions about satisfying everyone in this complicated set of relations, but approaches each set with the goal of achieving the best outcome for both his audiences and his employer. This requires a sensitive and flexible approach, and Funky D explains that he has a particular way of handling this aspect of his job. "My performance is always up close and personal. I like to look you right in the eye. And then you get to learn . . . how far to push somebody. 'Cause you could tell. So it comes with experience." He uses this information both to determine his set (which is never fixed before a show) and to select the individuals with whom he will be able to have particular kinds of fun that the whole audience will vicariously be able to enjoy (efforts that also reinforce the branding of the property). This fun can include having individuals demonstrate sexualized dance moves (such as wining)[41] after he teaches them to the audience, making particular audience members the subject of slightly off-color jokes, or inviting women to dance with him.

A brief example illustrates this point well. On Friday, February 19, 2016, toward the end of his first set, Funky D taught everyone in the audience how to wine by using the famous 1980s soca tune "Dollar Wine" by Collin Lucas. When he was satisfied that everyone in the audience had explored this particular use of their bodies, he called on one woman, in particular, with whom he had been interacting from very early on in the show. He invited her up onto the stage with the band in order to be more clearly seen by all.⁴² Funky D then explained that there is another move, in addition to wining, called a jook (a stabbing pelvic thrust). He demonstrated it for her to loud laughter and applause from the audience. Then he had her try it, and, as she worked through her motions, he looked knowingly at the audience, generating another loud response. The teaching completed, he stood close to her and, playing on the lyrics of Collin Lucas's song, told her that he wanted her to be like a cash machine and that, when he asked her, she should give him all her dollars. This delighted the crowd, and, because he had carefully selected his dancing partner, resulted in a fun, sexualized, and very funny moment that he then repeated by, in turn, giving her all of his dollars. But it is important to recognize the skill in reading people and his audiences without which Funky D might have made everyone quite uncomfortable in the course of that series of events. He explains his approach and his priorities as follows:

> I shift my set on what I see. First thing I do, when I come to work at night, is I look in the audience. I look in the audience to see who's there. I don't know the first song I'm going to sing. Never in my career has there been a set list. What I do, I come to work and I look at the audience. Look at the age group, look at the amount of couples. So I say okay, tonight's going to be a lot of lovey-dovey stuff. Some nights you get a lot of Bahamians in there. So I know okay, going to be plenty of scraping and raking tonight. . . . But if you have a script and your audience is not into that you could lose them. (Funky D, interview with the author, February 20, 2016)

He goes on to point out that "when you have the older audience, they want the Harry Belafonte stuff, because that's what they knew as island . . . can you do 'MaryAnn' or 'Island in the Sun'? There are still some people that that's what they know as island music. Some of them believe if it doesn't have a steel pan in it, it isn't island, either." But he also struggles with the limited musical horizons of many of his audience members. So, for instance, as he points out, "it'll be so strange. . . . I'll play a Bob Marley song, right? Somebody come up, how come you ain't play no Bob Marley yet? 'cause they only know 'One Love,' 'Three Little Birds,' that's it. . . . [If] You don't play one of those, they figure you ain't played no reggae. So you deal with stuff like that with the audience, so my repertory is really wide" (Funky D, interview with the author, February 20, 2016).

Depending on the makeup of the audience and the kinds of requests they are making as he walks through the crowd, Funky D will chart a path through the evening, and his band follows him on that journey, knowing from long experience the cues and comments pointing to a particular song or a shift in repertory. Perhaps the most complicated audience management issue for Funky D to navigate in the course of a week's performances is the relationship between repeat visitors who are returning to hear Funky D play and those guests who are staying a bit longer than an average tourist might. The overlap between these two constituencies can sometimes cause guests to hear the same song multiple times over the course of a week. And if the guests complain about this in a public review forum such as tripadvisor.com, then the expectations of the management become an issue for Funky D. Funky D explains this dilemma as follows:

Management here are very testy about tripadvisor.com. So the hotel brought me in, said well there were a couple of comments [on tripadvisor.com] saying that you play the same song. So I said . . . let me tell you what's happening . . . we have a lot of return guests coming in. So if I play "Hello" tonight, for somebody, and this European sitting all the way in the back [hears it]. Then when someone come, "Man, last time we were here you played 'Hello' for us, please play that for us!" So I play that again, the fella in the back is like, "Jesus Christ, I just heard that song last night, man!" . . . That's going to happen no matter what . . . dealing with repeat guests, you're going to get that. Do you want me to tell the guests that I played that song last night so I can't play it tonight? Eventually they said, you know what, we see what you're talking about. (Funky D, interview with the author, February 20, 2016)

Expectations, expectations! And even as this brings him into the crosshairs of management at Breezes, it is precisely this aspect of Funky D's day-to-day performative reality that also engenders the most interesting and vexing *repertorial* dilemma for Funky D. That is, expectations also inform decisions about how much "Bahamian" music to play on a given night. Audiences tend to have a sense of what island music is — that is, they recognize soca, calypso, and reggae, in particular, as Caribbean genres. They are also likely to have encountered these genres more readily before arriving in Nassau than any Bahamian sounds. As such, the trick for Funky D is that, as he characterizes it, "I sneak in Bahamian music." And if locals in attendance ask him why he isn't playing much Bahamian music, he responds by pointing out that "you can't just play Bahamian music, 'cause the audience is so wide." It is deeply ironic that the albums that Funky D records and sells to tourists (he has released five over the years) are thoroughgoing musical tributes to the Bahamas, featuring rake-n-scrape and junkanoo rhythms and a deeply local sensibility throughout. So tourists head home from their vacations, having encountered very little in the way of what Funky D would consider Bahamian music in live settings, but in possession of a souvenir album that is the embodiment of current Bahamian popular music.

And this brings me back to one of the central dilemmas at issue in this chapter—the difficulty of identifying the musical "it" that the Bahamas is selling to tourists. For starters, the musical soundtrack to these encounters is today much more likely to be soca or reggae than any "Bahamian" music. The joy of these shared cosmopolitanisms notwithstanding, even though both Carlton and Funky D want more local music to be part of the tourist experience, both are caught in the reality that expectations drive reviews, and that reviews directly impact their employment. The best Funky D can do is to send tourists home with recordings of the sounds he wishes he could offer them in person. The best Carlton can do is to hire local musicians, organize nostalgia-driven "local nights," and hope for the best. And yet the open question here revolves around what qualifies as Bahamian music in the first place. It strikes me that this is an excellent illustration of some of the frictions that accompany global connections.

In order to continue exploring this question, I turn now to the career of Alia Coley, which offers a counterexample to that of Funky D. Born March 15, 1974, Alia grew up singing in church, and by the time she was in high school she had developed a passion for music. She knew much earlier than did Funky D that she wanted to make music a career.

> By high school I pretty much knew that that's what my profession would be. And then to top it off, I actually entered a song competition called On-Stage (that was in 1991). I graduated in 1992. So the finalists had the opportunity to go off and perform at the Apollo. And I went to the Apollo, and I was on that stage . . . and I think the song that I performed was "His Eye Is on the Sparrow." . . . So I was sent into the semifinals and I came in fourth overall in the Caribbean. (Alia Coley, interview with the author, February 21, 2016)

Two years after graduating from high school, Alia matriculated at Berklee College of Music and completed two spring semesters there, returning to Nassau in between. When she returned the second time, she was hired to sing in a large production at the Crystal Palace Casino. "It was called the Caribe show. It was like a combination of Cuban and Bahamian fused . . . at the Crystal Palace Ball . . . that was my first gig in 1996. I went right into the hotel scene. That was it for Berklee, I didn't go back."[43] From that moment on, she has never worked a day job in Nassau, preferring to focus on being a full-time professional singer. This involved networking, singing in multiple venues each week, and generally being willing to play under a wider range of circumstances than Funky D.

In 1997, when the Caribe show ended, Alia secured two nights at Sandals Royal Bahamian resort, where she was backed for hour-long sets by the VIP Band (still in residence there at the time) and another night at the Crystal Palace. She also added a night at Breezes and stayed on there for several years. Reflecting on her approach to sets in these early years, she remembers that "it was more about what I liked to perform, but I also kept in mind that these were guests so [I had to] at least give them an experience of some Bahamian music. So I would throw a little Bahamian music in there. But for the most part R&B — I was known as a balladeer. I did a lot of ballads back then." She also points out that this was the period when she began "to grow as an entertainer. Because initially when I came out I was very reserved on stage. Don't move too much, just very all about the voice . . . but to be as comfortable as I am now, I've grown to be that way over time." By 2002, she had added a show at Atlantis to her weekly schedule, playing five nights a week in four different venues.

In 2005, she briefly moved to Detroit to record her first album. She recorded her second album in Los Angeles in 2008. On both occasions, the hotels where she had been employed were happy to let her rotate off for a few months and then bring her back into the mix upon her return. She describes her current work week as follows:

> My typical week starts with Sunday at Ocean Club from 6 to 9. Monday . . . I'm off. And then on Tuesdays I go to Sandals Exuma, forty-five-minute show. I come back on Wednesday morning and then I'm off that day. And then Thursday nights I'm at Atlantis from eight to twelve. That's my longest gig . . . at the Coral Towers in the lobby there . . . lots of kids. . . . And then Friday nights I'm at Breezes. . . .

Surprisingly, I work twice on Saturdays but one is only every other Saturday. So every other Saturday I'm at Atlantis during the day at [the] poolside. Well you know no one really gives a damn that much. So I mean they're just having a great day at the beach or whatever, they do enjoy, they do engage, but for the most part they're just kinda hanging around the pool. But I try to do more Caribbean, more Bahamian [there], and then I throw in some Adele and that's when they're like [what?!] and all the cameras come out. And then [every Saturday] evening I'm back at Sandals [Royal Bahamian] . . . forty-five-minute show. (Alia Coley, interview with the author, February 21, 2016)

What is striking about this list of venues is how very different they are from each other. Nightclub main stages at all-inclusive resorts (Sandals Exuma, Breezes, and Sandals Royal Bahamian) are interspersed with lobbies (Atlantis Coral Towers) and pools (Atlantis) at full-service resorts and a restaurant at a high-end hotel (Ocean Club). She thus also plays for very different constituencies throughout the week, often to indifferent (pool, restaurant) or raucous (kids) audiences. She is, moreover, keenly aware that her ability to perform mainstream pop is, in itself, a form of exoticism for her audiences and also a vehicle for developing shared cosmopolitanisms. Her typical work week thus requires a different set of skills than does Funky D's. And this fact informs her approach to her craft. Because she plays for such different audiences, she has focused on making sure that she is, herself, ready to bring the same energy to each performance, regardless of context or audience. "The way I approach when I'm about to perform is pretty much the same. My standards remain the same. I don't care if it's one person, they're going to have a ball, because I'm having a ball."[44]

A major difference between Alia's approach to performance and entertainment and that of Funky D is that, as the epigraphs to this section point out, while Funky D is willing to perform songs that he does not enjoy in order to serve his audience, Alia makes her personal enjoyment of the material a principal criterion for performing it in the first place. Another stark contrast between these two musicians can be drawn along lines of self-identification. Although Alia knows the Bahamian catalogue and is steeped in rake-n-scrape and junkanoo styles (over the years, she has sung backup vocals on and composed many of the most popular local songs), she considers herself a popular musician who happens to be Bahamian. As such, she approaches her audiences not primarily as tourists, but rather as potential fans—her concerts not as encounters between locals and nonlocals, but as occasions to perform for the widest possible public. "I don't think about playing for tourists. I am just performing for people. First and foremost I do it because I love it. I am extremely passionate about it and I get really a sense of fulfillment when I see the response on people's faces and their reaction to what I do. So I never looked at it like that."[45] This perspective is also reflected in the materials she chooses to record for herself. Both of her albums are deeply influenced by R&B, and stake a claim as mainstream popular music. The Bahamas are not sonically significant in either project, and neither album is designed as a souvenir recording.

This does not mean, however, that Alia doesn't take audience expectations seriously. She recalls a recent show in Exuma: "Last week Tuesday, these people, I don't know what they were on. 'Cause sometimes the crowd is like that. Sometimes they're hyped, and then sometimes they just want to sit and listen and just appreciate whatever. But some are like rowdy and they're like let's go, and they can't wait for the next fast song. So . . . it depends, okay, my crowd is into that, I'll switch up like on the spur of the moment, switch up the repertoire, 'cause if they wanna party then let's keep going to the fast ones." She continues, pointing out that "it's important for you to be able to read your audience and feed off them. Because you want the energy to be reciprocated, if you know what I mean. If I'm giving off something, and you feel it, then it comes back, vice versa." Alia currently plays at three different all-inclusive sites on three different days of the week, eliminating some of the challenges faced by Funky D, who performs in the same venue six days a week. As such, she has a fresh audience virtually every time she takes the stage and could, conceivably, play a very similar set every week. Even so, she chooses to mix things up, claiming, "I don't really like to be so predictable that when I do come in on Thursday nights they're [the staff] like well we kinda know what she's going to sing next, I hate that. . . . So I like to be spontaneous and do different things and keep it fresh. I like to feed off the energy of what's happening in front of me."[46]

A final point of contrast between Alia and Funky D is the fact that, since around 2004, she has played almost exclusively to tracked accompaniment. This preference has developed out of her experience, during the late 1990s and early 2000s, of playing with multiple bands (VIP Band at Sandals, G Notes at Atlantis, Summer Breeze Band at Breezes) and not always being satisfied with the results. On several occasions she found the bands simply unprofessional or, alternatively, unwilling to learn new material (Alia incorporates at least ten new songs into her repertory each year). She grew tired of subpar performances and a lack of enthusiasm for her material on the part of the bands. "That for me killed the band concept . . . unless I'm 100 percent sure that I have musicians that are professional . . . let me just use the tracks." She recalls her relief when, a few years after starting her weekly performances at Sandals Exuma, she was able to move to tracked accompaniment.

But performing to tracked accompaniment brings with it other potential challenges. Alia acknowledges as much when talking about her craft. She takes pride in knowing the lyrics to all of her songs by heart and points out that it is important to her to be able to switch effortlessly between very different repertories in a given set and by request, not least because her audiences sometimes view her performances as a sort of karaoke-like show. Flawless execution is, for her, a mark of professionalism that counteracts this perception.

Another significant risk is reliance on technology for the faithful reproduction of her backing tracks, coupled with a loss of control over the spontaneity that an artist like Funky D is able to command from song to song and even within a given song. This is the case because, although she works from iTunes on her Mac laptop whenever possible, she is not always in close proximity to it in the course of performance. On Sunday, February 20, 2016, she performed at the Ocean Club and stood right next to her computer, which was plugged into her own portable PA system, which she also controlled as needed. The setting at the Ocean Club is fairly low-tech (no lights, no stage, no built-in sound system) and therefore rather easy to manage. It also affords Alia a great deal of flexibility should she need to shift up her set. Skipping or adding a song is as easy as sifting through a playlist in iTunes.

When I saw her two nights earlier at Breezes, however, Alia faced a rather more complicated and much less ideal scenario for performance. The control room for the sound system is located behind the stage and there is no direct access to it (although there is a window through which the engineer can see the stage, there is no way to open it). She must, therefore, get a set list together before even heading out on stage and then use hand signals to indicate any changes to the running order.

Another concern related to tracked accompaniment is the quality and reliability of the technology itself. During her performance, the digital audio converter was evidently failing and made a hash of several moments during two of her tracks, forcing her to forge through on the strength of her vocal performance even as the backing track was chopped up and compromised. There can be no doubt that tracks offer a sense of certainty often absent when a band is playing live, but it is also true that they introduce other challenges to performance that make it necessary to strike a different set of accommodations and compromises along the way. What is clear, however, is that, for Alia, the question of *what* is better in the Bahamas isn't the right question. For her, it is a matter first of performing a brand of professionalism and an identification with mainstream popular music, and only secondarily a matter of connecting performance to a recognition of Bahamian cultural production. In fact, for her, R&B and pop music are as integral to the contemporary Bahamian cultural scene as are rake-n-scrape or junkanoo.

Conclusion

Although the careers and approaches of Funky D and Alia Coley are divergent, they connect within the larger context of music touristics in the Bahamas to illustrate the centrality of the all-inclusive hotel as a space within which questions about the political economy of music and sound are being raised. The all-inclusive hotel is the space within which the significance and value of local musical production is being weighed. It is also the space that is illustrating the local importance of genres such as R&B, soca, reggae, and pop music — illustrating the frictions attendant to global connections in that the definition of "local" in a space as cosmopolitan as Nassau is complicated at best.

For most hotels, the idea of a resident band has today become untenable. This is the case not only because of the relatively high cost of securing such a band, but also because there are several attractive alternatives available to the hotels, including small combos (two or three people) and soloists performing to tracked accompaniment, both of which can be rotated regularly for variety. In this climate it is, in fact, a solo artist such as Alia who stands the best chance of getting hired to entertain guests. But the challenge is to envision what the future of music looks like in Bahamian hotels. As hotelier George Myers sees it,

The entertainment industry will have to adapt to meet the requirements of the modern visitor and the new tourism industry. Today, the band is not nearly the attraction it was back in the olden days. Therefore the entertainment today has to become an attraction for the visitor to want to be able to participate in it; otherwise it doesn't do any good. Whereas hotels used to have one main dining room with a captive audience, major hotels today have six to eight restaurants. Each one is themed differently, which suggests you wouldn't have the same kind of music in each one. In the age of technology, where hotels make widespread use of electronic sound systems, bands are no longer cost effective if they are only serving as a means of providing background music. Those are the kinds of things that have changed. Today, a guest who comes here for seven days does not want to eat in the same place every night. They want a variety of restaurant offerings, a variety of menus, and likewise a variety of entertainment. There has to be a least four, five different things. It can't be the same thing every night. (BHTA 2012)

And these comments point to the larger issues circulating around the political economy of music already outlined in this chapter. Myers is correct in asserting that sound systems can provide background music quite cost-effectively. Musicians, therefore, need to offer additional entertainment value to their audiences if they want a chance at being hired. But what it means to entertain, what a contemporary "attraction" might sound like in an era when all-inclusive hotels are the primary venues within which tourists are likely to hear any live music, is a question likely worthy of some scrutiny in the Bahamas—and this regardless of whether an articulated cultural policy is ultimately found to be necessary, desirable, or practical.

As the case studies of Funky D and Alia Coley have illustrated, musicians performing in all-inclusive hotels necessarily continue to play to their audience's expectations, looking to generate positive reviews and, along with these, happy entertainment managers. In this environment, as Funky D's career illustrates, one option is that Bahamian music must be "snuck in." Funky D is concerned, here, with a particular kind of authenticity tied to place (Taylor 1997), and also committed to a particular vision of the history of entertainment in the Bahamas. But, viewed from the perspective of Alia's career, the all-inclusive hotel can also lead to an expansion of the range of what might be considered Bahamian, or local, music. Alia is quite convinced that her performances are all Bahamian, regardless of genre, primarily because she herself is Bahamian. This quite different approach to defining "local" music is an extension of the deeply cosmopolitan musical exchanges that have marked Bahamian entertainment since at least the 1950s and that have continued to be shaped by new sonic possibilities and shifts into new performative contexts.

In the contemporary moment, then, the entire definition of what entertainment should be is an open question, intimately related to the much larger issue of globalization but focused through and highlighted in the particular frictions that animate musical performances in all-inclusive hotels. This chapter, then, affords both an affirmation of and a partial response to Anna Tsing's useful statement and query, "Global connections are everywhere. So how does one study the global?" (2005, 1). One option, it seems to me, is to work with one (hotel) musician at a time. In answering in this fashion, I have moved, in this final section, beyond the frame of the all-inclusive hotel or even of the Bahamas in order to connect these ideas more generally to musicians working in tourist venues. And this is because, and here I am paraphrasing Jocelyne Guilbault,[47] "how to locate oneself in this globalized tourism industry" remains a pressing question for all musicians working in today's tourism sector.

ACKNOWLEDGMENTS

This chapter could not have been completed without the generous support of Carlton McPhee, entertainment manager at Breezes. I am very grateful both for his willingness to grant me access to the property and for taking the time to entertain my questions while there. Many thanks are also due to Funky D and Alia Coley, who both afforded me access to their busy lives and found time to discuss their careers with me. Finally, I owe a debt of gratitude to my dear friend Fred Ferguson for his support and assistance throughout this project.

NOTES

1. By shared cosmopolitanisms, I suggest that some encounters between musicians and vacationers are mediated through a range of engagements with transnational forms of popular culture (whether music, dance, film, or art) that can provide the foundation for temporary solidarities and afford moments of connection that transcend the all-inclusive hotel's production of difference. On this subject, see Guilbault in this volume.

2. Focusing on identity has also, of course, been fairly critiqued for the ways in

which it can slip into essentialist arguments or uncritical approaches to authenticity, and many scholars working in the Caribbean have found in Edouard Glissant's insistence on relation (1997) a powerful means of productively resisting such pitfalls.

3. For more information on this topic, see Leslie Meier's *Popular Music as Promotion: Music and Branding in the Digital Age* (2017), and Joel Beckerman and Tyler Gray's *Sonic Boom: How Sound Transforms the Way We Think, Feel, and Buy* (2014).

4. These frictions are also animated and exacerbated by the colonial specters and the neocolonial dependencies that remain ingrained in the political economy of the tourism industry. See Polly Pattullo (2005) and Mimi Sheller (2003).

5. For more exhaustive treatments of this topic, see Rommen (2011), Cleare (2007), and Craton and Saunders (1998). In addition, although the Family Islands and Grand Bahama were developed as destinations as well, for the purposes of this study, I will focus on events and developments in Nassau.

6. The Bahamas advertised widely in print media, opened tourism offices in major cities, and partnered with travel agencies for special promotions.

7. Figures excerpted from Cleare (2007, 148–49).

8. In 2012, the organization changed its name to the Bahamas Hotel and Tourism Association.

9. Cleare notes that, between 1953 and 1959, seven new hotels were completed in Nassau.

10. Labor unions, too, coalesced and became more active during this moment, advocating for the rights and benefits of their memberships. Constituencies variously taking advantage of organized union representation included hotel workers and caterers, taxi drivers, nightclub owners, musicians and entertainers, and restaurant owners, among others.

11. This resolution was made by Sir Etienne Dupuch on January 23, 1956.

12. The following promotional passage from *Nassau Magazine* is rather typical of these marketing strategies: "The tribal tone beats of Africa, handed down through a half dozen generations, mingle here with the sophisticated rhythms of Broadway and the London Music Halls as Nassau tunes up for another record season. The hotels large and small, the Bay Street 'hot spots,' and the native 'Over-the-Hill' emporiums of goombay and calypso have tuned pianos and tightened skinheads of bongo drums to entertain what the travel world has predicted will be the biggest invasion yet of music-hungry, fun-seeking vacationers." This preview of the 1957 season goes on to describe the "tribal tone beats" offered at many of the venues around Nassau, going on to cast Bahamian musicians and singers variously as "penetrat[ing] the eardrums," "jungle queens," and "brash," while contrasting these with the "sophisticated rhythms" of the white foreign artists and "maestros" hired to play at the hotels" (quoted in Rommen 2011, 95).

13. George Symonette, for instance, sold albums that described his music in the following terms: "Strolling troubadours have long been one of the romantic features of the Nassau background, which especially appeals to the visitor and temporary resident in the Bahamas. The *untutored, inbred talent of these rhythm-conscious 'natives'* expresses itself, much like old folk-songs, in lyrics with local appeal and native dialect" (Symonette 1955, emphasis mine).

14. Peanuts Taylor, interview by Charles Carter, *Bahamians*, Island 102.9 FM, May 3, 2003.

15. Tourism figures excerpted from Cleare (2007).

16. According to Andrew Barnett, George Myers, and Robert Sands (all members of the Bahamas Hotel and Tourism Association), "during the 50s and 60s, particularly, live music generally flourished. It was standard for hotels to have live music during the day and night. There was a band by the pool and a band by the bar. . . . The Nassau Beach Hotel had bands inside and outside; bands at dinner time and bands late at night. . . . The hotel employed live bands on a full time basis in 1967. . . . The Nassau Beach hotel also had five to six local bands as an integral part of its operation in the 70s and 80s" (BHTA 2012).

17. See Rommen (2011).

18. For a more detailed account of this moment in Bahamian entertainment, see Rommen (2011).

19. Remembering the Over-the-Hill scene, Freddy Munnings Jr. points out that "artists not only appeared on the Cat and Fiddle stage, but they mastered the art of performance in that space. They were also nurtured at the Central Highway Inn, established by Percy Munnings, and the nightclub Hatch on Wulff Road. . . . Nightclubs were incubators of excellence" (BHTA 2012).

20. It is worth pointing out here that many musicians have found alternative spaces within which to train, including church bands. It is also the case that vocalists have not suffered from the lack of venues to the same degree as instrumentalists. Finally, with the increasing reliance of musicians on software and technology during their live performances, the need to rehearse a band to perfection, or to exhibit a particular skill set on an instrument, have become less pressing markers of excellence than the entertainment value offered by their sets.

21. It was during these years that the property eventually purchased and renovated by Breezes was first built. In its first incarnation it was called the Sonesta Beach Hotel and Golf Club. It would later become the Ambassador Beach Hotel before being acquired by Breezes in 1995.

22. Another example of the government's pragmatic and short-term approach to issues involving musicians and entertainers concerns a series of decisions relating to how the cruise ship industry was regulated. Until 1968, cruise ships were required by their contracts to shut down their onboard shops and entertainment before they reached port and to keep them closed until they were again on their way. This policy ensured that passengers would frequent restaurants, nightclubs, and shops while in Nassau. In 1968, however, under increasing pressure from cruise companies, and in need of additional revenues, the government renegotiated the terms of these contracts, allowing cruise ships more autonomy. Musicians, entertainers, nightclub owners, restaurateurs, and taxi drivers were livid, and the debate raged for several years—especially because the Over-the-Hill scene was, at that moment, on its last legs. There was a growing conviction among these constituencies that the government and the Ministry of Tourism had failed them and did not, in fact, have their best interests in mind. This belief was confirmed in 1975 when, over the loud objections of those stake-

holders most directly affected, the Ministry of Tourism announced that it would begin sponsoring native shows on cruise ships while they were in port. This decision provided a few jobs for musicians and entertainers, but nevertheless also contributed to the eventual death of the remaining nightclubs in Nassau, even those located on Bay Street. This set of decisions illustrates well the pressures that drove policy at the Ministry of Tourism during these years.

23. The famous entertainer Ronnie Butler, for instance, pioneered a dance band version of rake-n-scrape, which he then performed as an explicitly nationalist musical style.

24. Ronnie Butler, interview with the author, June 27, 2007.

25. Ray Munnings, interview with the author, July 11, 2009.

26. Nicolette Bethel, interview with Larry Smith, April 22, 2009.

27. Ronald Simms, musician, radio host, and entertainment entrepreneur, puts it as follows: "The musicians' union of today is a very wanting body. The musicians' union that I was a part of back in the 1970s up through the mid-1980s was a very vibrant and very powerful body. Nothing happened in this country musically without the say-so of the musicians' union. Whether that was people coming in to perform, people working on hotel properties, or anything, the musicians' union was a very powerful body. They have lost their clout over the years . . . and the membership of the musicians' union coming along did not feel that they were being sufficiently represented by the musicians' union. They felt they were only paying their levies and their dues and not getting just due. So, as a result, the new musicians that were coming on to the scene simply turned their eyes away from the musicians' union" (Ronald Simms, interview with the author, 2016).

28. Figures excerpted from Cleare (2007).

29. The progressive privatization of sectors formerly run by state governments and the neoliberal influence over economic policy (often precipitated by a need to seek assistance from the International Monetary Fund) were not unique to the Bahamas. In fact, these trends affected the entire Caribbean region (and the entire world) during these years.

30. "They've been talking for too many years now about this program called culture in the classroom where they're supposed to integrate culture into the educational curriculum. They've been talking about it since I was a fuckin' kid! I'm an old fuckin' man now and they're still talking about it! There's no commitment to getting it done. It goes even beyond that. For many, many, many years we've been talking about a national cultural policy. There's fuckin' none! It's still in the discussion stages . . . for years now . . . so there's no national commitment to this happening, there's no sense of urgency to these things happening" (Ronald Simms, interview with the author, 2016).

31. A recent initiative called Junkanoo Carnival (operating since 2015), along with a handful of musicians hired to perform at ports of call and markets, constitute the bulk of the efforts currently sponsored by the Ministry of Tourism. Local entrepreneurs have also abandoned the prospect of programming live music.

32. This fun vibe is also reflected generally in the age of employees and staff at Breezes. I searched carefully but could not find among the exceptionally energetic hos-

pitality staff (bartenders, pool and activity attendants, lobby receptionists, etc.) a single individual who looked a day over twenty-five. It is only among the musicians and entertainers (and the management) that one finds more seasoned individuals.

33. Carlton's caveat regarding management teams is important to emphasize here. While many departments across Sandals properties are headed by Jamaican nationals, Sandals resorts in St. Lucia, for instance, are managed mainly by St. Lucians.

34. Carlton McPhee, interview with the author, February 19, 2016.

35. Carlton McPhee, interview with the author, February 19, 2016.

36. For a classic philosophical engagement with this question of inclusion/exclusion, see Agamben (1998).

37. Here we might consider how Bourdieu's meditations on class distinction (1987) might be usefully invoked to analyze the dynamics in play. For Bahamians who can afford the price of entry, attending a night of entertainment at Breezes accomplishes several things at once: it confirms their economic capital; it increases their cultural capital, and this in both the objective (being at Breezes) and embodied (being a Bahamian at Breezes) domains; it also affords them encounters with foreign nationals and other Bahamians of similar or higher economic means, thereby opening new possibilities for expanding their social capital; finally, it also offers an opportunity to increase their symbolic capital.

38. Importantly, access is a two-way street (as is exclusivity). Thus, all-inclusive can, in some instances, mean that guests are encouraged implicitly or even explicitly to spend their entire vacation exclusively on resort grounds. In other contexts, however, hotels foster a more open relationship to the surrounding community and treat the island's nightlife, shopping, and general atmosphere as a value-added (and no cost to the hotel) benefit for their guests. Although each resort manages their policies regarding off-site access to suit their own economic interests, the relative mobility of hotel guests and the access they enjoy—not just to hotel property, but also to the nation at large—is a stark reminder of the privileged position they occupy in relation to local populations.

39. Funky D, interview with the author, February 20, 2016.

40. Funky D, interview with the author, February 20, 2016.

41. In Caribbean dancing, wining (from winding) refers to gyrating the midsection of the body, specifically the waist and hips (pelvis).

42. This marked a significant moment in the set, because he is, himself, almost never up on the stage, but rather down with the audience during his performances.

43. Alia Coley, interview with the author, February 21, 2016.

44. Alia Coley, interview with the author, February 21, 2016.

45. Alia Coley, interview with the author, February 21, 2016.

46. Alia Coley, interview with the author, February 21, 2016.

47. See Jocelyne Guilbault's (2017) chapter entitled "The Politics of Musical Bonding: New Prospects for Cosmopolitan Music Studies" in *Ethnomusicology or Transcultural Musicology? Perspectives on a 21st Century Comparative Musicology*, edited by Francesco Giannattasio and Giovanni Giuriati, for an extended exploration of this crucial question.

2 · TOURISTIC RHYTHMS

The Club Remix

JEROME CAMAL

Do you have "l'esprit Club?"

Perhaps you have read Jamaica Kincaid (2000) and you have convinced yourself that you are not that kind of tourist.[1] Or perhaps you feel like Lévi-Strauss: you hate travel and travelers, and yet you are still looking for your own *tristes tropiques*.[2] You care, you want to learn. Most of all, you seek an authentic experience. You want to do the things that local people do. You want to eat real local food in some out-of-the-way joint (MacCannell 1973; see also MacCannell 2008). You could never imagine yourself at an all-inclusive resort. You are like me and — although I don't like to tell myself that — I am like you. I may be what you would like to be: an outsider with some amount of insider knowledge. You see, I come often and I stay longer than you will. I know the shortcuts and the best place to get a *bokit*, the local fry bread sandwich. I speak the language. I have friends. But when I arrive, my friends greet me with a smile and then ask *"Tu repars quand?"* (When are you leaving?). We don't operate on the same rhythm, they, you, and I. They, too, know travel and often even migration. But theirs is a long cycle compared to mine. My comings and goings cut into their ongoing. I'd like to believe that in their eyes, perhaps, I am what they hope you would be. But I suspect that they possibly view me as they view you, and they are just too nice to tell me. In fact, you are the part of me that I try to fend off when I travel to the Caribbean and decide to take some time off. I imagine myself as more than a tourist, more than another white European male getting his groove on, but perhaps there is always and still a bit of the tourist in every ethnographer.

You can probably tell that there is a lot of anxiety here. Anthropologists do not like to think of themselves as tourists (Bruner 1995; Crang 2011; Crick 1995). Both MacCannell in his classic study and Kincaid in her bit-ing essay describe tourists as a product of modernity which they explore and construct even as they try to escape it through their exotic vacations (Crick 1995; MacCannell 2013). Mimi Sheller, for her part, discusses the tourist as consuming the Caribbean, which has never been real but rather a place that he/she (the Global North?) has constructed as a fantasy (Sheller 2003; see also Pattullo 2005). We anthropologists, ethnomusicologists, and other ethnographers would like to think ourselves above this, but we also know better. James Clifford has long reminded us that we collect data and "culture" the way tourists collect souvenirs (Clifford 1988). While Sheller kindly left scholars out of her lists of cannibals and vampires, she nonetheless urges us to reckon with our own consumption of the Caribbean. We consume the Caribbean to produce what we like to call "knowledge," but is really, concretely, articles and books that help us advance our careers (Crang 2011; Crick 1995; Sheller 2003). It seems, therefore, that ethics may not offer a solid ground on which to stand as I try to distance myself from you. What then? I need an answer, you see, because my colleagues could not help but chuckle when I mentioned that I was going to do fieldwork at an all-inclusive resort. It was hard enough to get them to take me seriously when I worked on Caribbean music and dance; working on tourism made me all the more suspect. It seems that studying what is supposed to be fun is perceived as somewhat less than working.[3] Is this what distinguishes me from you, then? I work while you play? But what if I work at the place where you play while doing the activities you do to enjoy yourself? Maybe, again, this is just a question of rhythm: you come for a week to ten days. I expand and repeat that experience. In this repetition, I become different from you. Or at least, I hope I do.

When I arrived on the Island in December 2015, it marked the eighth anniversary of my first visit there, right before Christmas 2007. I remember the first time I landed at my destination after a series of flights through Miami and Puerto Rico. I — maybe like you — had imagined the French Antilles long before I got there. Growing up in a white middle-class family in France, the Antilles existed only as an ill-defined idea, an exotic outpost of the nation, rather than a specific place. In the seventies and early eighties, pop music periodically revived the circulation of *doudouiste* tropes, most notably in the ubiquitous songs of the Compagnie Créole.[4] (*Tu grimaces.*[5] You also remember their 1983 exoticist ear-worm "Vive le douanier Rousseau.") Things changed in the 1980s with the fast-growing popularity of *zouk*. Groups like Kassav' and Zouk Machine put Creole in the ears of many French teenagers like myself and helped us locate Martinique and Guadeloupe on a map. But it wasn't until much later, after I migrated to the United States, that I started to take a real interest in the Caribbean. The novels and essays of the Martiniquan creolists opened new imaginary and intellectual horizons for me. The slums of *Texaco* (Chamoiseau 1994) displaced the postcard pictures of luxury hotels and sun-soaked beaches. As a budding ethnomusicologist—before I ever got on that first Caribbean-bound plane—music scholarship, fiction, and sound recordings combined to fuel my imagination of Caribbean soundscapes. At the same time, my training in the American academy exposed me to postcolonial theory and cultural studies, further framing the region for me. It was this Caribbean— "an effect, a fantasy, a set of practices and a context" that "defies the separation between the real versus the imagined"—that I went looking for on my first voyage (Sheller 2003, 5).[6]

And, of course, I found it. Soon after my initial arrival on the Island, I was thrown into what I described in my field notes as "*un vieux car en mauvais états*" (an old bus in bad shape) whose stereo played a mix of zouk and other genres of Caribbean pop "*à fond*" (at top volume). (Was it really that loud, or was that the way I wanted to hear it? Was I exoticizing loudness?) The next day, I stumbled upon my first drum performance, and I remember the shivers I got upon hearing those sounds bounce through the urban environment. A few days later, I found myself sitting in an empty tiled fountain at a funeral parlor, camera in hand, taking in the songs and sights of a wake. Then came the *chantè nwel*, the Christmas caroling typical of this part of the Caribbean. Sheller is right: the Caribbean is produced by our imagination just as much as it is consumed. But, you see, visitors' sensory engagement with the Caribbean is not limited to sight and taste.[7] It is complete. It involves all of our senses: sight, smell, taste, but also touch, kinesthesia, and, of course, sound.

In our ocular-centric world, sonic experiences often take a back seat to the visual. While some people—like myself—undeniably travel to the Caribbean in search of musical thrills, the region is more likely to first evoke images involving white sand, emerald water, and palm trees than the sounds of *merengue*, *bomba*, or even *calypso*. In fact, when I recently asked my students to imagine themselves listening to Caribbean music, this is exactly what they came up with: sun, sand, and smiling faces. Caribbean music, to most of them, sounds like a cocktail on the beach. Of its actual sounds, they had almost nothing to say. And so the camera—rather than the sound recorder—remains the quintessential tourist accessory. In fact, a man taking a photograph adorns the cover of MacCannell's classic *The Tourist*, highlighting tourism studies' privileging of sight and visual culture.[8] Of course, music has in fact played an important role in "tropicalizing" the Caribbean for tourists' consumption. For example, Timothy Rommen exposes the complex role that both recorded music and live musical performances have played in promoting the Bahamas as a tourist destination while also participating in the creation of a racialized geography (Rommen 2011).[9] Similarly, long before the Compagnie Créole, *biguine* did much to construct the *doudouiste* image of the French Antilles during the interwar period (Hill 2013, chapter 2).[10] Yet if my students can associate reggae or steelpan with the Caribbean, these are little more than tropes in their minds. They do not necessarily evoke specific sounds: these students tellingly struggled when, in the first meeting of a class on Caribbean music, I prompted them to describe what instruments they were hearing as they fantasized sipping cocktails on the beach.

Even on the resort, visitors do not pay much attention to the soundscape surrounding them, as long as it doesn't become obtrusive. As Jonathan Sterne has already pointed out, doing an ethnography of listening is a challenging exercise. When I asked resort guests and staff about their auditory experience, I mostly got blank stares or amused looks. They only heard the soundscape of the resort when it forced itself into their consciousness—when, for example, the music coming from the sound systems became too loud or when the lovemaking in the room next door kept them up at night. My experience confirms Sterne's conclusion: refocusing somebody's attention to their ears during an interview could not reveal what they typically heard as they went through their day (Sterne 1997, 26). This chapter is largely, then, an auto-ethnography. It is, most of all, an attempt to make sense of my experience as a (white, male, French) anthropologist staying in an all-inclusive resort and the deep unease that it provoked.

Have you heard of rhythmanalysis? With this concept (method? theory?), Henri Lefebvre (2004) invites us to listen to and otherwise observe the rhythms of the *quotidien*, meaning both the everyday and the ordinary. Paying attention to rhythms enables us to bridge the somatic with the mechanical, the natural with the industrial, the individual with the social. Rhythms encompass both our biological rhythms (for example, waking and sleeping), the natural rhythms of our environment (day and night, seasonal change), as well as mechanical and industrial rhythms (think of the rhythms of traffic or factory shifts). Here I want to pay particular attention to those rhythms that have a sonic manifestation in order to investigate the ways in which sounds define space and organize social life. Sounds do not only "mediate sociality" or curate space, as Guilbault demonstrates in this volume; they are also symptomatic of particular social structures. For Lefebvre, rhythms are constituted by repetition in time and space. But he is quick to point out that there can never be an absolute repetition: the unavoidable introduction of the unforeseen in repetition necessarily entails the creation of difference. Therefore, rhythms can help us move beyond the sonic production of space to understand how these sounds are also productive and symptomatic of social hierarchies.[11] Moreover, rhythmanalysis brings to light the interplay between different rhythms, for example, the linearity of your vacation (you arrive, you stay, you leave) with the circularity of the flow of visitors through the resort or the daily repetition of activities. Thus, for Lefebvre, social life is inherently polyrhythmic. Rhythms can work together to create eurythmia—as they do in a healthy body. But they can also become discordant; the resulting arrhythmia is then both cause and symptom of a pathology or suffering.

Of course, the metaphor of polyrhythm rings through the Caribbean. *Souviens-toi*, Antonio Benítez-Rojo famously characterized Caribbean societies as polyrhythmic.[12] They are the product of various rhythms and interruptions in ways that echo Lefebvre's theory. Most notably, colonialism is the imposition of one rhythm over others, with slavery a brutal interruption. But, in a Deleuzian move, Benítez-Rojo also suggests that polyrhythms offer a sort of decentering structure (I am tempted to call it an *un*-structure) to Caribbean life.[13] The polyrhythmic and improvised performances of Caribbeanness (walking, dancing, moving "in a certain kind of way") diffuse colonial violence, sublimate it. In its polyrhythms, the Caribbean can absorb the rational epistemology of the Enlightenment and capitalism (with their dualisms, diachronicity and linearity) and preserve its own (though syncretic) flows, folds, double folds, circularity, and (most importantly) opacity. Of course, according to Benítez-Rojo's fractal-inspired frame, the Caribbean is itself a rhythm, a meta-archipelago in which a "repeating island" generates difference as it steps "toward nothingness" (Benítez-Rojo 1996). The rhythms of the resort, for their part, are both constitutive and interruptive of the rhythms of the Caribbean repeating island.

Tu t'endors? Non? Bien.[14] Allow me a last rhetorical and theoretical flourish. I want to pursue Benítez-Rojo's chaos theory–inspired metaphor a bit further. I see the Caribbean all-inclusive resort as a repeating machine, which is itself the repetition, or more precisely a remix, of the plantation machine. The remix is not a copy of the original: parts are added, others muted. What is removed leaves an "absent presence," the traces or ghostly presence of the original that listeners must fill in for themselves. Meanwhile, the additive side of mixing creates a kind of contamination or synthesis (depending on the light one might want to shed on the process) that makes the original increasingly difficult to locate or re-create.[15] As the point of origin disappears within new sonic, historical, and economic entanglements, the imagination is free to re-create new utopian (as in the diasporic longing for home; Veal 2007, chapter 8) or, in this case, dystopian trajectories.

I see you shake your head. You wouldn't go to an all-inclusive to start with. You seek a more authentic experience. I understand the allure of authenticity as a counterweight to our postmodern existence (MacCannell 1973; see also MacCannell 2008). And you're right: the resort—this resort in particular—does not pretend to be authentic of anything other than itself. It is a simulacrum, hyperreal. Fine. Sheller and others have told us that much already. My interest here is in conducting a kind of archaeology of tourists' sonic experience of the Caribbean. Most of all, I argue that labor structures and their histories are audible. Though dialectical, labor and leisure form an oxymoronic pair. As a result, the tourism industry endeavors to keep labor invisible. In fact, on the resort, labor is often hidden or disguised as play. Moreover, many tourists—complicit in the practice—would sooner remain blind to the work that their leisure demands. Listening, then, offers a way to apprehend what would rather remain hidden: alienating labor practices and the long history of colonialism that informs them in the Caribbean.

To do so, I will first expose the aurality—a socially constructed and power-inflected field of sound production, perception, and interpretation—of the plantation, the original mix, before turning to the ways this aurality gets remixed in and around the all-inclusive.[16] Paying attention to the rhythms of the resort, I listen for the traces of their antecedents on the plantation but also for what they reveal about a contemporary labor regime intended to extract capital from the production of "happiness." Yet the resort doesn't simply remix the sonic culture and proto-industrial regime of the plantation. The third section of this essay considers how its sounds overflow its boundaries, remixing the space around it. Finally, I conclude by reflecting on how my stay on the resort—literally a few hundred meters away from where I had conducted countless hours of fieldwork on music and cultural nationalism—has remixed and destabilized the Caribbean of my imagination (Camal 2014).

You probably don't really care about any of this anyway. You just want to know about the resort. Unfortunately, I can't tell you exactly where it is. You see, when I contacted its management to inquire about conducting research at their hotel, they reacted as if I were trying to sell them a marketing campaign and told me "*nous ne sommes pas intéressés*" (we are not interested). They let me know that there was nothing stopping me from coming to their establishment and that I was free to waste my vacation away by taking notes, but they wanted nothing to do with it. Not every corporation is as open to collaboration as those with which Paul Rabinow has worked (cf. Rabinow 2007). This hotel belongs to a company—itself owned by a Chinese investment firm—with offices in both Europe and North America; no one could tell me who to contact to get official permission to conduct my fieldwork. To make matters more difficult, the management of the resort itself rotates, making it challenging to build a relationship with anyone. Plus, these people had the bad habit of not returning my phone calls. Maybe this is not so surprising of a company that Polly Pattullo describes as a "self-supporting little empire in the sun . . . tucked away and a law unto itself" (Pattullo 2005, 74).

So let's just call the hotel "Club Poseidon." It is located by a beautiful beach on the southern coast of an island that I know well. This island is an overseas French department in the Lesser Antilles, a little administrative piece of Europe in the Americas. This has important consequences. First, tourism represents about 7 percent of this island's GDP—an important economic sector but not the primary source of economic activity.[17] Second, because they are part of the eurozone, the French Antilles remain expensive destinations compared to their CARICOM neighbors. As a result, most visitors (about 88 percent in 2014, according to the INSEE) come from metropolitan France.[18] Finally, if the implantation of European-owned or North American–owned hotels in the independent Caribbean has often been analyzed as a form of neocolonialism, the situation is a bit more complicated in territories that are not truly postcolonial and whose economies are so deeply entangled with those of a European state (Crick 1989; Gmelch 2003, 35–36).

I know you'd like to know: Where exactly is this resort? It doesn't really matter. In fact, the paper holder for my room's keycard offered a map of the resort, its buildings, swimming pool, tennis courts, and boat docks surrounded by, on one side, a homogeneous blue sea and, on the other, an equally homogeneous forest of palm trees. This resort, you see, is like the luxury haven that Robinson Crusoe built for himself on his desert island. Mind you, this is not quite the "resort that shame forgot" that Junot Díaz wrote about (2013, 13–15).[19] There is no private golf course here and certainly no private airstrip. And the only people moving around in electric golf carts are the staff. *Au fait*, have you noticed that electric golf carts emit almost no sound?[20] You won't be bothered by the noise of an internal combustion engine while you relax on the beach. This is actually remarkable. As it turns out, the resort is not really tucked away on the scenic cove of a desert island. It is located about five hundred meters from one of the busiest roads on the whole island. If you come in on one of the shuttles, you may be surprised to see how long it takes to drive the twenty kilometers or so from the airport, especially during rush hour. I spent several months living in a bungalow off this road several years ago, maybe a little less than a kilometer from the Club, sandwiched between the sounds of *konpa* coming from the restaurant next door, the goats in the backyard, the barking of feral dogs, and the constant traffic noise (engines, car stereos, shout-outs to friends, friendly and not-so-friendly honking). Remarkably, as I sat on the beach adjacent to Club Poseidon one afternoon last January, I realized that I couldn't hear any of that. Only the faint siren of an ambulance managed to find its way to my ears from time to time. Architecture and landscaping work wonders. I'll get back to these absent sounds later.

I should probably tell you a few words about the people who dwell in the Club Poseidon that I (ironically) came to regard as "my village." (In French, the resort is also referred to as a *village de vacances*, a holiday village.) There are basically four categories of people here. The guests are all club members (your reservation includes your membership fees) and are addressed as such by the staff. They are easy to identify: they all wear a bracelet around their wrist—pink if you are new to the club, blue otherwise. The bracelet is the linchpin of the entire disciplining regime of the resort. It determines who eats, sleeps, and has access to the restrooms at the hotel. It also determines who gets greeted with a smile and a warm hello as they walk on the beach . . . and who doesn't. I was on the resort after the New Year and most of the guests were older. There were a few families with very young children (too young to go to school), some younger couples with no kids, but the majority of the guests were retirees. Some staff members informed me that the clientele was slightly different between Christmas and New Year, in the middle of school holidays. Clientele types cycle through the year.

The Club is rather expensive and caters to professionals who, based on their table conversations, alternate their winter vacations between skiing in the Alps and traveling to tropical destinations. Many of them circulate through the different Club resorts around the world. I met a couple at a restaurant outside the Club (the one I told you about, with the good bokits — you'd love this place) before I went there. They were still wearing their blue bracelets and earnestly discussing their experience with a friend. I couldn't help but introduce myself and ask them a few questions. It turns out they were lawyers who lived in Paris but whose families were from the Island. We had a nice chat and, at some point, the young woman told me that she had gone to several Club Poseidon locations. *"C'est bien pour les célibataires, on sait qu'on va y rencontrer quelqu'un"* (it is good if you're single, you know that you will meet someone), she explained as her husband threw me uncomfortable glances. Indeed, the Club is designed to facilitate interactions between members, with long communal tables in the restaurant and many group activities. The Club is where upper-middle-class (mostly European) professionals go to meet each other. As this couple explained to me, to get the full experience of the Club, you have to get into *l'esprit Club* (the Club spirit): sit at other people's tables, partake in activities, join in the dances, even if they seem silly. (I can see from your half-cocked smile that you've read Díaz too and you're thinking: "The average asshole would love this place." I guess that also makes me the only "budget Foucault" on the beach [Díaz 2013, 14–15].)

But let's return to our "villagers." When you wear a bracelet, the people greeting you are staff members, referred to on-site as "organizers." During my stay, they were nearly all white and, with one exception, none of them were from the island. Most of them were under thirty. Organizers are seasonal workers, flown in for several months. Many of the ones I spoke with rotated through various locations. Others were just doing this in between more permanent jobs. At the time of my visit, most of the organizers were from France or francophone Canada, with the exception of a team of staff photographers who were all from Italy. During a previous visit in the summer, the staff seemed to come from a greater variety of European countries, including Italy and the Netherlands. This island being administratively part of France facilitates the circulation of a European workforce.

The management, entirely white, is made up of people whom Antilleans call *métros*, meaning that they have come in from metropolitan France to take jobs in the overseas departments. Lest you forget how this operation is structured, there is a large display by the reception with photos of everyone: a white man (in his late forties or early fifties, perfectly cut silvery hair, and a smile that would be the envy of a Cadillac car dealer) sits at the top of a pyramid. He is the *chef de village*. (I kid you not: *tristes tropiques*, indeed.) Below him you will find the first names and pictures of the management staff, several women among them. Then a couple rows of their "children," the seasonal staff who interact more frequently and directly with guests, ten to twenty years younger than management.

Absent from this tableau are the local employees who cook, serve food, and clean the rooms, all of them from the island, all of them with dark skin.[21] Women wait on guests in the dining room, wearing madras skirts and white *chemisiers* in a rough imitation of a Creole dress. Other women engage in the Sisyphus-like task of keeping the rooms looking as if no one had slept, showered, or eaten there the night before. I never got much of a look at the kitchen. It seems to me that the head chef was white, but the stations along the buffet line were all manned by Antillean men.

I have left out one category of village dwellers: the black men who patrol the outskirts of the resort's grounds. They all work for a private security company; we wouldn't want the name of the resort associated with such obvious discipline and surveillance. (I told you: budget Foucault.) Regardless, I hope you get the parallels here: welcome to the plantation!

Sounds and Rhythms of the Plantation—The Original Mix

I am not the first scholar to compare all-inclusive resorts and plantations. When many tourists and tourism providers imagine the Caribbean, they do it by recycling myths and fantasies that go a long way back (Feldman 2011; Sheller 2003; Strachan 2003).[22] Although it took place in another tropical paradise, there are good reasons why the Reverend Abraham Akaka described tourism as a "new kind of sugar" as he blessed a new hotel in Oahu (Finney and Watson 1977). Before there were big hotels, there were big houses, and as Sheller, Feldman, and others suggest, the practices, hierarchies, and fantasies of Caribbean tourism are informed by the long history of colonialism, plantation economies, European travel writing, and photography (Crick 1989; Feldman 2011; Sheller 2003; Strachan 2003).[23]

Likewise, the plantation casts its shadow over those who labor on Caribbean resorts, blurring the distinction "between service and servitude" (Jean Holder, quoted in Pattullo 2005, 63–64).

Polly Pattullo, in a broad-ranging accusation, writes: "From the outset, there were the echoes of slavery in the dynamics of the tourist industry" (2005, 64). I want to take this metaphor literally and return, if I may, to this echo's initial sounding point, to the colonial plantation. I want to show you how its rhythms participated in the creation of a colonial aurality. I build on Ochoa Gautier's concept of aurality to discuss colonial efforts both to make sense of the world through the acoustic but also to control the sonic environment (Ochoa Gautier 2014). An emergent colonial aurality informed which sounds were heard as valuable and/or productive, which as desirable, and which as threatening, both on and off the plantation. If the acoustic was a key element in the construction of European colonial epistemologies and ontologies, we should also acknowledge that any colonial aurality was by nature a sphere of contestation. Sounds marked the rhythms of the plantation, but they were experienced in very different ways by those who owned the plantation and those who were enslaved there. Because enslaved Africans' own experiences and understandings of the plantation are absent from the French colonial record, the following paragraphs focus on European ears as they encountered tropical, proto-industrial, and black sounds.[24]

From the first European encounter with the natural soundscapes of the New World, sounds have revealed the shortcomings of the Enlightenment epistemological project. When Europeans arrived in the New World, they set out to map it, to reference its people, flora, and fauna, all in an effort to control and dominate. However, tropical sounds resisted mapping or sketching and could not easily be made to fit into encyclopedic taxonomies. As Edwin Hill points out, they thus pointed to the limitations of the "imperial gaze" and forced European chroniclers out of their quantifying enterprise and into a qualitative apprehension of the world they were colonizing. It is from this initial encounter with a sonic incommensurability—mixed with fear, fascination, and desire—that Europeans developed their "imperial ears" (Hill 2013).[25]

The plantation itself offered European chroniclers a soundscape that was as wondrous as tropical nature, but a soundscape that, ultimately, reverberated with the contradictions of their own philosophies. In their efforts to maximize profits by imposing an industrial rhythm of production on the cyclical vagaries of nature, planters regulated time closely using mechanical watches and clocks (Munro 2010, 16–17). A new soundscape emerged alongside the nascent industrial agriculture as sonic signals (the cracking of a whip, the ringing of a bell, or the blowing of a conch shell) relayed the rhythms of clocks in order to organize slave labor. Moreover, the sounds of the plantation—the grinding of the mill, the cracking of the whip, the crying of enslaved bodies—made audible the dehumanizing nature of the European colonial enterprise. These sounds, Hill concludes, exposed the *ratés*, the backfirings, of European modernity. They were the "sonic symbol[s] of slippage, excess, waste in the colonial machine" (Hill 2013, 353). In fact, to return to rhythmanalysis, rather than simply polyrhythmic, the sounds of the plantation reverberate with the arrhythmia created by the brutal imposition of linear and teleological time (moving inexorably toward "progress") of Enlightenment philosophy and proto-industrial production onto the cyclical rhythms of nature, animist religions, and task-oriented labor that exist in a "here-and-now" (Munro 2010).[26]

The "imperial ear" that emerged as a product and tool of European colonialism has provided the templates through which North American and European visitors construct and consume the soundscapes of Caribbean destinations. The myths that first came to life on the plantation continue to inform which sounds should be included, even foregrounded, on the resort and which should be eliminated. Some tropical sounds remain wondrous (the rushing of waterfalls, the gentle rolling of waves), while other still prove incommensurable (the shrilling of nighttime tree frogs—or are they crickets?) or threatening (the buzzing of mosquitoes). Moreover, just as the proto-industrial sounds of the plantation made audible the abuses and contradictions of modernity, the resort is designed to eschew the mechanical sounds of labor that could remind visitors not only of their modern lifestyle "at home" but also of the abuses of a transnational liberal economy that exploits the labor of some for the pleasure and profit of others. Moreover, the "listening ear" shaped by colonialism and exoticism recasts roots reggae, steelpan, calypso, or zouk (all musical styles that have, at some point, carried an anticolonialist or anti-imperialist message; Dudley 2007; Guilbault 1993, 2007; Stolzoff, 2000) as evidence of the inherent warmth, happiness, and laid-back personalities of Caribbean people. Slavery apologists pointed to slaves' singing as evidence that the plantation was a humane and happy place. Similarly, Caribbean musics are enlisted to mask the exploitation of both people and the environment by touristic corporations. As Bobby McFerrin sang with an affected West Indian accent to the vicarious tourists watching the movie *Cocktail*: "Don't worry, be happy." I will now take you inside the Club Poseidon to show you how it remixes the plantation's aurality. I will focus on the rhythms that define the experience of three groups of village dwellers: the guests, the seasonal staff, and the local employees.

The Rhythms of Work and Leisure—Remix

The Tourists' Perspective

"Imagine yourself . . . alone on a tropical beach close to a native village" (Malinowski 2014, 4). Except this time the village has few natives, the beach is far from deserted, and all your belongings are safely stored in your air-conditioned room. In fact, the only things you took to the beach with you were your towel (a pastel green that immediately identifies you as a hotel guest in contrast to the brightly colored towels of other tourists), your keycard, and your cell phone. Or, depending on your age and propensity, you left the electronics in the room and brought down a book instead. Also, unlike Malinowski, you did not arrive on the resort by boat. You, like me, most likely flew in. Did you notice, as I did, the music playing in the airport hall as we waited to get through customs? It was steelpan—an instrument that originated in Trinidad—an odd choice for a Francophone island, one that recasts this Island as just another island. This is particularly striking since—in a context in which tropical destinations increasingly try to differentiate themselves from one another—this island recently successfully lobbied UNESCO to have its traditional drum music recognized as an intangible heritage of humanity, a telling effort to define its cultural specificity.[27]

From the airport, you most likely took a shuttle to get to the resort. If you did decide to drive yourself—as I did—and you didn't know where to go, it could be hard to find. Off the main road (always busy), you have to make a right-hand turn onto a smaller road hidden behind a bus stop. There is only one small sign to indicate the way. It would be easy to miss the turn. (If you see the *boulangerie* [bakery], you've gone too far.) The road will lead you to a gate with a *vigile* (security guard) sporting navy blue fatigue pants, black boots, and a white polo shirt. He is an older gentleman. In a courteous but firm exchange, he will ask you for your name and instruct you to wait while he checks his registration log. He is Saint Peter, guarding the gates to Paradise. Without cracking a smile, he will instruct you to head to the right at the fork in the road to drop off your luggage at the reception, then go back, take the other road, and park your car by the tennis courts. So few people drive themselves to the Club, there is no actual parking lot there.

When you arrive at the entrance to the long, covered path that leads to reception, you will hear some zouk playing somewhere. In a telling example of how the resort curates its soundscape, this music was turned on just for your benefit. The rest of the time the area—which is to the back of the resort, facing away from the beach and all the other buildings save the administrative offices—is quiet and quite deserted.

Once you are inside the Club, you are quickly introduced to its most frequent ritual: as you pass every single staff member, they greet you with a warm—and frequently *répété*, meaning both rehearsed and repeated— "*bonjour*" or "*bonsoir*" depending on the time of day. Variations are frequent: "*Ça va bien?*" (How are you?) Or more casual, using the informal French second person singular to signal real intimacy: "*Tu vas bien?*" Or my favorite, experienced once from the chef de village, no less than three times in a row: "*Bonjour, ça va bien?*" with a smile and a wink for extra flourish. Three times. Within five to ten minutes.

Checking in is a very intimate experience: a staff member will offer some juice and a towel to freshen up. Then she will fasten your bracelet to your wrist and show you to your room, where you can transform yourself, put on a new persona. As a guest explained to me, upon your arrival: "*On enlève nos habits professionnels de parisiens et on devient [membres du Club]. On devient [membres] comme les autres, quoi*" (You take off the professional attire of a Parisian and you become a Club member. You become a Club member like the others). Which most likely means that you slip on a pair of flip-flops. The slapping sound of sandals give the basic tempo of the day. They combine with the obligatory greeting to sonically define the relationship between staff and guests. The latter wear sandals. The former wear closed-toe shoes and greet everyone they pass.

The other (but perhaps most distinctive and sonically significant) ritual punctuating a day at the Club are the Mad Moves. These are choreographed dances (think line dancing) set to various forms of dance music that stick close to the 120 bpm mark. The most important feature is for the music to provide a clearly marked section when everyone can "go crazy." Songs used for zumba are particularly effective. Leading to these moments of exuberance are a sequence of steps, led by one of the young staff members, that remains basically the same regardless of the music: "*En haut! En haut! En bas! En bas! Arriba! Arriba! Abajo! Abajo!*" as people point up or down. People step right and left, spin, clap their hands, move forward and backward. And then everyone is let loose as the dance leader cheers: "*Allez! Allez! Poseidon allez!*" (Go! Go! Poseidon, go!)

If you arrive on a Saturday, you will be introduced to the Mad Moves that very night. You may be reluctant to join in at first but the "kind organizers"—who are always present for evening activities—will come to you, grab your hand, and cheerfully coerce you to join in. *C'est ça, l'esprit Club.*[28] From then on, the Mad Moves will happen at predictable times every day: first before lunch, usually held on the beach; then one or more times during the evening. In the morning, they are used as a high note to conclude the morning sports activities, generally growing out of the aquagym or zumba class. In the evening, Mad Moves mainly happen after the show to get people into a party mood. No one will ever teach you the Mad Moves, but you will probably pick them up on your own. The relentless 120 bpm beats and regular cheering "Allez! Allez! Poseidon allez!" came to define the sonic environment of the Club for me, heard with a mix of amusement and dread. I must not have been the only one feeling that way. These dances are actually poorly attended: a look around the lines of dancers reveals that they are mostly "organizers."

The days at the Club Poseidon all follow the same basic schedule. Breakfast is served until about 9 AM, when most classes start. These include things like sailing, trapeze, Pilates, aquagym, zumba, wind surfing, or archery lessons. The morning events conclude with a group activity, often a game pitting the staff against a group of guests. Lunch, in typical French fashion, is scheduled from 12:15 to 2:15. Activities pick back up until 5:30. Dinner is served from around 7:30 until about 9 PM, then an evening show at 9:30, and finally some sort of party at 10:30. The beach fills up and empties according to this schedule.

Two things jump out looking at these daily cycles. First, I couldn't help but be surprised by the fact that, on vacation, people would stick to such a work-like schedule. The restricted restaurant hours mean that one has to adopt the overall rhythm of the resort. This is especially true because— and this is my second point—everything runs with industrial punctuality. There is, in the daily rhythm of the resort, something of the efficient but dehumanizing experience of modern homogeneous empty time. This is in contrast to my experience of the flexible passage of time on the island, which is characterized by periods of stretching and speeding up, of waiting and rushing. I never waited at the Club. But I also never felt like I had the possibility (permission?) of being late.

I use the word *permission* here because there is a sense that the resort is a self-disciplining institution. Because it interfaces with a public beach, the staff members (and security guards) are constantly checking people's wrists for a bracelet. Guests often do the same. On the day my companion and I arrived, we were a bit late to have lunch at the restaurant, so the person who checked us in let us go get some food before taking the time to give us our bracelets. As we were eating, a young staff member came to our table, originally to ask how our meal was, but upon noticing that my companion was not wearing a bracelet, he inquired, suddenly less bubbly: "*Madame, pourquoi ne portez-vous pas de bracelet?*" (Madam, why are you not wearing a bracelet?) We had failed to properly display our identifying "branding," the company's logo not yet properly displayed on our bodies. Conversely, *avoir l'esprit Club* is also inscribing its brand on you, and it is common for guests to wear apparel purchased at various Clubs Poseidons around the world. As I will show later, guests sometimes also involve themselves in policing the beach. Being on the resort, one is constantly aware of being watched, just as one engages in the act of gazing. This was made clear by an announcement during one of the competitive games: "*Le chef de village vous observe, alors soyez vigilants!*" (The village chief is observing you, so be vigilant!) The young bodies of the staff are offered to the members' gazes; but they also gaze back and discipline the guests.[29]

Most visitors stay at the resort a week, although I met some who were there for a lot longer, including a retired pharmacist from Quebec who was planning on staying six weeks.[30] As a result, activities are structured to repeat on a weekly basis, starting on Saturdays, the day when most people arrive. Panels lining the path from the main bar to the dining area detail the themes of each day's activities and dress code. (You look amused. Yes, there is a dress code.) Photographs of two Club employees (the typical white and blond heteronormative young couple) model the daily costumes: strolling down the pier in their "white" attire on Tuesday; hugging and looking into the distance (the satisfied look of the landowner surveying his estate) in their "black and *fluo*" outfits on Thursday; on the beach, her sitting on his lap, looking each other in the eyes in their "smart" apparel on Friday. Monday is "beachwear," and I won't even describe that photo for you. I think you get the idea. In practice, not everyone dresses the part, of course, but many people do. The themes are relatively easy to accommodate and, if you have stayed at another Club Poseidon before, you will know what to bring. Besides, if you don't have the appropriate costume, the gift shop rotates through its stock to match the daily themes. (Another way in which branding is facilitated.) And so it will quickly become part of your daily routine to check what the theme for the next day will be.

Likewise, your weeklong stay will be punctuated by a series of nighttime shows put on by the staff. These generally take place in the theater, and the best way to describe them would be that they oscillate between karaoke and Cirque du Soleil. The Tuesday night show was on the Cirque side, with a succession of trapeze and dance routines organized to tell some sort of Manichaean story about the struggles between white and dark forces for control over a sacred stone. (I think you know who won.) The music that night consisted of a mix of trip-hop and metal for the trapeze acts and New Age sounds for the narrative scenes in between. Thursday, we were treated to the "History" show, a large-scale karaoke in which the young organizers lip-synced and danced their way through music of the 1970s, 1980s, 1990s, and a few recent hits. The big screens on each side of the stage showed the original videos with the lyrics of the song so that audiences could participate. The selection that night included the Village People, Queen, Kiss, Claude François, Michel Sardou, Prince, Michael Jackson, George Michael, the Gipsy Kings, Umberto Tozzi, and "Oh Happy Day," taken from the *Sister Act 2* soundtrack. (How do I know? The costumes made it obvious . . . and the fact that the only black staff member "sang" the lead.) The poster announced Madonna but she didn't show up.[31]

The music for all these shows is prerecorded, blasted through the theater's sound system. As the DJ explained to me, the musical selection is designed to build up so that people feel like dancing by the end of the show and thus are more likely to join the party scheduled for 10:30, either by the pool or at one of the bars. Like the shows, these parties are held to recorded music.[32]

On Thursday night, following the "History" show, I joined my fellow guests as we marched from the theater behind a golf cart broadcasting party music, alongside the beach to the Biguine restaurant at the western edge of the resort. There we were to attend a fluo (neon) party, which, the staff had informed me for most of the day, was going to be fun and last until 2 or 3 AM. When we arrived, the restaurant had been decorated with neon-colored signs. Three big white letters transformed the deck into a "VIP" area. There were a few Moët & Chandon lights to add to the aura of exclusivity and conspicuous consumption. (Where's the Cristal, you ask? It was available for sale, although I didn't see anyone actually purchase any.) The DJ had set up his gear on a second-floor balcony. The evening started with three Mad Moves to get the crowd going. This seemed to work while it lasted, but as soon as the staff stopped encouraging people to dance, most people retreated to the bar. The guests who had followed the golf cart from the theater were mostly of retirement age. They seemed unmoved by the Latin-flavored EDM that the DJ had selected. A few staff members kept dancing by themselves. But I was mostly treated to the familiar spectacle of white bodies not dancing (Craig 2013). The Club management and the DJ never quite managed to get "in tune" with the guests (cf. Guilbault, this volume). The dance floor was soon empty. The chef de village's decision to turn up the volume could not reverse this dynamic and, by 12:30, the DJ gave up and packed up his gear. If the Mad Moves—like the colonial *quadrille* that they echo—allow for safe socializing through scripted, group dancing, EDM remix and their individual dance moves did not suit the spirit of my fellow Club goers.

The whole cycle of evening shows is organized to climax on Friday evenings with a party on the beach that closes with a fountain of champagne. The next day, people pack up, enjoy one last outing on a sailboat, one last swing on the trapeze, or simply catch more sun on the beach before grabbing a ride to the airport and their flight back home. Meanwhile, a new group arrives. That night a game and their first Mad Moves will give them the opportunity to get into *l'esprit Club*. For the staff, the cycle starts all over again.

The Seasonal Staff's Perspective

As mentioned, the seasonal staff stays on the resort for several months before rotating to another Club. Although, per French law, they are prevented from working more than thirty-five hours a week (at the time of my stay), their working days stretch much beyond that. Essentially, because their primary job is to interact with the guests, they start their day when they first arrive at the restaurant for a quick breakfast in the morning. There, they sit with guests to provide company and conversation, a role they fulfill for each meal. Depending on the particulars of their job, they then move on to supervise a sport, organize the restaurant for the next meal, rehearse the evening's show, or work as lifeguards or at reception. In the evening, they participate in the show, then most of them stay up until the end of that night's party or later, having drinks with each other and with late stragglers at the beach bar. And every time they pass a guest, they offer a smile and a cheerful greeting. A large sign in the hotel lobby reads: "The goal in life is to be happy. The place to be happy is here. The time to be happy is now." The seasonal staff is there to turn this into a reality for every person who visits the resort.

For some, a job at Club Poseidon is a bit like a year-round camp counselor position. For others, it becomes a drag. One staff member—who was doing his first season with the Club supervising archery—described the boredom of days spent doing the same thing all day long. The music played throughout the resort structured his day: zouk coming from the main bar during the day, then 1970s and 1980s hits in the first part of the evening, moving through the 1990s, and finally more recent selections. "You know what to expect," he concluded. "It's very predictable."

The rhythm of long, repetitive working days is hard to maintain, explained another staff member in his early thirties. "*Il faut de l'endurance*" (You need endurance). He was trying to limit the partying in his first couple of months at the resort, but he had already had a few *nuits blanches* (sleepless nights). On my first evening at the Club, I couldn't help but notice the tired looks of many staff members as they partook in a Mad Moves routine. Their movements were mechanical, their faces haggard. Gone were the smiles and the energy they had displayed only moments earlier. Their labor and even entertainment subsumed by a machine designed to produce "happiness" (and euros), these staff members are forced into arrhythmia, their work rhythm clashing with their biological needs.

The Local Staff's Perspective

The local staff are the only people who are openly referred to as employees within the Club structure. These employees are also the only people who do not stay at the resort overnight. They come in to clean the rooms, cook, and wait on tables every day. During my stay, these employees were all Afro- and Indo-Caribbean. Although they are ever-present, they have very few direct interactions with Club members. Most guests ignore them and get ignored in return. In contrast to the team of "organizers" and their rehearsed smiles and bonjours, the employees very rarely greet anyone. On the island, not greeting folks as you walk into a bar or restaurant, or even as you pass them on the street, is considered rather rude. On the resort, however, it becomes a rare privilege for this class of workers.

In addition to their actual labor, these employees are there to provide *une touche de couleur locale* (a touch of local color) as the French goes. (Feel free to take *couleur* literally here.) As you may have gathered, the Club serves up a tropical experience that makes almost no attempt at specificity, save for the syrupy zouk music that is broadcast in the bar area throughout the day. Otherwise, there is nothing to indicate that you are on a specific Caribbean island, with its distinctive cultural practices. The dance parties do not feature any Caribbean couple dances. Local musicians rarely perform at the resort, and the only band I have heard there played Bob Marley covers. And although the buffet line always offers a few local specialties (along with the pizza, pasta, steaks, fries, and other standard buffet food), they are unusually bland by local standards, as a station attendant once warned me about an underwhelming *sauce chien* (pepper sauce). In this context, the local employees, especially those working the dining hall and buffet line, are little more than embodied tropical tropes, incarnations of the *doudou* figurines (complete with fat lips, fruity hats, and exaggeratedly curvy bodies) on display by the reception. While the seasonal staff—the organizers—are known by their first names and their respective specialties, the local employees do not wear name tags and they have no announced specialty. They are the anonymous, alienated black bodies working in the big house.

Their alienation was audible. It was audible in the silences that often responded to my efforts to salute the women busing tables. It was audible in the too many occasions on which I heard one of the men working the buffet line address a guest as "doudou," this most tired of colonial clichés. It was audible, loud and clear, in a laugh. One evening, at the end of the dinner service, I went back to the line to get some fruit. As I was looking at the display, the man working the fruit station asked me what I would like.

"*J'aimerais un* maracuja" (I would like a *maracuja*), I replied, using the Creole word for passion fruit. He looked at me and declared, very seriously, as if I had offended him: "*Il ne faut pas utiliser ce mot-là. C'est mal poli*" (You shouldn't use this word. It is impolite). I was taken aback.

"*Ah bon?*" (really?) was all I could muster.

"*Oui*," he replied. "*Ça veut dire, 'je vous aime madame'*" (It means "I love you, madam").

I tried to defuse the situation.

"*Ah, et bien, ce n'est pas forcément une mauvaise chose*" (That's not such a bad thing, then).

But he insisted: "*Il ne faut pas dire ça*" (You shouldn't say this).

Then he started muttering to himself as he cut open a passion fruit for me. The muttering turned into a chuckle. The chuckle grew into quiet, uncontrolled laughter. There was something deep in this laugh. "I wanted to kid around until I choked," writes Fanon, "but it had become impossible" (Fanon 1971, 90).[33] If the waiter's remark had originally been intended as a *maskò*—a feint, a ruse, or a trick—the laugh was both its conclusion (laughing at the gullible tourist) and an expression of his own impotence. Regardless of my ignorance, I remained solidly in my position of relative power, free to consume the fruit of the Caribbean which he was serving me. This laugh has haunted me since. I heard its echoes in the quiet muttering of one of the women cleaning up breakfast tables one morning. The laugh was the neurotic extension of a comment that the local head bartender shared with me one evening: "*Moi, je regarde mais je ne dis rien*" (Me, I observe but I say nothing).

Maybe I am pushing the plantation metaphor too far. I am quite certain that the employees I was just describing may not like the comparison, regardless of how they feel about their jobs.[34] In addition, we need to keep in mind that the plantation—while a repressive and restrictive structure of power—also created conditions for resistance and creative manipulation (Trouillot 2002). Likewise, within the neocolonial context of the resort, Creole regains its resistant and disruptive quality. For local employees and contract workers, the opacity of Creole offers a refuge. If the women working the dining hall seldom talk with Club members, they chat freely with one another, secure in the knowledge that neither most of the guests nor the management are likely to understand them.

Now, *écoutes*.[35] Do you hear in my analysis my own deafness, the silencing that comes with my position and with the particular analytical frame that I have chosen? Listening to the resort as a remix of the plantation sets up a perhaps clichéd narrative of oppression and resistance. It silences the fact that, for its employees, the Club is first and foremost a place to work and that labor cannot be reduced to colonial oppression. This frame of analysis ignores the "background sounds" that could not reach my ears—either by design or because I was not attuned to them—but that would give this ethnography more depth (see Harewood, this volume). What could be learned from listening to the background sounds of the kitchen? Would they reveal the kind of camaraderie that Gmelch, and Harewood in this volume, describe? How would the kitchen staff's laughing ("we get lots of laugh, lots of laugh"),[36] contained in a kind of intimacy behind closed doors, compare with my interaction with the fruit station attendant? What would I hear if, instead of following other guests, I hung around the bedrooms and hallways during the day while the staff makes the beds and cleans the rooms? How would these local workers describe their sonic environment and what would their descriptions reveal of the daily rhythm of their labor?

Nonetheless, as we contrast the rhythms of the quotidien of both local employees and seasonal workers, an important feature of the all-inclusive comes to the fore. Whereas the local employees provide a service that is comparable to what one would expect at any hotel around the world (cooking, cleaning, providing security, etc.) and therefore hold an unambiguous position within tourism's political economy, the organizers (who for the most part come from Europe) occupy a peculiar position, one that has no precedent prior to the development of a leisure economy. In Marxist terms, as our rhythmanalysis revealed, those "kind organizers" are classically exploited: Their working day extends long past their contractual labor (their primary activities as DJ, sailing instructor, or restaurant manager). Outside their contractual working hours, "kind organizers" performed a sort of unrecognized affective labor—by which I mean the performance of sociality that enhances feelings of hospitality—that is central to the creation of value in a "happiness" economy (Hardt 1999).[37] Even within their primary, contractual, job function, kind organizers' labor is most often experienced as play as they teach trapeze or take you out on a quick boat outing. The element of play is reinforced by the fact that no financial transaction ever takes place between the hotel staff and its guests. The virtue of the all-inclusive is that guests have paid for everything weeks, if not months, prior to setting foot on the resort. Whereas other hotels encourage guests to leave during the day, outsourcing activities on the island, the "organizers" are there to make sure that everyone stays on-site. They are also responsible for maintaining a similar experience across the chain's many locations. "Kind organizers" contribute a form of unrecognized affective labor—providing company and entertainment past their standard working hours—that is central to creating value in a happiness economy. They make the "Club spirit" manifest.

The Club, then, does not echo the plantation but remixes its rhythms to produce something new, a structure where labor is either hidden or disguised as play. Yet an analysis of its rhythms reveals its arrhythmia, its alienating and exploitative nature. The resort remixes the exploitative system of the plantation and even its racializing structure, but it complicates it. Indeed, it is the white and youthful bodies of the organizers that are subjected to the most blatant efforts to maximize surplus value and that become the objects—mostly through their athletic performances—of tourists' erotic gaze. Overall, although putatively oriented to producing happiness, Club Poseidon imposes an industrial rhythm onto the somatic rhythms of its employees and guests, all in order to maximize profits and keep its members within the confines of the hotel. Loud music and incessant rhythms stimulate the bodies of both to keep them engaged in the task of producing "fun." But this is not the only way in which music is used. Let me tell you how it contributes to reshaping the physical environment and the experience of visitors.

Sounds Remixing Space

At this point, you may not want to ever set foot in a Club Poseidon. I don't blame you. I felt uncomfortable the whole time I was there—all the more so because I was there during carnival. The distance between the street and the resort never seemed so great. Carnival on the Island does not center on fancy floats or elaborate costumes as it does in New Orleans or Brazil. Rather, this particular carnival is all about the *gwoup a pò*, the drum groups who rush the streets, marching briskly through the urban environment accompanied by the syncopated polyrhythms of a battery of handheld drums. The larger of these groups can have several hundred members. One of them—one of the oldest and largest—is generally accompanied by a flock of adolescents on their scooters and motorcycles who speed through the streets, revving their engines, ahead and around the official *déboulé* (procession). Each group is also preceded by a small squad of young boys carrying long whips to which are attached firecrackers. In an inversion of the symbols of slavery, as well as a cathartic performance of its violence, they crack these whips in flamboyant displays, clearing the roads for the oncoming group. Carnival offers a most noisy and joyous atmosphere. Sounds and movements redraw the normally sedate urban environment. Driving becomes impossible and to walk with one of the groups is to experience being swept away by its energy as its members push one another along with loud "*Woulé!*" (Go!) The sounds of drums and songs reverberate on buildings, through boulevards, streets, and alleys. Their rhythms alter both the urban landscape and soundscape.

Remarkably, the people I spoke with at the Club did not know about carnival. For the whips of Antillean carnival, they substituted the feathery costume of a Brazil-themed evening show. Although, one night, I was able to hear the distant sounds of a gwoup a pò, the Club is designed to keep not only the musicians themselves but also their black sounds at bay. As I have already mentioned, the Club is built away from the main road, with a buffer of trees that helps keep urban noises to a minimum. The buildings were constructed to face toward the ocean: their mass in itself shields the adjacent beach from the sounds of what goes on further inland.

I say the beach adjacent to the resort because, by law, beaches on the island cannot be private. The Club tried, though. Some of my friends from this area have recounted the fights that went on as locals fought to protect their access to the beach from the encroaching hotel. Eventually a compromise of sorts was reached and anyone can still access the beach. There is, however, a metal revolving gate, about 2 meters high, at the head of the access trail. On the right is a fence; on the left, the sea. It is difficult for, say, a street vendor to access the beach with their wares. All along the path and the beach, a wooden fence and security guards make sure that the resort remains the privilege of those who can pay for access.

The resort has found ways to dominate and control the public beach using sound to privatize a public space. The hotel has installed sound systems in four locations: in its theater, in the main bar, and in the pool area. These three locations are next to one another and border the eastern edge of the beach, the one from which a visitor would arrive. On the beach itself, the beach bar also has a sound system. In addition, if need be, portable speakers can be installed in the restaurant at the western edge of the beach, as happened for the *fluo* party. Music played at either one of these locations is loud enough to be heard on most of the beach. Thus, just as the muzak played inside stores participates in defining their physical space within the mall, the Club's mixes push the boundaries of the private hotel outward to claim the public space (Sterne 1997). The loudness of the Club's sound systems establishes a "wall of sound" around the public beach (Deleuze and Guattari 1987, quoted in Sterne 1997, 31). These sounds work to discourage non-club members from coming to the beach. They represent a sonic equivalent to the myriad plastic chaises lounge that cover the beach but are reserved for hotel guests. The loud stereos also serve to contain other sounds, both natural and human-made. Indeed, the music broadcast throughout the resort covers natural sounds in open spaces (such as the bar) where thick glass windows and the humming of air conditioning cannot serve this function.

While the hotel can sonically claim the public beach, there is little tolerance for counteroffensives. One afternoon, as I sat on the beach, I observed the interactions of a hotel guest and a group of local teenagers. These boys had claimed one of the hotel's *transats* (chaises lounge) and created a small space for themselves with a cooler and a folding chair. They chatted enthusiastically, their banter punctuated by *timal* (literally "young guy," generally used in the same way as "man" in American English) and "*awa!*" (no). They had a small Bluetooth speaker with them, and they listened to some dancehall as they spoke. Next to me was an older, white, hotel guest who was reading a travel guide. As the teenagers got more animated, they turned the volume up on their speaker. At their first attempt to claim the sonic space, the older club member turned around to look at them. They retreated and lowered the volume. However, a few minutes later, they tried again. This time, they increased the volume and then left to go swim. The woman next to me scanned the beach. Unable to locate them, she got up and went searching for them. I saw her, several minutes later, walking back from the water accompanied by two of the teenagers. They smiled at her, looking rather smug. They returned to their seats and turned down their music.

Their small speaker was, of course, no match for the sound systems of the resort. I see this episode as an illustration of the different levels of tolerance for different styles of music evaluated within a racialized aurality. The only genres of black musics that enter the Club mix are those genres, such as reggae, that have a history of white appropriation, that have to some extent been alienated from the black bodies that produce them, or that, at the very least, can be construed as hybrid. Zouk on the resort functions a bit like the biguines of the colonial era. Conversely, those sounds that index oppositional expressions of "modern blackness" (like dancehall) are not tolerated (Thomas 2004).

The sound politics of the Club result in what the couple I met before my stay described as an impoverished sonic environment, a complaint I heard repeated many times in different guises. While some people complained that the music was simply too loud, others regretted not being able to hear the songs of birds, the sounds of waves, or the singing of tree frogs at night.

Others longed for more distinctive local music. For my part, I came to miss the barking of dogs and the maddeningly random crowing of roosters. In their places, residents of the village de vacances are surrounded by the overwhelming and relentless soundtrack of the Mad Moves, the regular pit-pat of flip-flops, and the repetitive and disingenuous greetings of the staff.

Touristic Rhythms in the Age of Ethnographic Reproduction—The Final Mix

Tu vois, as I reflect on my sonic encounter with the Club, I realize that my reluctance to enter the resort resulted from my intense discomfort with its labor structure.[38] But my discomfort was also heightened by the contrast between life on the resort and my previous experiences on the Island, experiences that, as I described earlier, had been shaped by my own trajectory as a scholar and my subject position as a French expatriate ethnographer. As much as a geographic area, my field has also been an ideological problem-space in which I muse over anti- and postcolonialism within the French nation-state. I brought these concerns with me to the Club, amplified by what was then—on the part of many Antilleans—a renewed interest in the heritage of slavery.[39] The Club remixed these experiences and concerns with the results that you see here. Oh, you my tourist alter ego, you who I have been speaking to (and against) throughout these pages, how I tried to distance myself from you while at the Club! But the Club lifted the persona of the postcolonial American scholar and sent me back the image of my own French white body. I wanted to be different from you, from the other guests vacationing on this Island. I know the shortcuts and the best place to get a bokit. I speak the language. I have friends. But in the end, there I was, just like you, more inconspicuous on the beach than my French-American self at a nationalist event. Situated just a few hundred meters from where I had spent many weeks conducting fieldwork on cultural nationalism, the Club had remixed my field site, revealing things—about the Island, about myself—that I had worked hard to ignore.

On my last night at the resort, this all proved too hard to take and I decided to escape, to become a touristic maroon, to dive back. As the Brazilian show was finishing in the theater, and before the beach party claimed that space, my companion and I headed east along the trail, toward the town. Once we got into town, we rolled down our sleeves to cover our bracelets and we walked to a local restaurant that we knew often had live music. A small jazz combo was playing that night, weaving a mix of American standards, biguines, and original compositions. I ordered a *ti punch* (rum with sugar and lime juice) and no one asked if I wanted ice (a heresy in this very simple cocktail; remember that when you go looking for an authentic experience). We settled at a table, soaking in the live music and the surrounding mix of French and Creole conversations.

As we walked back toward the resort later that night, a car was cruising the boulevard pumping some dancehall. A few teenagers still lined the seaside boulevard, chatting in Creole. The power generator of a lone food truck selling late-night bokit was still humming. A motorcyclist roared his way past us. Further down, we had to chase away a couple of wild dogs that barked their discontent as we encroached on their territory. And all around us, invisible frogs blanketed the night with their drone-like chant. On this last night, I left behind the controlled space of the resort and embraced the gritty polyrhythm of the Island. I listened with my academic "listening ears." These sounds have come to make sense to me and reminded me that I still have much work to do here.

NOTES

1. The style of this essay was inspired by Jamaica Kincaid's combative address to tourist visitors to Antigua. I was also inspired by—and make several references to—Junot Díaz. Kincaid's provocative description of the tourist as "an ugly human being" resonated with my own discomfort, as a tourist and ethnographer, while I researched and wrote this project. In response to Kincaid's harangue, I chose to address myself in this essay, or rather an alter ego, or rather the part of myself that I try to keep at bay—but is nonetheless always present—as I conduct fieldwork in the Caribbean. This essay is then best understood as an interior dialogue. It is in this spirit that I directly intervene in the text using the second person singular in French (*tu*) or English (*you*). Tu, here, does not actually refer to you, the reader, but rather to this imagined alter ego. This also informs my choice to address this alter ego in French in the text. Emboldened by Díaz's own strategic use of untranslated Spanish, I have decided to let my native language erupt to mark structural transitions in the text. While I acknowledge that the intrusion of a foreign language can be frustrating for some readers, this strategy is meant to evoke two essential aspects of the touristic and ethnographic encounter. First, at a simple and direct level, touristic and ethnographic spaces are often bi- or even multilingual spaces. As I hope this essay demonstrates, the hierarchical interplay between French and Creole is a central sonic feature of a French Caribbean resort. This multilingualism opens the door for partial understanding and, more impor-

tantly, for strategies to resist understanding. This is my second point: the multilingual encounter is ripe for the play of opacity between service providers and tourists or between ethnographers and collaborators. Edouard Glissant views opacity as an essential right within what he calls the "poetics of Relation." For Glissant, opacity is not only a right not to be understood—and thus to protect one's subjectivity, to exist outside of the play of Hegelian dialectics—but it is also inherent to our own psychology, an admission that we may not entirely understand or know our selves, another point that I try to make in this essay. To mitigate the reader's potential frustration, I have provided translations of these French interjections in endnotes. For those dialogues taken from my field observations, I provide a translation in the main body of the text.

2. Lévi-Strauss famously opened *Tristes Tropiques* with the declaration: "Travel and travelers are two things I loathed—and yet here I am, all set to tell the story of my expeditions" (Lévi-Strauss 1971).

3. Crang highlights that research institutions are themselves often suspicious of disbursing funds for tourism research. In my own experience, the University of Wisconsin–Madison financial system did not recognize a resort as a suitable hotel, forcing me to find workarounds to get research expenses reimbursed (Crang 2011, 209).

4. *Doudouisme* critically refers to poems and songs marked by colonial ideology and exoticist aesthetics. The term alludes to the *doudou* (Creole for darling), the tragic Creole woman abandoned by her French lover.

5. *Tu grimaces*: You wince.

6. These remarks highlight once again that travel destinations—whether for tourism or research—are not reducible to fixed geographical points, but are rather "in play," constructed through social practice from previous experiences. See Crang (2011); Sheller and Urry (2004).

7. Sheller does mention other senses in her later book (Sheller 2012).

8. The continued popularity of John Urry's *The Tourist Gaze* further illustrates this point (Urry and Larsen 2011). There are, of course, a number of important studies of music and tourism prior to this one. See, for example, Baumann and Fujie (1999); Desroches et al. (2011); Gibson and Connell (2005).

9. For further examples, refer to Rommen and Neely (2014).

10. The term *doudouisme* is used to critically describe any exoticist artistic representation of the French Antilles. The term derives from the trope of the *doudou* (Creole for darling or beloved), the *mulâtre* woman who is helplessly in love with a Frenchman. As Hill so brilliantly demonstrates, this trope feminizes Caribbean hybridity, which is then subjugated to colonial masculinist paternalism.

11. On the role of sounds in producing space, see Sterne (1997). Munro reprises Lefebvre's argument about the importance of rhythm in "bonding societies and groups and in structuring the collective experience of time" (Munro 2010, 5).

12. *Souviens-toi*: Remember.

13. Michaeline Crichlow offers a similar analysis using the metaphor of "limboing techniques" (Crichlow and Northover 2009).

14. Are you falling asleep? No? Good.

15. On cutting and mixing as cultural metaphors, see Hebdige (1987); Henriques (2011, 149–57).

16. My understanding of aurality builds on the recent work of Ana Maria Ochoa Gautier (2014).

17. Statistics are for 2012 according to the Cours des Comptes's Rapport Public Annuel, "Le tourisme en outre mer: Un indispensable sursaut" (Paris, 2014).

18. INSEE: Institut National de la Statistique et des Études Économiques.

19. It may be worth quoting Díaz's description of a Dominican resort at length here: "I don't even want to tell you where we're at. We're in Casa de Campo. The Resort That Shame Forgot. The average asshole would love this place. It's the largest, wealthiest resort on the Island, which means it's a goddamn fortress, walled away from everybody else. Guachimanes and peacocks and ambitious topiaries everywhere. Advertises itself in the States as its own country, and it might as well be. Has its own airport, thirty-six holes of golf, beaches so white they ache to be trampled, and the only Island Dominicans you're guaranteed to see are either caked up or changing your sheets. Let's just say my abuelo has never been here, and neither has yours. This is where the Garcías and the Colóns come to relax after a long month of oppressing the masses, where the tutumpotes can trade tips with their colleagues from abroad. Chill here too long and you'll be sure to have your ghetto pass revoked, no questions asked. . . . The sun is blazing and the blue of the ocean is an overload on the brain. Casa de Campo has got beaches the way the rest of the Island has got problems. These, though, have no merengue, no little kids, nobody trying to sell you chicharrones, and there's a massive melanin deficit in evidence. Every fifty feet there's at least one Eurofuck beached out on a towel like some scary pale monster that the sea's vomited up. They look like philosophy professors, like budget Foucaults, and too many of them are in the company of a dark-assed Dominican girl."

20. Au fait: by the way.

21. Like many Caribbean islands, the population here descends mostly from Africa, South Asia, and Europe. Vernacular racial taxonomies do not map comfortably onto U.S. racial formations.

22. For a broader view, beyond the Caribbean, see Amirou (2012).

23. For a discussion of the Hawaiian context, see Desmond (1999).

24. If slave narratives exist for nineteenth-century North America, no similar documents are available for the French Caribbean.

25. Hill borrows the concept of the "imperial gaze" from Pratt (1992).

26. "Here-and-now" is a translation of Benjamin's concept of *Jetztzeit*, which contrasts with the homogeneous empty time of modernity.

27. On the "global beach" and the need to differentiate tourist destinations, see Löfgren (2004); Sharpley (2004). About the process of heritage-making in this particular case, see Camal (2016).

28. That's the Club spirit.

29. Sheller develops the idea of gazing back in, *Citizenship from Below* (2012).

30. My stay was a brief four nights, plus a prior visit with an evening pass on one night, and many hours spent conducting observations on the beach before that.

31. These shows offer a complex erotic encounter between staff and guests that demands a closer analysis.

32. On some Mondays, a live band performs. I was not able to be at the resort on a Monday night, but I did hear a group play Bob Marley covers from the beach.

33. My translation of "*Je voulus m'amuser jusqu'à m'étouffer, mais cela m'était devenu impossible.*" The verb s'amuser is difficult to translate in this context. It simultaneously carries the idea of playing around and enjoying oneself.

34. The hotel employees whom Gmelch interviewed seemed reluctant to make the connection themselves, although one can wonder how likely they would be to enter this line of discussion while being interviewed at their place of employment (Gmelch 2003, 35–36).

35. Écoutes: Listen.

36. Bovell quoted in Gmelch (2003, 78).

37. Hardt (1999, 89–100). While I build on Hardt's definition here, I do not mean to adopt his and Negri's overall conceptualization of "immaterial labor." My main focus is on drawing a distinction between those activities that constitute the primary job of the Club employees, those that constitute their wage labor, and the secondary—affective and unwaged—labor of hospitality.

38. Tu vois: You see.

39. Since my return, I have learned that a slave cemetery had been exposed when the Club built its swimming pool in the late 1990s. An archaeologist was given only a day to examine the site before construction started again, in violation of French law.

3 · LISTENING FOR NOISE

Seeking Disturbing Sounds in Tourist Spaces

SUSAN HAREWOOD

The task of the critic would be to call attention to the cultural voices at play not only those heard in aural close up but also those distorted or drowned out by the text.

—*Shohat and Stam (2014)*

I want to disturb my neighbour

—*Bob Marley (1980)*

On Monday evenings at about 7:30 PM during the tourist season, hotel circuit veteran Richard Layne strides into the beautiful courtyard of the small all-inclusive hotel on the south coast of Barbados. The guests and wait staff are already quietly busy in the choreography of the evening meal. Tall, handsome, and immaculately dressed, Richard carries his guitars and pulls a trolley containing his amplifier and a small laptop computer loaded with the backing tracks he created to use in his hotel shows. In a very short time Richard is set up. In hushed tones he introduces himself to the diners, promising them an eclectic repertoire: "Good evening, ladies and gentlemen, my name is Richard Layne and tonight I'll be playing a little bit of this and a little bit of that. . . ." "A little bit of this, and a little bit of that." It's a phrase he will come back to over and again between songs in his repertoire. And indeed Layne covers a lot of musical ground—from John Denver to Beres Hammond, from the Merrymen to Typically Tropical.

Layne has a very clear understanding of his job: "It's my job to please the guest. I provide background whilst they are dining and having conversation . . . I see my job as pleasing management by pleasing the guests." Layne is an important, though unobtrusive, part of the sounds of the all-inclusive. Specifically, he is a significant element in the creation of the overall "peace and quiet" in the hotel. During the day the hotel is almost silent, and most nights' entertainment, like Richard's, provides a quiet, harmonious background to tourists' dining and conversation.

There is a way in which this beautiful courtyard, with its ready rum punches and carefully tended mini-palms, fulfills one version of the dream of a perfect Caribbean island vacation. This is a dream cultivated in European travelogues and tourism literature over the centuries (Sheller 2003). Here is the idealized space of European idleness. In such a space, work and leisure come together in specific ways: away from the hurly-burly of "modern" life and labor, the travelers have earned their time to surrender to the peace and quiet, barely having to stretch to reach the cooling sustenance of a tropical cocktail. Though much of the research on tourism has analyzed these tropical fantasies through visual culture (Sheller 2003; Urry and Larsen 2011; Waterton and Watson 2014), the fantasy is constructed as much in the auditory realm as it is in the visual realm—near silence or "peace and quiet" is as necessary for some versions of the fantasy as the mental postcards of sunsets, pristine sands, and fruit that at one time would have been exotic but now can be found at any local grocery store.

Adam Jaworski and Crispin Thurlow (2010) argue that silence is deployed as an ideal in the promotion of super-elite tourism. Silence is a trope, they suggest, that is used to signal exclusivity, and it assists would-be travelers in previsualizing their vacation. In other words, it is through representation of quiet and the absence of other people's noise that tourism advertising seeks to produce "exclusivity" and thereby beckon to the would-be tourist. Jaworski and Thurlow are focused on visual representations together with the attendant (or, indeed, absent) text, yet their point can be materially experienced in exploring the actual sounds of all-inclusive tourism. The all-inclusive hotel, the cruise ship, the gated community, and the media feedback loop or echo chamber all highlight ways in which people, to differing degrees and for a variety of reasons, seek to section themselves into like-minded or similar groups. However, the Barbadian case that forms the focus of this chapter illustrates that the construction of these enclaves of peace and quiet requires not only the curation of sounds inside the hotel, but also the curation of the soundscape outside.

The all-inclusive hotel concept in the Caribbean first emerged in Jamaica as a response to the political and economic problems the island was facing (Crick and Campbell 2007; Issa and Jayawardena 2003). These problems made it difficult to market the Jamaican hotels abroad, and thus the creation of all-inclusive hotels, one might argue, began as a way to shield tourists—and for tourists to shield themselves—from any sensory awareness of the sounds, tastes, smells, or feel of political and economic upheaval. The upheaval derived from the growing pains of a postindependence nation caught between its colonial past and neocolonial present— a situation that exacerbated poverty and political clientism. The original Caribbean all-inclusive hotels, then, were an effort to construct a destination that was delinked as much as possible from the island nation in which it was located. Claudio Minca (2010) demonstrates just how important "the island" as a utopian space has been to European writers. The island, he points out, has been constructed in the European archive as this ideal space of re-creation. The tourist industry has consistently made use of this ideal, and it has been especially important to enclavic tourist properties like all-inclusive hotels. Mimi Sheller states, "the creation of the gated, security-guarded, 'all-inclusive resort' throughout the Caribbean has long served as a way of creating spatial/temporal enclaves that carved out tourist territories and performances largely cut off from the surrounding locality, and from local inhabitants" (Sheller 2009, 1395). She, like other writers (Kingsbury 2011; Minca 2010), highlights the role that private security forces, surveillance, and walls have played in the construction of an island within the island. However, I argue in this chapter that the ever-expanding nature of contemporary globalization has seen the extension of the disciplinary effects of tourism beyond the enclave. The notion of a protected "inside" of the hotel that developed in Jamaica in the 1970s and 1980s is modified somewhat in the Barbadian case, in which it is possible to see and hear the extension of the disciplinary project of tourism beyond the brick walls of the hotel. In fact, I contend that, perhaps especially on an island like Barbados with its debatable reputation for placidity, it is particularly important to examine the way colonial and postcolonial narratives produce a sound environment that converts some of the more disturbing noises of history into the more muted tones of Heritage. I argue that the production of a particular version of the peaceful tourist island outside of the hotel reinforces the peace and quiet inside the hotel. In other words, sonic walls replace the militarized walls. Finally, I also suggest that listening to the muted, though ever-present, critique embedded in Caribbean performance might offer a way to come to terms with the disturbing noises of persistent coloniality.

In what follows I pay close attention to the sounds in the background in and around an all-inclusive hotel in Barbados. Specifically, I move out from the "peace and quiet" in the courtyard into the surrounding neighborhood and back again, listening all the while. As the hotel is located within the UNESCO World Heritage Site of Historic Bridgetown and Its Garrison, I use this movement outward as an opportunity to listen for and analyze sounds that seek to reenact particular sonic versions of the Barbadian and British pasts in the creation of Barbados as both nation and destination. I contend that listening to these background sounds helps us explore the ongoing questions that a postindependence tourism destination is constantly engaged in asking. What historical narratives are emphasized and what narratives are muted in the production of the "tourist island"? How does this sound environment facilitate the production of the all-inclusive island within the tourist island? What might be gained in tourism studies by amplifying and listening attentively to the disturbing sounds of past and present coloniality?

Sound and the Structuring of Quiet

Sonic meaning-making practices are a useful cultural site at which to explore both Barbados's determination to be an independent nation and its status as a tourist destination. The citizen desires that culminated on November 30, 1966, with the ceremony at the Garrison Savannah celebrating Barbados's constitutional independence from Britain do not necessarily coincide at all times with tourist desires, set in motion by the ever-expanding global tourism industry. By the same token, of course, these desires do not necessarily diverge either. This is the complexity of human relations that is perhaps most starkly observable within the colonial/postcolonial context. Though colonialism is built on the production of an idea of absolute differences, the enforced proximity of colonizer and colonized produces forms of kinship—even if that proximity is produced less in the segregated spaces that imperialism produces and more in the imperialist pedagogy that (in the case of European colonialism) continues to infuse pervasive Eurocentric narratives.

Research in critical tourism studies has highlighted the potential conflict and contradiction at the heart of tourism, especially heritage tourism, and, perhaps, particularly for state actors and heritage practitioners working in the formerly colonized world. The concept of "heritage" has been viewed with skepticism. One of the major critiques has been that heritage is a process that, though it supposedly highlights the old and the ancient, in fact creates something new (Kirshenblatt-Gimblett 1995), a version of history that fails to serve the needs of anything much more than the commercial interests in society. Thus, for example, Bella Dicks (2004) identifies the competing forces in contention within tourism destinations: on the one hand, she suggests, there is the desire to stage and affirm "authentic" culture, while on the other hand there is also the need to cater to a market that might be more interested in its fantasy version of the destination. Hazel Tucker and Elizabeth Carnegie (2014) point out similarly conflicting objectives, suggesting that heritage sites might be identified as important for the community or people whose culture is being preserved, but that the *real* audience for any heritage site is the tourist, and this results in the commodification of heritage. Such explorations of heritage highlight time and again how history is converted into "heritage." By this the writers mean that historical research gets stripped of its complexity and packaged in ways that make it easily consumable and commodifiable. For those places where colonialism existed and, indeed, continues to exist in various configurations, this has frequently meant revivifying again and again a colonial past conveniently emptied of the imperialists' violence. It is often a history that marginalizes the very same populations exploited during colonialism. And it is often a history that caters to the wish fulfillment of the tourists who bear some kinship with the colonizers.

Many of the tourists, of course, do not have a direct familial connection, and recognizing that is important to providing nuance to any analysis. For example, one important way to complicate the idea of kinship is to recognize that the growth and relative ease of international tourist travel today means that many of the white European and Anglo-American tourists traveling to places like Barbados are likely to be descendants of those who were press-ganged into maritime service or disenfranchised by vagrancy laws. Yet the presence (or absence) of a direct line of biological lineage is not necessarily the end of the story told and retold in the heritage tourism site. Scholars exploring tourism have highlighted that tourism and world heritage tourism revalue colonial narratives and iconography through a variety of (often visual) media. These images become the archives by which sons and daughters and cousins of plantation owners and sons and daughters and cousins of indentured servants can both imagine their kinship to imperial power and its aftermaths. And indeed, sons and daughters of the enslaved, as is demonstrated below, are often invited to do the same, with limited consideration of what is at stake. One of the challenges facing citizens in the colonized and colonizing world is how to interrupt the making and remaking of these lines of kinship within the context of an expanding tourism industry that relies on those lineages.

In a series of articles, Christine Buzinde and her coauthors have examined the Eurocentric ideologies at play in heritage sites in Canada and plantation America (Buzinde et al. 2006; Buzinde and Santos 2008; Buzinde and Osagie 2011). Relatedly, for the English-speaking Caribbean, Polly Pattullo (2005), Jamaica Kincaid (2000), and Mimi Sheller (2003) have, in different ways, examined the persistence of colonial tropes and colonial relations in contemporary advertising and tourist practices. Sheller, whose scholarship is an important node from which a rich body of tourism research emerges, traces the changing Eurocentric discourses about the Caribbean from the seventeenth century through to the nineteenth century, which become folded into contemporary tourist iconography and then present the region and its people as perpetually available for European consumption. Sheller, therefore, leads a significant group of scholars exploring the importance of tourist imaginings to the construction, maintenance, repair, and transformation of locations into the type of tourist destinations that reproduce colonial power relations. There is a similarly important body of literature that is giving thought to how the imagination might be deployed to challenge these colonial narratives. For example, Keith Hollinshead's work (2002, 2004, 2009) has focused on tourism as a world-making practice. He turns his attention from tracing the development of tropes and icons to asking how these acts of imagination might be put to more hopeful purposes. Hollinshead has been a catalyst to others examining the world-making imaginative practices of tourism (Ateljevic, Hollinshead, and Ali 2009). However, Chambers and Buzinde (2015) argue that this branch of tourism research clustered under the heading "hopeful tourism" remains lodged in colonial thinking itself. They suggest that the critical turn in tourism has not addressed the questions of structural power and inequality in tourism and that hopeful tourism maintains its focus on both European lives and European knowledge. Their contention that there remains a great deal of work to be done in order to change the habits of thinking in and around tourism is an extremely useful critique. However, Chambers and Buzinde's call for radical epistemological delinking from Western ways of thinking relies on easily identifiable, absolute, and bounded categories of Western thought and non-Western thought that are impossible to maintain. In fact, the condition of Caribbean postcoloniality is such that it is always already hybrid.

Thus it becomes necessary to find ways to simultaneously acknowledge the domination and depravity of colonialism while also paying attention to the entanglements and complex forms of belonging that exist. I believe that sound may offer one way to do this. Tourism research has maintained quite a fixed focus on visual culture and text produced in Europe and North America for European and North American travelers. It has to be acknowledged that this research has been extremely fruitful. However, because the images in tourism advertising are often produced in the North for northern would-be travelers, this can also lead to the Eurocentric focus Chambers and Buzinde are challenging. In this chapter, the focus on sound complicates this somewhat. It focuses on sounds produced within the nation and intended for both nationals and vacationers. This focus on sound highlights the complex position of Caribbean postcoloniality: in the West but not of the West; constantly engaged in negotiations over what is authored by historical and contemporary conditions of coloniality and what is authored by the historical and contemporary impulses toward independence and freedom.

The contribution that the analysis of sound can make to these efforts to challenge Eurocentrism is suggested, for me, in the Shohat and Stam quotation that heads this chapter. In its context within their book (2014), this quotation links sound and space as methods to challenge the habits of Eurocentric thinking. Shohat and Stam's engagement with voice as a metaphor to represent identity and representation (Novak 2015) makes its anti-imperialist challenge by taking the visual medium of film and approaching it sonically, at least provisionally. In so doing, they seek to rethink the taken-for-granted categories of analysis. The same approach can be valuable for seeking an anti-imperial analysis of tourism, as tourism research itself has been so visual in its focus. Thus I am using Shohat and Stam as a jumping-off point and linking this chapter to their project of "adversary scholarship" even as I extend their use of sonic metaphors to a more direct engagement both with the entangled uses of sound metaphors and with the material experiences of sound. This chapter builds on research in *Audible Empire: Music, Global Politics and Critique* (Radano and Olaniyan 2016) that demonstrates the importance of music in the construction of empire and suggests that taking up Shohat and Stam's adversarial project can best be undertaken by utilizing sound studies' commitment to investigating the sound practices and the discourses and institutions that describe those sound practices (Sterne 2012). Shohat and Stam's brief exploration of the metaphors of sound is concerned with questions of sound and space in that they are interested in the power dynamics that shape which voices are heard in the foreground and which voices get drowned out.

In this chapter I take up similar interests by examining the ways in which sounds are experienced as being in the background. However, "being in the background" challenges the rather assured politics of voices "drowned out by the text." Drowned out voices indicate those positions that have been marginalized in some way. This chapter is deeply concerned with those voices but also approaches this by considering sounds that might be experienced as being in the background for different reasons. The chapter thus begins by examining sounds that are experienced as being in the background because they are somewhat at a physical distance from the listener in the courtyard, and by doing this I seek to demonstrate the blurring of the lines that divide the peace and quiet in the all-inclusive from the supposed outside soundscape. The chapter also examines sounds that are experienced as being in the background because they have become so naturalized that we pay little attention to them and yet, as the research on background music demonstrates (Sterne 1997), these sounds have the ability to shape our affective responses and behaviors. When these sounds are not just the canned music of the mall but rather are the reenactment of colonial power relations, I argue that they are deployed in order to produce a version of innocent Englishness that both shapes the postcolony and helps preserve the indolence of the courtyard.

In the pages that follow I also listen carefully for at least three versions of sounds experienced as deep background "noise," if we take noise to be sounds deemed to be out of place (Cooper 1995; Novak 2015). First, I explore the imperial noises of colonial brutality, which are often shoved aside by the repetitive return to the idea of English innocence. Second, I explore the deep background insurgent noises; these resemble Shohat and Stam's drowned out voices—sounds that are experienced as noises to be refused by touristic pleasure and disciplined by state and economic elites. And, finally, I attend to the moments when these "neighborhood sounds" quietly seep into the courtyard, and I ask how the politics of these sounds might be heard and amplified in the courtyard. By paying attention to the sounds of the courtyard and the performance of veteran hotel musician Richard

Layne, I seek to link these sounds more firmly to the insurgent sounds of Barbadian history as a way to disturb some forms of coloniality that remain unchallenged in touristic relations.

The Main Guard Clock Tower and the
Ordering of Post/Colonial Time

Is that the one with a lot of history?

—*A comment from a conversation I had with an American who had taken a Caribbean cruise. She was trying to remember if one of the many islands she had visited on her cruise had been Barbados.*

Seated in the quiet of the courtyard in the very late morning, I try listening for the striking of the clock of the Main Guard clock tower. In the Nomination Document that successfully resulted in Barbados' Historic Bridgetown and Its Garrison being listed as a UNESCO World Heritage Site on June 25, 2011, the Main Guard clock tower is described in the following manner: "The most notable and recognizable building facing onto the Savannah is the 'Main Guard' (or 'Clock Tower'), built in 1804, situated to the west of the Savannah and near geographical center of the entire Garrison area" (Ministry of Community Development and Culture 2010, 44). The Main Guard is just a few yards from the all-inclusive hotel, but I could only faintly hear the clock in the courtyard. When I *did* hear it, the indistinct sounds of the Westminster Quarters barely breached the walls of the hotel. All of the notes did not quite make it to my ears, yet the tune was still recognizable. I wondered if the tourists heard the clock and recognized its familiar chimes. The clock at the Main Guard chimes the Westminster Quarters from 6 AM to 6 PM weekdays, every fifteen minutes. The Westminster Quarters or Cambridge Quarters was composed at Cambridge University by organ student William Crotch in 1793 ("Bell Chime" 2016). It is the chime that has been associated with the English Houses of Parliament since 1859 ("Bell Chime" 2016). The *Encyclopedia Britannica* states that the chime is the most commonly heard chime in English-speaking countries. Indeed, it is one of the alarms on my cell phone, reminding me that it is healthier if I break from writing this and get up and move every hour. The sounds of the Westminster Quarters in the Historic Bridgetown and Its Garrison UNESCO World Heritage Site are part of the overall sonic pedagogy of this site. The alarm on my phone is simply entitled "old clock." The

Quarters, their very ubiquity and ability to simply signify "clock," together with the other music played by the clock tower, perform a regular and regulating type of work that produces the version of Barbados as nation and destination that makes the peace and quiet in the courtyard possible.

It takes less than five minutes to walk to the Main Guard clock tower in the heart of the Historic Bridgetown and Its Garrison area. Signage dots the area marking its significance as a site to be gazed upon (Urry and Larsen 2011). Multiple signs announce the buildings that are important to the heritage site, in most cases specifically referencing its military heritage. These signs seek to anchor the meaning of the area. The signs not only highlight the fact that heritage and tourism are inextricably entangled, but also suggest why the cruise passenger whose comment heads this section views Barbados in terms of quantifiable amounts of history. In a global tourism industry in which each destination is seeking to advance a brand, it would seem that part of Barbados's brand is that it is the location where one can sample history because somehow they "have a lot of it."

The signage displays logos from the private sector, government agencies, and UNESCO as an international organization, and highlights the public and private, national and supranational institutions that invest in and are invested in the site and its portrayal of a particular notion of Barbadian history. For example, the signs ringing the UNESCO World Heritage Site state: "Historic Bridgetown and its Garrison exhibits an important interchange of human values in the diversity of African, European and other ethnicities, and the confluence of cultural practices of free and enslaved persons who created a hybridized culture and creolized architecture, over the span of almost three centuries." This blurb tweaks "history" into "heritage." The blurb is certainly not blind to the history of imperial power and enslavement. Whereas earlier histories largely erased the contributions of non-Europeans, particularly Africans, to the construction and development of the Caribbean, contemporary historians have been engaged in the processes of researching and writing scholarly historical narratives that recognize those contributions (Shepherd 2010), and the sign's blurb must be recognized as part of ongoing efforts to draw local and global attention to the creative and intellectual labors of people of African descent in making, not just the Americas, but also European prosperity (Beckles 2013; Williams 1994). Nevertheless, the blurb, as a tiny narrative of progress and human collaboration, places a great deal of emphasis on equal contributions while providing only limited attention to the significant power differentials of those taking part. Whereas the signs produce, in image and text, a version of Barbadian heritage that flattens the relations of power in Barbados slavery and its colonial past, the clock and its chimes further background that disturbing, noisy history by more assertively foregrounding Barbados as "Little England"—a historical narrative that has its own long history, including its persistent use by the tourism industry (Burrowes 2000). This narrative of Barbados as Little England is also replicated in the chimes of the Main Guard clock.

At 6 AM each morning, the clock, which stands not only in the historic Garrison, but also next to the current headquarters of the Barbados Defense Force, plays "Reveille" (the military wake-up call). The Main Guard is home to a number of military organizations including the Barbados Legion and Barbados Poppy League. At 7 AM the clock plays "Bunessan," also known as "Morning Has Broken." During November, the month in which Barbados celebrates its constitutional independence, the clock chimes the Barbados national anthem, the lyrics for which were composed by Irving Burgie, also known as Lord Burgess, a key figure in the 1950s calypso craze in the United States. Burgie penned songs like "The Banana Boat Song," "Island in the Sun," and "Don't Ever Love Me" (a song set to the music of the island song "Yellow Bird"). Also in November the clock plays "Beautiful Barbados" by the internationally recognized Barbadian hotel band The Merrymen. During Christmas season the clock plays Christmas carols and songs. Though these are the regular tunes that are played, the clock has an expandable repertoire of over 150 tunes. The chime mechanism is an electronic one imported from England as the original mechanism is awaiting restoration. Over half of the tunes in the potential repertoire of the clock are hymns and/or Christmas songs. In addition to the Barbadian national anthem, there are national anthems from the United Kingdom, United States, Canada, France, Israel, Italy, Japan, Wales, and Germany. In addition to "Beautiful Barbados" there are folk and popular songs from Ireland, England, Wales, and the Isle of Man. To understand the ways in which this repertoire produces the postcolony, it is helpful to very briefly examine research on the functions of public bells in sound studies.

Clock chimes and tower bells have long been important to the regulation of public life. Alain Corbin (1998), like Jonathan Sterne and Emily Raine (2006) and Mark Smith (1997), explores the ways in which public clock chimes would come to regulate life. In the nineteenth century public chimes imposed what Corbin refers to as "an empty, continuous, neutral time" (1998, 219). Similarly, Sterne and Raine (2006) describe the traditional public clock as a "social metronome" and argue that a community's recognition of themselves as a public is their recognition of themselves as sharing and consuming the same time. The balance of Sterne and Raine's article, however, highlights how the contemporary moment shifts time's regulating function from the public to the level of the private. They contend that today we have so many devices — cell phones, tablets, fitness trackers, computers — through which we keep our personalized schedule that the keeping of time has moved to the level of the self-regulation of the subject. Sterne and Raine suggest that acoustic markers of time have been silenced in the digital era — no ticking, no clicking as the clock arms sweep the clock face and, rather than the regular alarms of the public clock, we set a series of sonic alarm events — like the one telling me to get up and move — that have meaning within our personalized schedules.

Given this migration of sonic time-keeping into the imperceptible logics of self-regulation, then, the restoration of public acoustic time becomes a valuable cultural practice to unpack. The clock on the Main Guard, while simultaneously serving as an acoustic time marker for the specific audience that lives and works in the area of the Garrison, also marks the time of postcoloniality. By describing this as the time of postcoloniality I am highlighting the way in which Barbados's "postness" as postindependence is celebrated even as the sounds serve to suture Barbados back into its position as colony. Thus, the chimes on the clock are a historical reenactment sounded out every fifteen minutes that firmly weds the independent nation of Barbados to England, and not just any version of England; it is a spotless portrait of English inherent superiority. This is encoded into the narrative that identifies Barbados as Little England.

Barbados's designation as Little England is something that has been discussed in many contexts. Curwen Best has identified this narrative as a myth that has "stereotyped Barbados as a homogeneous entity: Protestant, prim and proper, transparent, noncomplex" (2000). Perhaps the most illuminating use made of Barbados's supposed Little Englishness can be found in Jamaican author John Hearne's essay "What the Barbadian Means to Me" (1967). In this essay, written, ironically enough, to mark Barbados's independence, Hearne says he is fascinated by the dissimilarity he identifies between Barbados and its neighbors. Though he feels affinity with Trinidadians and Guyanese, he views Barbadians as an elusive "problem." The mystery of Barbadians, he says, is that they are more English than other

West Indians: In the first place, he is English in a way that the rest of us are not. "History Englished him by giving him an exclusive association with that potent and wonderful country just at the time when it was in one of its most creative phases (Hearne 1967, 6). This "Englishing," Hearne suggests, provides Barbadians with a broad range of positive character traits: he (and Hearne uses the male pronoun throughout) has "real psychic strength," "flexibility of the mind"; is industrious, thrifty, honest, and orderly; and has compassion, integrity, and a well-established educational foundation in the Classics. Note that even as Hearne offers his backhanded compliment, he reinscribes Barbados and the entire Caribbean into the British imperial narrative of English superiority. Though he suggests toward the end of his essay that the Englishing has made Barbadians particularly petty and cruel, Hearne's overall argument about the Barbadian is that he is strange but wonderful, and the reason he is wonderful is that he has been exposed to the wonderful English at their most creative phase. Note that this supposedly creative phase, 1627 to 1966, includes the era of imperialism, which of course includes enslavement and indentureship.

One can imagine that this type of myth invites certain "Protestant" sounds but rejects others as noise. Thus, returning to the clock's repertoire, there are clear ways that it produces Barbados as a Christian nation-state closer to its English colonial roots than its Caribbean neighbors. The Westminster Quarters, the traditional songs, and the hymns produce a particular form of (both religious and secular) Anglicanism, though this is firmly linked to Barbadian independence by the playing of the Barbadian national anthem as well as the popular ballad, "Beautiful Barbados." However, the list of other available national anthems is made conspicuous by the fact that, despite the importance of regional integration to economic, political, and cultural futures for Barbadians and all other members of CARICOM, not one anthem from a Caribbean neighbor is on the list. These orientations are in many ways unremarkable; one does not have to suggest nefarious intent in accounting for this repertoire. In fact, its very ordinariness highlights how colonial discourses continue to curate the archive and the fact that nationalist discourses can often be entwined in colonial ones. Nevertheless, though the repertoire is unremarkable, it is helpful for understanding the relationship between the Barbadian island destination and its relationship to the all-inclusive island within an island. The repertoire of the clock and the signs work together to repeatedly produce, every fifteen minutes at least, the island destination that provides the peaceful home for the all-inclusive island within the island. These are the sonic walls of the hotel. Even if tourists within the hotel are largely unaware of the chimes—as I have already suggested, the chimes hardly penetrate the actual walls of the hotel and, even if they did, the Westminster Chimes have become ordinary in their ability to simply signify "clock" or even "time"—I would argue that the visitors' awareness or lack of it is less important for us to think about than the fact that the labor of orienting Barbados to Little England is perpetually being sounded. In the next section I argue that this narrative quells the noisy colonial anxieties of both the postcolonial elites and the tourists and their remembrances of colonial violence.

The Sounds of Drums and the Production of Innocence

Norfolk didn't have anything to do with the slave trade though.

—*An assertion from a British cruise passenger in relation to nothing we had been discussing*

You may be surprised to know that Norfolk played an important role in all parts of the Slave Trade.

—*From the website Norfolk's Hidden Treasures*

Each Thursday beginning in June and ending in March of the next year, as the clock on the Main Guard clock tower chimes noon, the Changing of the Sentry is performed. This is a military ritual that would have been executed at guardhouses throughout Barbados during the nineteenth century. Described as "the Barbadian version of the Changing of the Guard at Buckingham Palace" (Barbados Garrison 2015), the reenactment participates, then, in the same sonic construction of space that positions Barbados closer to the version of England described above. If listening intently to the legitimated public sounds of the clock draws our attention to a persistent effort to construct Barbados's "wonderful" Little Englishness, then listening to the military/militaristic rituals of the Changing of the Sentry might draw our attention not only to the violence and imperial race-thinking at the core of this myth, but also to the links between World Heritage Sites and the neocolonial desire to be absolved of any wrongdoing. This desire for absolution haunts the Norfolk cruise ship passenger's comment that heads this section. His words seem to be a blurted effort to distance his ancestors from any involvement in slavery, and yet, as I have suggested already, this craving for absolution is contradictorily located within the tourism industry's reliance on the affirmation of colonial heritage. This visitor's contradictory feelings are not merely a personal discomfiture, however; writers from different points along the routes that crisscross the colonial/postcolonial world have highlighted the challenges attendant to "coming to terms" with the brutal past of imperialism. Two scholars, Paul Gilroy and Percy Hintzen, seem particularly relevant to understanding World Heritage Sites in the postcolonial world, as part of the processes by which claims to white innocence and the questioning of blacks' rights to freedom are replicated.

Paul Gilroy (2005), writing from an English perspective, describes a "postcolonial melancholia" that haunts the formerly imperial states. Colonizing nations like Britain, he says, are unable to address their loss of imperial prestige. Their melancholia makes them unable to move on from their grief at that loss. This gives rise to particular forms of racism and xenophobia and also to the writing of revisionist histories. The revisionist histories seek to separate the colonists and those who are perceived to have some kinship with the colonists (either directly or through the kinship work performed by tourism advertising described above) from the brutal past and thereby to whitewash history. This effort at rewriting history, which Gilroy sees occurring within the academy and popular histories, replicates itself outside of the academy from the compulsion to deny a personal link to the slavery past, to the ways in which heritage sites make and remake history. Percy Hintzen (2005), writing from a Caribbean perspective, identifies what I see as a related malady, which he describes as "colonial nostalgia" and which he says haunts some members of the Caribbean ruling classes. These postcolonial elites are desperate to think of themselves as modern but are confronted by two problems. First, Eurocentric discourses have repeatedly narrated Europe's exclusive claims to being modern. Second, therefore, the only way that postcolonial elites can claim to be modern, especially in the face of the poverty and decline that the Caribbean experiences (largely because of its hinterland status to the economies of the overdeveloped world), is to yearn for some sort of supervisory position in a new (impossible) version of the colonial past. Listening carefully to the Changing of the Sentry, this difficulty in "coming to terms" with the colonial past can be heard in the performance.

The ceremony begins with two sentries and a noncommissioned officer (NCO) marching into position below the Main Guard clock tower. The officer addresses the sentries in the tones we, the gathered tourists and locals, would easily recognize as the genre of command. Not every single word makes it through the breeze blowing across the Garrison, but it is clear that the sentries are given a long list of things they must and must not do. The black shiny boots under brilliant white spats click on the asphalt as the NCO marches off. The voice of the narrator comes over the loud speaker. *His* voice, amplified by the public address system, easily cuts through the breeze as he welcomes the gathered audience to the Changing of the Sentry on behalf of the Garrison Consortium — the nonprofit organization that produces the reenactment, a night tour, and maintains the signage and the Main Guard clock. The narrator tells us that the ceremony "is an authentic staging of an activity that took place every hour daily during the nineteenth century at five other guard rooms and eight sentry posts through this Garrison." He identifies the Main Guard building as one of the historic buildings and part of the UNESCO World Heritage Site. He draws attention to the white Coade stone coat of arms of King George III that adorns the Main Guard, explaining that Coade stone is "a long-lasting ceramic stone perfected by Eleanor Coade in the late 1700s in England." He invites us to look closely to see that, in King George's royal coat of arms, one of the lion's legs is missing, having fallen victim to "an enthusiastic cricket ball hit out of the Garrison field."

The narrator's script, therefore, anchors the reenactment to a narrative that emphasizes British royalty, English invention, and sport. Though the words of the narration serve as an anchor for the reenactment, the content of the words must also be heard to be anchored by the tone and the contexts of performance. Thus, though "invention" seems relatively uncontroversial as a value, "royalty" and "cricket" seem more open. As a rich body of literature has demonstrated, cricket for the Caribbean, and for much of the formerly colonized world of the British Empire, served not only as a key site at which British colonial superiority was performed, but, because of that very symbolic importance, cricket also has been fundamentally important to anticolonial politics (see, for example, Beckles 1999, 2000; Downes 2005; James 2005). It is thus very likely that the meaning of "cricket" in the narrative accommodates both of these meanings. An oppositional listening to "royalty" might understand the use of royalty in a similar mode — one in which the absurd human ordering of monarchical rule is brought to the foreground. However, the tone of the narration indicates that the dominant messages encoded in the use of royalty link it more closely to the pageantry of the Changing of the Guard and the version of a "wonderful" monarchy found in *Royal* and *Hello* magazines than to any "subversive" republicanism.

Perhaps it is in the sound of the drums played during the reenactment more than anywhere else that the cultural politics described above might be listened for. The drum has persistently been the instrument where racial politics are heard (Radano 2000). The march of the military drum booms through the reenactment, muting, though not altogether silencing, insurgent drums. At this site the aesthetic racial hierarchy set in train in the metropole was refined and rationalized in Barbados into the 1661 Slave Codes. The codes controlled "the social activities of the enslaved limiting cultural expression, movement, marketing activities and several other aspects of their lives — entrenching their unfreedom and dependence in plantation society" (Ministry of Community Development and Culture 2010, 105). The Slave Codes were replicated in Jamaica, South Carolina, and Antigua. The control included the prohibition of drumming — though how strictly the codes were enforced depended on a range of factors (Goveia 1970). It is commonly held that the ethos of prohibition and control of drumming and other cultural practices led to the development of Barbados's indigenous music, tuk.[1] In any case, the enactment of the codes sought to determine which sounds were dangerous, and dangerous to whom. The military drum is presented as the sound of legitimate violence, while the Slave Codes positioned black culture as inherently threatening.

Military service stood at the nexus of the definition of blackness, whiteness, class, and citizenship. In the early plantation period white Barbadian planters used the enslaved in the militia. Militia service was a right of citizenship (Handler 1984). But, of course, the slaves were not citizens, and their inclusion in the Barbados militia was both an indication of the need for militia men and the "super citizen" status of the white elite classes, who were able to fulfill their citizenship through the bodies of others. Similar shifting borders of race, class, and freedom also played out in the recruitment of blacks to serve in the West India Regiment (WIR). Alfred B. Ellis's *History of the First West India Regiment* (1885) is an argument for increasing the size of the WIR in order to have a force that could serve the vast British Empire. In discussing the suitability of the West Indians to serve as a force in tropical locations, Ellis maps out the imperial racial structuring of humanity. This involved the categorizing of different forms of "subject people" and the construction of different versions of whiteness. Thus black

West Indians were compared favorably to Africans because of the positive influence of their close proximity to white role models. A West Indian regiment, it was suggested, would work well in India because of the enmity between "the Hindoo" and the West Indian. The white working classes were deemed too susceptible to tropical diseases, but blacks were seen as better able to withstand them. The argument about black and white soldiers and tropical diseases should not be understood as an argument about which soldier had developed immunological resistance to diseases. Rather, the discussion highlighted what the upper classes saw as black and working-class white unsuitability for self-governance. While the attention given to the physiques of the black soldiers bordered at times on the homoerotic, attention to poor white physiques seemed to provide the upper classes with evidence of the working white poor's inferior status (Daye, Chambers, and Roberts 2008).

While the command, duty, or privilege of serving in the military mapped out the gradations of male humanness allowed by the imperial powers, the campaigns that the West India Regiment fought tell us even more about the brutality of colonial power and the ways in which the reenactment quiets (again, does not silence) the noisy viciousness of imperialism. Although the black soldiers were manumitted upon joining the army, not only was that freedom precarious if the soldiers went into the larger slave society (Daye et al. 2008), but of course, as soldiers in a regiment of the British Army, their primary task was to assert British imperial power. This entailed crushing the freedom and justice uprisings of others, including the Carib War in St. Vincent 1795, the 1816 Bussa's Rebellion in Barbados, and, in the post-Emancipation period, the Morant Bay Rebellion in Jamaica in 1865, to name just a few. Thus military service in the slave colony used black enlisted bodies and constrained freedom as the "tip of the spear" to deny black and Carib freedom.

The sounds of the Changing of the Sentry, then, like the sounds of the Main Guard clock, are part of the way that the island destination is produced by its orientation to a particular version of Little Englishness. Yet I would suggest that whereas the sounds of the clock might seem quite innocent, the Changing of the Sentry highlights the violence and hierarchizing of humanity that were at the heart of the imperial project. These performances are replicated as if they also were innocent. However, they cannot be accepted as innocent if there is no way to confront the violence and brutality. In the next section, I return to the courtyard and, by linking the sounds in the courtyard to those in the UNESCO World Heritage Site, I attempt to explore whether a type of listening that is active and attuned to the lineages of Caribbean political performances might challenge the constant return to a singular Little England narrative.

To Listen and to Hear: Returning to the Courtyard

A little bit of this, a little bit of that

—*Musician Richard Layne*

Waiting in the courtyard for the evening's entertainment, the near-silence of the morning has given way to the hushed sounds of dinner. The female wait staff, dressed in polo shirts and black skirts, are putting the final touches on the place settings: plates, glasses, and cutlery clink into precise place. Every once in a while, the women will murmur directions to each other as they flit between the tables. Guests appear dressed in the "evening resort wear" insisted upon by all-inclusives. Pastel-colored sundresses, collared shirts, and slacks contrast with the fiery redness of sunburned skin. As guests sit, they begin conversations with each other and with the waiters. Both waiters and guests use the polite tones of the routine service encounter as they cover the basics of the vacation script: daytime tourist activities completed and planned, and meal choices. The waiters speak their Barbadian accents with precision, wanting to ensure that they are clearly understood. The visitors speak their regional English accents with precision too, also wanting to ensure that they are clearly understood. Their respective accents, Barbadian and English, suggest that perhaps the distant sons, daughters, and cousins of English indentured servants and the distant sons, daughters, and cousins of enslaved Africans are meeting in this space once again. These performances of tourism work and tourism leisure maintain the peace and quiet of the courtyard.

These are not the only sounds heard in the courtyard in the evening, however. Other sounds seep through. In contrast to the murmuring wait staff, every now and then the more garrulous interactions of the kitchen staff stutter through the quiet. Laughter and loud conversations bounce off the clanging pots and pans. Both backstage and frontstage sounds are accompanied by music from a small sound system that seems midway between frontstage and offstage. Red buttons glow from a dark corner, and the sound system is tuned to local hit radio. Dancehall reggae sporadically breaks through into the courtyard. The slight distortion from the speakers means that it is not fully clear which songs are playing. What makes it through occasionally, then, is a sensation of the driving though quieted beats of dancehall accompanied by the indistinct Americanized-Bajan speech patterns of the contemporary Barbadian radio announcer/ DJ. In the rise and fall of dinnertime conversation, the kitchen sounds and dancehall rhythms occasionally come to the foreground. I am put in mind of Carolyn Cooper's description of dancehall from Jamaica's inner city invading the space and power of middle-class neighborhoods: "Night noises . . . pollute middle-class neighborhoods, disturbing a neighbor's sleep, [and] are a threatening challenge to those uneasily awake in comfortable beds" (Cooper 1995, 5).

However, neither guests nor waiters appear to notice the backstage sounds. Of course, just because they do not give any outward sign of hearing does not mean that they have not heard. Hearing does not necessarily provide an outward indication. Or perhaps the tourists and the frontstage tourism workers are intent upon the scripts of their respective performances (Edensor, 2001). Possibly, as Minca (2010) suggests, backstage performances like these, rather than challenging the serene holiday illusion, are, in fact, a necessary part of that illusion. He suggests that the moment when the tourist catches a glimpse of the toil involved in maintaining the tourist illusion, or the tourism worker behaving differently from the required touristic script, permits the tourist to recognize her/his participation in the suspension of disbelief. This, Minca suggests, "allows tourists not to be embarrassed or annoyed but actually rather amused by their involvement in what would otherwise be perceived as unacceptable public performances and forms of control" (Minca 2010, 97). Minca's analysis, which is ocular, highlights the way this "look behind the curtain" serves the tourism industry and satisfies, even as it disciplines the tourist and the tourism worker. However, embarrassment, annoyance, or amusement do not exhaust the possible responses to those aspects of tourism work that, as referenced above, reiterate colonial relations.[2] A key question must be whether different ways of listening to the touristic performance might offer different ways of accessing responses — responses that repudiate the imperialist resonances. Listening implies a willingness to attend to the concerns of others: "Listening here is, first and foremost, the act of recognizing what others have to say, recognizing that they have something to say, or better, that they like all human beings have the capacity to give an account of their lives that is reflexive and continuous, an ongoing, embodied process of reflection" (Couldry 2009, 579–80).

This type of listening, of course, is in no way easy. Listening practices are structured by power, and inviting those who travel to listen in ways that move them beyond the touristic soundscape, with its sounds muted or silenced for their comfort, is particularly challenging. Still, tourism is often viewed as a pedagogical project. This can be witnessed in the ways that governments, cultural workers, tourists, and tourism managers write about the history lessons that are to be gleaned from heritage tourism. Indeed, it is heard in the commonly expressed aphorism that travel broadens the mind. Thus, progressive lessons of travel must challenge the dampening sounds of colonial power and seek out the noise that disturbs. In what follows I seek to explore just a little of the complexity of the performances of a veteran hotel musician.

Richard Layne is a twenty-year veteran of the hotel circuits. He performs at different hotels different nights of the week and has consistently performed at one of those hotels for thirteen years. His success and experience over the years illustrate that Layne has been an integral part of the nationalist efforts to craft a postindependence national Barbadian cultural identity. He has won a number of awards including the Musicians and Entertainers Guild of Barbados (MEGOB) award in 1985, has a number of National Independence Festival of Creative Arts (NIFCA) medals, and has performed at the NIFCA Gala many times. Layne represented Barbados at the Caribbean Broadcasting Union (CBU) Awards and, in 1992, he represented Barbados at Lancaster House in London at the Royal Festival. Layne started singing on the hotel circuit with some friends, one of whom heard him practicing in front of his house. "I am a self-taught guitarist. I would sit on the neighbor's step for hours. . . . A fella from the neighborhood approached me and asked me if I would like to sing in the hotels. I was worried at first, I said 'the type of confidence you have in me, I don't know if I have in myself.'" (R. Layne, interview with the author, April 21, 2015).

Layne has created a number of folk songs that are very popular with Barbadians. Some of his most well-known folk songs focus on the insurgent history of Barbados and, as such, can link us back to the muted voices of Historic Bridgetown and Its Garrison. For example, one of his songs celebrates a national hero, Bussa—the enslaved man who led the 1816 slave rebellion crushed by the West Indian Regiment referenced earlier. Another of Layne's songs celebrates another national hero, Clement Payne, whose efforts to win union representation for workers in Barbados can be linked to the muted narratives of the Garrison. Although the emphasis on the Changing of the Sentry is on the pageantry of the imperial forces, a muted part of the performance is the significance of the West Indian Regiment soldiers to the black labor politics in the Caribbean and United States (Elkins 1970; Howe 2001). Many black leaders and soldiers saw participation in World War I as a means of gaining representative government in the Caribbean. Those who enlisted soon found that institutional racism was alive and well in the armed forces overseas. By the end of the war, large numbers of disaffected former soldiers returning to the Caribbean were viewed with alarm by the colonial authorities. Many of the former soldiers had fought for equal rights in the armed forces and were returning to a region that was rife with strikes and other forms of labor unrest. A number of them did precisely what the colonial authorities feared: they became vocal, active, leading members of local and regional political organizations, including the Universal Negro Improvement Association (UNIA) and the Working-men's Association. The "noise" of this line of Barbadian history is muted in the narratives of Little England, yet Clement Payne is the heir of this line of activism, and Richard Layne's song celebrates this line. Layne also composed a song that celebrates the indigenous cultural and saving organization, the Landship, which is generally accompanied in its public performances by the tuk band, also referenced above. However, Layne rarely performs these songs in his hotel performances. He says: "You could say that there are two sides to Richard Layne: the one who plays in the hotels and the one who plays at the cultural shows and that the Barbadians who hear me at cultural shows might not know about my hotel circuit self, and the tourists don't know about my cultural show performances" (R. Layne, interview with the author, April 21, 2015).

In his performances at the all-inclusive hotel, Layne says that his job is to form part of the background. His current repertoire is wide-ranging and deliberately diverse. At the beginning of his performance and in between sets he tells his audience that he will be playing a "little bit of this, a little bit of that." This includes country, pop, ballads, island songs, calypsos, and reggae tunes from different eras. He developed the repertoire from being an attentive scholar of tourist wishes: "There is no set formula of how to please the tourist audience. I worked it out by trial and error. You play the island songs and there is a reaction. It has a nostalgic effect. It's my job to please the guest" (R. Layne, interview with the author, April 21, 2015).

When he first started singing, he was strongly influenced by Harry Belafonte and the calypso craze in the United States. He taught himself to play guitar by learning island songs such as those penned by Irving Burgie. When a friend invited him to begin singing on the hotel circuit, these island songs were, and they still remain, an important part of his repertoire. However, he pointed out that not every hotel worker likes his decision to play island songs. "I see my job as pleasing management by pleasing the guests. Sometimes a hotel worker might compare me to another performer or tell me something like, 'You, you Richard Layne, you can only play 'Yellow Bird'! I tell them that 'Yellow Bird' is one of the tools of my job. It is what my audience wants" (R. Layne, interview with the author, April 21, 2015). Layne's response draws our attention to two important issues: first, how he theorizes his job, and second, some of the ways that parts of his repertoire are viewed. In relation to how he understands his job, Layne is keenly focused on his audience; however, he also recognizes that they are not necessarily the primary audience—the hotel management is. In some ways, Layne is explaining that the tourists listening to his performance are produced for the tourism industry, that they form a type of commodity audience, if you will (Smythe 1977).

Moreover, the critique from some hotel workers who claim that all he can play is "Yellow Bird" is not a reference to Layne having a limited repertoire. I have already indicated that his song choice covers a range of eras and genres. Rather, the comment is a critique of the island song genre, with "Yellow Bird" standing in for all of those songs. Like the hotel workers, some academics and cultural workers have been skeptical of island songs (Crowley 1959). Olive Lewin, in a 1986 presentation at the International Council for Traditional Music (ICTM) Colloquium in Jamaica entitled "Banana Boat Song Forever?," worried that the public relations image of the Caribbean presented in island music and tourism advertising would fix the Caribbean forever into the image of "sun, sea, and sand—with a dash of rum thrown in" (Lewin 1986, 2). Additionally, Stephanie Williams at the same conference, in a presentation entitled "Yellow Bird—Ai Zuzuwah: Stagnation or Growth?," worried that Caribbean tourism performers were serving tourists "schooled on Belafonte" inauthentic musical compromises

(Williams 1988, 18). Williams is particularly concerned about the pedagogical role of tourism, which I mentioned earlier, and her presentation suggests that, like good teachers, Caribbean musicians must challenge their students/tourists.

Although I agree wholeheartedly with the push to challenge the audience, I think it is a mistake to dismiss island songs such as those played by Layne too quickly. The separation of the island song from its Caribbean roots is not as easy as might at first be suggested in the discussions of inauthenticity. In fact, the island songs that Richard Layne plays can invite us to think about the Caribbean in different registers—national, regional, and diasporic, and across racial boundaries that often go underexamined. Rather than a simple inauthentic expression, these songs trace the constant routes of the Caribbean diaspora back and forth between the region and metropolitan centers in the United States and Britain. Additionally, Layne performs songs that Irving Burgie, the same artist who wrote Barbados's national anthem, either made popular as Lord Burgess or produced for Harry Belafonte. Thus the genealogy of Irving Burgie's island songs emerges from his own lived experience as a professional musician interested in his identity as a member of the Caribbean diaspora as well as the commercial potential in that music. Important to that identity as an African American with a Barbadian mother is his participation in the insurgent politics of the civil rights movement (Burgie 2006). Equally, it would be a mistake within the tourism context to permit those travelers "schooled on Belafonte" to remain tethered exclusively to the image of Belafonte as the handsome man who popularized the sounds of the islands when his contributions to broad-level activism are so significant. Thus a song such as "Yellow Bird/Don't Ever Love Me" can and should be heard as a popular song circulated and reworked by the international music industry—we should not blind ourselves to the commodification of Caribbean music.

But, in keeping with arguments I have made above about finding, crafting, and bringing to the fore muted histories, it might also be usefully listened to through its links to the original source material: the nineteenth-century song composed by Michel Mauleart Monton using lyrics from the poem *Chouchoune* by Haiti's national poet Oswald Durand (Dash 1998). Rather than drawing on the specifics of *Chouchoune*, what I think can be useful for the arguments of this chapter are that the lines traveling from Layne to Burgie to Monton to Durand might suggest ways in which the sonic mapping of Little England is always accompanied and critiqued by transnational sonic references to differing engagements with black radical politics.

A large part of Layne's repertoire consists of reggae. Songs from UB40's internationally successful 1983 album *Labor of Love*—an album of cover songs—feature prominently, as well as songs of reggae and love by artists such as Beres Hammond and Tarrus Riley. As with the island songs, there are those who express concern about the ways in which major-label reggae decontextualizes reggae from its source (Alleyne 1994, 1998, 2000). This argument seems particularly appropriate to one of the songs in Layne's repertoire—the novelty song "Barbados" by Typically Tropical. Yet, to perhaps an even greater degree than in the case of the island song, the roots of reggae—though they certainly move through the commodification of the music industry—are rarely fully shorn of their potential to signal or cite reggae's significance in black radical politics and aesthetics. Indeed, like the island songs, global reggae draws together national, regional, and diasporic Caribbean lives and interests.

Yet the question remains: How much of this can be heard, and how much of it is listened to?[3] In the Caribbean presentations at the 1986 ICTM Colloquium, tourism is represented as a teaching tool, and the tourist is largely represented as a strangely delicate,[4] yet nevertheless eager, student. The capacity to hear these sounds takes us straight to the problem of how imperial knowledges crowd out all other forms of knowing. For visitors to have the capacity to hear these sounds, the pedagogy of advertising materials that most tourism research has analyzed (as well as the everyday pedagogy of sound that I have sought to analyze here) would have to change by foregrounding the insurgent and drowning out the Eurocentric knowledge. For these sounds to be listened to requires yet other moves. One move is suggested particularly in my analysis of the Changing of the Sentry and its links to postcolonial melancholia and postcolonial nostalgia. Another move is suggested in my analysis of Richard Layne's performance of island songs and reggae songs that, almost unconsciously, draw upon black postcolonial critique. Thus the sounds of rebellion are present, but truly listening to these noises of insurgency requires that the traveler "come to terms" with the disturbing noises of imperial violence and its continuing residues.

Conclusion

I am tourism.

—*Slogan for the latest campaign of the Barbados Tourism Product Authority*

In this chapter I have sought to listen carefully to the background of the all-inclusive hotel. Doing so has required an extensive engagement with the "outside" of the hotel. However, it is my contention that the peace and quiet *inside* the hotel might best be understood by recognizing that the contemporary construction of tourism destinations in a postcolony such as Barbados means that a simple delineation of "outside" and "inside" is not possible. In the 1970s and 1980s, early all-inclusives in Jamaica were set up to create an island within the island. However, in this moment, it is possible for places such as Barbados to experience what one might call the "touristification of everything." Thus the hotel and its environs are subject to persistent colonial discourses that curate sounds that seek to cancel out the more disturbing noises of Caribbean history. The iterative construction of Little and Big Englishness as innocent, quiet, regular, and genteel sets aside the noise of historical death and violence. Thus the chapter explores how the Main Guard clock serves as a barely heard, though regulating, aspect of public life that simultaneously celebrates Barbados as an independent nation even as it resutures the island firmly into its Little Englishness. And the Changing of the Sentry, which is beautiful to watch and listen to, is a ritual that foregrounds military pageantry and, although it does not ignore the attendant violence that is inherent in any reference to the military, it does not necessarily engage with what is at stake in asking visitors and locals to participate in the reenactment of military power that was used to assert the illegitimacy of nonwhite freedom and violently crush black and Amerindian efforts at freedom.

But of course, even though I suggest that this represents the touristification of everything, it is not truly *everything*—it is not absolute. The chapter has argued that the insurgent noises are always present or can be made present by drawing them out from their background position. Even within the all-inclusive courtyard, sounds seep in. The noises of kitchen labor make their way to the foreground, offering a lively counterpoint to the polite, whispered dance of wait staff and visitors alike. Additionally, Richard Layne, veteran musical performer, consistently demonstrates his ability to read his audience and construct their island fantasies. Yet there remain genealogies, in Richard's performances at the hotel and in the wider Barbadian society, in the sounds of the clock tower and the reenactments of the Changing of the Sentry of the West Indies Regiment at the site of the signing of the Slave Codes, that suggest that there are multiple ways to remember the history of Barbados. Thus the question becomes, how might the capacity to hear and the will to listen be cultivated? Those moves require a significant reordering of the political, economic, and cultural processes that persistently place Eurocentric knowledge and European comfort at the center.

NOTES

1. Tuk is a traditional Barbadian music. The music was traditionally played at public events such as public holidays. It can still be found at some of those events; however, one is more likely to see tuk bands in hotels and at tourist events, and it has become an extremely important part of the national celebrations of Barbadian culture. Usually, the tuk band consists of a bass drum, sometimes called the bum-drum; snare, called the "kittle"; pennywhistle, which plays the melody; and steel or triangle, and sometimes a cowbell. Generally, tuk is described as a music genre that fuses the African and European elements of Barbadian culture (Best 2001; Meredith 2014; Walcott 2014).

2. Indeed, Minca himself maps out one of the winding paths that leads from the concentration camp to the all-inclusive hotel.

3. Though the differences between "hearing" and "listening" are not settled (Novak 2015), here I am using them to signal in the first instance the question of capacity to attend to, and in the second instance the intention to pay attention.

4. Tourists seemed to be represented as often "hurt" and feeling deceived when they were presented with "inauthentic" Caribbean culture.

4 · ALL-INCLUSIVE RESORTS IN SINT MAARTEN AND OUR COMMON DECOLONIAL STATE

On Butterflies That Are Caterpillars Still in Chrysalis

FRANCIO GUADELOUPE AND JORDI HALFMAN

READER'S NOTE

Four concerns animate the chapter you are about the read. The first concern is the importance of presenting Sint Maarten as a case that furthers our understanding of how political economic analyses of all-inclusive hotels in the Caribbean enable us to think and do our politics of decoloniality in the wake of the continuing impact of the twin forces of capitalism and Western imperialism in the region. Sint Maarten, after all, is still constitutionally part of the Kingdom of the Netherlands, and thus an overseas country and territory of the European Union. It is exemplary of the continuing political presence of the West in the region. In addition, the specificity of the Sint Maarten case is that the entire island functions as an all-inclusive site. Tourism is the only economic pillar; as such, everyone's livelihood depends on the hospitality sector. Moreover, the vast majority of the inhabitants—more than 70 percent of the population—are recently arrived newcomers who migrated to the island to work or invest in the tourism industry. Aware of their collective dependence on making sure guests have the time of their lives, Sint Maarteners of all social stations socialize and encourage each other to promote the island as a place where engaging tourists on a daily basis is a pleasant matter of fact. Everyone must be inducted into a cosmopolitan ethic friendly to the machinations of capital. Sint Maarteners do this with relative ease given that it is the history and contemporary dynamics of the twin forces of capitalism and Western imperialism that brought them and keep them on the island. In tandem with this first concern, you will encounter not solely hotel workers but also schoolchildren, priests, and civil servants exemplifying this process of making the entire island an all-inclusive site.

This has implications for the Sonesta Great Bay, the only actual all-inclusive hotel on the island. Expectedly, it functions as but one entrance point into Sint

Maarten. Management, personnel, and regular islanders that tourists encounter enjoying lunch or doing a staycation in this supposedly all-inclusive hotel promote venturing out and exploring the entire island at leisure. By focusing on the sound of the Sonesta Great Bay, we demonstrate how enticing tourists to appreciate Sint Maarten as an all-inclusive is done sensuously.

This brings us to our second concern, which is our attempt to take on board what has become a standard Marxist critique, namely to pay more serious attention to the senses. The work of capitalist enterprises and government apparatuses on the senses, in an effort to shape our sensibilities, renders the clear-cut distinction between the institutional and the everyday rather spurious. Walter Benjamin and the other icons of the Frankfurt School, as well as Stuart Hall and the other luminaries of the Birmingham School of Cultural Studies, are presented as early pioneers who sought to take the sensuous on board in their critiques of capital and the state. We take these critiques to heart in this chapter.

Third, the question that then arises is how this critique should be done. We recognize that the writerly styles of Benjamin and Hall are worlds apart. In his florid writings on, say, flâneurs, or on the aura of cinema, Benjamin performs what he conveys (Benjamin 1968). He renders dominant notions of the everyday unstable, seeking to unsettle his readers and thereby make them aware of the taken-for-granted dichotomy between the systemic that structures institutional life and the supposedly less coerced everyday. Benjamin's denotative style is quite different from the appealing yet more constative prose of Stuart Hall. With Hall we are invited into analytical texts that tell us how political economy works (Hall and O'Shea 2013). On the one hand, we have a scholar who does a critique of life in a world structured by capitalism and accompanying forms of injustice, and on the other hand, a social theorist who seeks to teach us how the mechanisms of alienation and dehumanization work. We have chosen to follow the option modeled by Benjamin, but in the Caribbean style of Edouard Glissant, the Martinican philosopher and ethnologist.

We take our cue from the Antiguan social theorist Paget Henry, who has noted a distinction similar to the one we sketched above between two Caribbean paradigmatic traditions of intellectual engagement with the political economic catastrophes that continue to befall the dominated in the region (Henry 2000). These modes of thinking and writing the Caribbean experience he terms the poeticist and the historicist schools. The latter is fully wedded to political economic analyses where Western historical impositions and the counter-moves of the dominated are privileged. The examples he cites are C. L. R. James and Frantz Fanon. In contradistinction, the poeticist tradition of Wilson Harris and Sylvia Wynter presents us with a language that seeks to enact the struggle to dismantle the certainties of common sense. It is the latter, structured by and facilitating hegemonic economic and political relations in the region through the work done on the senses, which renders the unjust somewhat acceptable.

The poeticist tradition exemplified in, say, the essays of Derek Walcott and Edouard Glissant, writers who, unlike Wynter and Harris, resided in the region while they did their intellectual work, are closer to our taste. What the Twilight Says (Walcott 1998) or Caribbean Discourse (Glissant 1989) does is to render Caribbean everyday life in ways that are unfamiliar while enacting the familiarity that persons who have experienced life on the islands can appreciate. In the writings of these authors you discover yourself anew in your quest to discover the wider Caribbean society of one's interest. Moreover, new vistas appear on how to appreciate the Caribbean in the emerging and ever-transforming (geo)-political economy of the world.

Fourth, given that, de facto, the entire island is promoted as an all-inclusive, and not solely a specific hotel, we have sought to enact in our writing the journey of our discovery and the possibilities that emerge when one fully engages the sensual order. The poetic mode of writing in our case has a political reason, as it does in Benjamin and Glissant. Our mode—call it methodology—is that of becoming object. This method should simply be understood as seeking to sensuously experience the machinations of life on Sint Maarten with as little interference as possible from the urge to immediately process. To become object, which, unlike a subject, does not think but experiences, is to encourage unprocessed experiencing.

Our sensuous engagement with Sint Maarten presented us with illuminations to think decoloniality in novel ways. In our case, the vision emerged of our world as butterfly (the outcome of the twin forces of capitalism and Western imperialism creating our emerging one-world) who was still a caterpillar (the incompleteness of this process that still enables us to envision the globe as consisting of competing worlds) in chrysalis (alerting us that our efforts in our competing worlds to transform this one-world into a just place can still have effect). We trust that this note enables you to appreciate the chapter below.

Attention that is beautiful allows one to witness and simultaneously create poetic truths. Such artistically constructed social facts are useful to enhance mindfulness of the emerging planetary Relation—the clash and "overstepping that grounds unity-diversity" (Glissant 1997, 1)—after the long nightmare of Western colonialism that continues to haunt the entire globe. The hauntings linked to that horror are: the genocide of Amer-indians and Aboriginals, which cannot be said to be a thing of the past, as their offspring are still seeking justice; the kidnapping and ideologically legitimized enslavement of Africans whose great-grandchildren continue to be plagued by antiblack racism; the orientalizing of Asians whereby the hardening of caste and sibling prejudice promoted in colonial times is a twenty-first-century public secret; the racialization of pink-skinned Europeans who defend their white status even as this increasingly does not translate to having job security or to accumulating wealth; and the in-fantilizing of women and discrimination against the LGBTQ community in a world of the Hillary Clintons, the Condoleezza Rices, Caithlins, and George Takeis. If the preferred discourse of colonialism and its hauntings is usually prose, might we not hope that poetic, metaphorical speech-writing can redirect meaning and awaken an ethic of loving each other without which none can ever truly be and properly become?

Anthropologists with a poetic attitude do a different kind of work than those wedded to a literalism that strictly obeys the law of noncontradic-tion steadfastly anchored in integral reality (Baudrillard 2005)—the hege-monic mediatic-techno-cultural real that all socioeconomic classes take for granted, yet which disproportionally benefits the privileged few of this world. We, the authors of this poetic dream, are rightfully considered as be-longing to the former tribe, and what you are about to read on the sound of the Sonesta Great Bay Beach Resort,[1] the all-inclusive hotel located on the island of Sint Maarten, is part of this tradition of scholarship.

Do not expect a breakdown; instead, be a participant in doing the poetic truth of this essay within and without these pages. And what might that be? Persuasive and at times effective as the "us" versus "them" discourses may be—blacks versus whites, colonized versus colonizers, women versus men, LGBT versus normative sexualities—all these discourses have to be consciously forgotten, sublated without full annihilation, sinking into the antidualist planetary imaginary of Relation, if we wish to turn a new leaf and create a new sense of humanness (Frantz Fanon's dream [2005, 2008], updated, desexualized, and further de-essentialized by Sylvia Wynter [cf. McKittrick 2015]; Edouard Glissant 1997; and Jean Baudrillard 2005). In short, we have to become butterflies.

A Butterfly Inspiring Other Ways of Making Sense

It was a butterfly, yellow like a pale version of the cartoonish depictions of the sun, that inspired this piece. Partially mesmerized, I[2] asked myself what this *Rhopalocera* was triggering in my imagination that would lead to the main argument of this contribution to the scholarship on the sound of all-inclusive hotels in the Caribbean. I let myself go.

Working from our preferred mode of doing anthropology, namely becoming object (Baudrillard 2005, 2007), letting oneself be seduced by the world—humans, plants, animals, microbes, minerals, artifacts—I was captivated by the song of this butterfly in Mary of the Star Catholic church in Grande Case, in Saint Martin. His song, which was a dance, which was movement, was actually sound. Sound was forbidden touch, and I responded to this butterfly by tasting, inhaling, viscerally seeing, and knowing Sint Maarten differently. By becoming object I did not just let myself be seduced by the song of the butterfly; I allowed myself to become a sensorial extension. Without boundaries, my senses gained new strengths and capacities, reminding me of the words of anthropology's newest romantic, Tim Ingold (2003, 2007, 2011, 2015), echoing Merleau-Ponty (1970) with a difference:

> If hearing is a mode of participatory engagement with the environment, it is not because it is opposed in this regard to vision, but because we "hear" with the eyes as well as the ears. In other words, *it is the very incorporation of vision into the process of auditory perception that transforms passive hearing into active listening.* But the converse also applies: it is the incorporation of audition into the process of visual perception that converts passive spectating into active looking or watching. (Ingold 2003, 277)

When one becomes object, one appreciates that the external and internal senses (sight, sound, taste, smell, hearing, touch, temperature, balance, kinesthesia, and nocioception) always work in tandem with the spiritual organizing sense known as reason. This triad deconstructs the common sense of mind and sense, and by extension the clear-cut distinction between subject and object—truthful, historically produced, pragmatically useful abstractions (Ingold 2003, 2015).[3]

Hearing and watching the dance of the butterfly, being touched by its movements, made Ingold's abstract reasoning and similarly radical philosophical anthropologies convincing (Baudrillard 2005, 2007; Benjamin 1968; Biemann 2002; Buber 1998; Glissant 1989, 1997; McKittrick 2015; Nancy 2000). One can only make sense and do anthropology differently by being wholly aware, and one cannot be wholly aware without becoming fully object, in other words, refusing the subject-object distinction within and without. One will always fail. But failing well leads to understanding. But where was I, exactly?

My Location

As I enjoyed the butterfly's dance and song in the Catholic church, it dawned on me that both of us were, so to speak, in a strange land. I wasn't on Sint Maarten. I was on Saint Martin. Both authors of this piece live on this thirty-seven-square-mile island, populated by approximately 80,000 inhabitants. It is part of the European Union and located in the Caribbean.

We are Dutch citizens registered on Sint Maarten, termed the southern side of the island by the activist few striving for political independence from the Netherlands. Sint Maarten is a constituent state of the Kingdom of the Netherlands. What this means is that, along with the Netherlands and the Caribbean islands of Aruba and Curacao, Sint Maarten hosts one of the four parliaments that legislate this transatlantic federation (De Jong and Kruijt 2008; Guadeloupe 2009, 2010; Oostindie 1998, 2006a, 2006b; Pijl and Guadeloupe 2015).

The country obtained this seemingly equal political status on the 10th of October 2010, yet like most extended statehood constructions in the Caribbean, the colonial mark remains. There is a democratic deficit, to use a euphemism, as the parliaments in the Caribbean only have autonomy with regard to internal governance. Law, defense, and foreign affairs are de facto regulated by the parliament in the Netherlands. The official body that handles these affairs, the so-called Kingdom government, consists of all the ministers of the Netherlands and a plenipotentiary representative of each island answerable to the legislators in The Hague.

A similar constitutional reality, only more explicitly unequal, obtains on Saint Martin, called the northern side of the island by the same activist few striving for political independence from France. Saint Martin is a *collectivité d'outre-mer*, an overseas municipality of the French republic. Saint Martin can send one representative to the Paris parliament and one to the Senate. These persons, however, get lost and their voices often go unheard among the hundreds of deputies and senators on the mainland. Moreover, they are expected to promote national interests above their own local concerns.

In short, both sides are dominated by European powers that, for pragmatic reasons, allow an open border policy. Sint Maarten and Saint Martin are free ports; people and goods travel freely. Yet the facts that whenever I make a call to someone on Saint Martin, I am making an overseas call to another European country, that the euro is the official currency on the northern side, and that I need a converter to use my electrical appliances as the voltage is 220 as opposed to the 110 on Sint Maarten, remind me that France actually borders the Netherlands in the Caribbean sea.

Colonialism was barbaric. It was barbaric, but it also created this place where today many industrious poor from the Caribbean and the wider world come to make a living. In fact, 80 percent of the population, consisting of more than a hundred nationalities, are newcomers who began arriving on the island in the 1960s. North American capitalists needed a new and politically reliable paradise after Cuba became communist, and chose this French and Dutch island where the bureaucratic machines of Paris and The Hague wielded less panoptic power (Guadeloupe 2009). The current social stratification is such that most investors are North Americans and Europeans, followed by Asians and Latin Americans. The workers are Caribbean, Asians, and working-class Europeans. The government and civil service are primarily dominated by old timers, who can be called locals. Everyone knows that everyone is directly or indirectly dependent on tourism, as agriculture and industry are virtually nonexistent.

The population is highly mobile, with a constant in- and outflow of persons who cocreate the island. One is hard pressed to meet Sint Maarteners who were born on the island, have spent most of their lives living there, or have plans to do so. Many relationships to the island seem peculiar: a nationalism for the good times as people cynically refer to their politics of belonging. They are pragmatically patriotic. As everyone is aware of their dependence on tourism, they are committed to the island as a means to their personal ends. Some disgruntled locals who feel that they aren't receiving enough of the generated wealth will occasionally refer to newcomers as parasites and predators. But they too exhibit this nationalism for the good times, as having that coveted EU passport allows them to fly in and out of the island depending on their fortunes. The ghastly word "parasite" referred to all.

We did not like the word. Too negative. Too inhuman.

Thinking about this amid the church benches, I began to see the islanders as human *Rhopaloceras*. Most come as weak eggs that turn into caterpillars (workers and petty entrepreneurs) feasting on the island. If they survive and go into chrysalis (attain stability and social assent), they are transformed into butterflies, dancing on the island as long as it benefits them.

What would Sint Maarteners make of us likening them to human butterflies? Would they appreciate our rather crude analysis of the island's dynamics? And what does this have to do with the sound of all-inclusive resorts on the island? What kind of sense are we making without being fully in control of what we are busy with? We tell ourselves not to be impatient. We must remain becoming object. Continue relating to the butterfly. True revelation is always deferred understanding.

The Meta-Story the Butterflies Tell to Themselves

As I sat in the church, the rational side of me reasoned that this butterfly singing and thus dancing in front of me, interpolating my imagination to venture into unknown territories of reimagining the island, and, as an extension, the world, cared nothing about my thoughts. But others might. Someone who did was one of the butterfly's human incarnations, Father Charles, the charismatic Catholic priest from Saint Lucia by way of Martinique.

As the butterfly danced, the congregation seemed fully taken up by Father Charles's performance. He professed that emancipating minds from mental slavery, Bob Marley's articulation of decoloniality, was the global theological-political agenda of the twenty-first century. The rich, not so rich, and those struggling to make ends meet, all occupied the church benches and loved him. He was the darling of the well off and of those whose labor made the former who they were.

Here was a contextual liberation theologist, if ever there was one. I had had many conversations with him. His library was filled with Catholic theological literature, along with an extensive collection of philosophy. Hegel and Pascal were his favorites. His Catholic Hegelianism was intriguing and almost convincing. For him, establishing God's Kingdom was synonymous with decolonizing the planet and thereby taming (not overcoming) capitalism. For Father Charles, the Imperial world wasn't the archenemy, for he argued that the good life on Sint Maarten and Saint Martin showed that God worked in mysterious ways. The real nemesis for him was the anti-Catholic mind-sets that worked against creating a universal where every I was part of a planetary We.

The Derridian counterargument that I brought to him, namely that Catholicism was only a particular, he entertained as a university idea, not an article of conviction. Like Derrida, I believe I should

> risk this proposition: each time forgiveness is at the service of a fi-nality, be it noble and spiritual (atonement or redemption, recon-ciliation, salvation), each time that it aims to re-establish a normality (social, national, political, psychological) by a work of mourning, by some therapy or ecology of memory, then the "forgiveness" is not pure—nor is its concept. Forgiveness is not, it *should not be*, normal, normative, normalising. It *should* remain exceptional and extraordi-nary, in the face of the impossible: as if it interrupted the ordinary course of historical temporality. (Derrida 2001, 31–32)

Catholicism was a universalizing tradition that changed in its exchange and recognition of other ways of world-making. One day it would be the ethical global community that it already was as an Idea. A Catholicism to come that would come. And for Father Charles the fact that the grandchild of a captured African, leading a multiracial church, could sit on what was unjustly described as a *Terra Nullius* conversing about this matter with the great-grandchild of another *katibu*, who worked as a more humanistically inclined anthropologist, was a testament to this.

In his weekly sermons Father Charles pragmatically denied the borders between Sint Maarten and Saint Martin. He averred that for Catholics na-tionality should never trump charity and love for God's creations. He min-istered to all on the island, reminding the islanders that in logical terms decolonizing the mind—through the institution of the Catholic Church—preceded the establishment of a new political arrangement.

As my attention moved from the butterfly to my memories of our con-versations, I heard Father Charles say that while Jesus had walked on water, he wished to run over the seas and rivers of the world. He continued that persons had come to him earlier and complimented him that he did such good for the community, to which he replied, "I do not do good, I am good." He ended his line of reasoning by stating that Sint Maarten people had to show reverence to the past by surpassing it; becoming Christ-like in their daily lives. It was interesting hearing Father Charles, paralyzed from his waist down due to a stroke, speak about running on water.

No one seemed to notice the irony as they understood his message that told them that reified versions of the past, while partially structuring their present, should not hold them captive. An elderly lady I later asked about the sermon claimed that Father Charles was talking about having confidence as a Christian and believing (in) yourself despite the odds. He echoed the meta-story most Sint Maarteners liked to believe about themselves: that they were a people inspired by teachings of Christ. Where he added a new twist to the meta-story was that he did not fall back on the ontological idea that being sinners Sint Maarteners would always be fallen. A decolonized world marked with decency was possible. It was up to Sint Maarteners to make this a reality on their island.

What I heard that Sunday was an echo, with a difference, of what is termed a prophetic vision of the past: doing the intellectual dance between history and fiction without privileging either in the service of decolonizing minds, bodies, and habits (Glissant 1997). The difference was that instead of borrowing from secular archival texts, Father Charles was combining the Bible with the Creole storytelling modes of doing truth.

A few days later I sat with Father Charles and discussed with him what I had experienced and my ideas on the theory of a prophetic vision of the past. I also told him about this essay I had to write on the sound of all-inclusive hotels on Sint Maarten. And I spoke about the butterfly and what thoughts it had triggered in me. How it had reminded me of my (being out of) place and how it had made me practice the art of becoming object. He smiled. He liked that kind of thing. He took some time to think it over and then said that for him the butterfly was symbolic of letting Grace participate in the authoring of this essay. Grace was God's providence happening in the text. Becoming object bore an uncanny resemblance to Pascal's appreciation of Grace. Our theological parlance was brief, as our conversation quickly switched to the beauty of butterflies on the island. Before leaving he asked me to consider that the metamorphosis of caterpillars into butterflies also pointed to the transformation that had taken place on the island and the world after Columbus's journey!

I found the word metamorphosis politically suspect, having been fed a steady diet of decolonial theories and anti-Western activism. It seemed a euphemism that obfuscated the imperial past and contemporary horrorism (Cavarero 2011) for many who inhabit today's world. Yet the memory of the butterflies, the literal one and Father Charles's, seduced me to temporarily put this theoretical vocabulary and my suspicion on hold; I had to continue becoming object and, as such, visit the island's all-inclusive resort.

An All-Inclusive Resort on an All-Inclusive Island

The Sonesta resorts, one located in Great Bay and the other in the low-lands, are the only all-inclusive hotels on Sint Maarten (their equivalent is Riu on Saint Martin). We chose the Sonesta Great Bay Beach resort, which is in Philipsburg, the capital of Sint Maarten. The hotel has been located here since 1976 but only became all-inclusive three years ago. When it did, it also became an adults-only resort, catering for peace and quiet and lux-ury. With 257 rooms, the hotel is not extremely large, but one cannot miss it at the end of the Philipsburg boardwalk. The hotel has a spa and a casino and is located right on the beach, supplying visitors with both a luscious view and easy access to the Caribbean water. Visitors can eat and drink at both the Sonesta resorts, thus opening up the two locations to a steady stream of happy tourists. They can explore the island, but, as in all other all-inclusives, theoretically, a person could leave the United States or Canada (mostly Canada in this case) with hardly a cent in their wallet and enjoy a great vacation for two weeks at the all-inclusive Great Bay resort.

We reasoned that Sonesta Great Bay would provide us with the ideal case to critically appreciate the idea that all-inclusive modes of vacationing create the forts of the twenty-first century—alien cells far removed from the rhythms and sounds of the islands where they are located. The natives did the menial labor, while the managers and visitors usually hailed from North Atlantic countries. All-inclusives were a mix of non-places (Augé 1995) with stereotypical caricatures of the Caribbean and the specific island to add some local flavor. This representation of all-inclusives was one we had discovered speaking to activists and scholars working in and on the Caribbean islands. How would this story hold up with an all-inclusive located in the capital of Sint Maarten?

Sonesta Great Bay, as an all-inclusive resort, remains a rarity on this island that annually hosts 2.5 million tourists. In conversations with Keith Graham, the general manager of the establishment, a Hong Kongese of British extraction, it became clear that it was highly unlikely that more all-inclusives would be established on the island. This is due to the fact that Sint Maarten is marketed as an all-inclusive island by investors and government officials alike. Every district on the island ought to be accessible to tourists. And all Sint Maarteners had to be socialized to expect and be hospitable to visitors arriving primarily from the United States, Canada, and Europe.

Even the University of Saint Martin, where both authors work, participates in this process. Two years ago we produced a song and video clip with working-class children celebrating tourism. The song starts with the question: "Who needs tourism?" And is answered by, "We do! Tourism is our business." The song, which brings together synthesizers, steelpans, and live guitar, is a syrupy mix of North American hip-hop, soca, and reggae that was featured on the local TV and radio, and now enjoys a continuous existence on YouTube.[4] The general marketing strategy of full access to the island, being all-inclusive, makes the idea of gated hotels, the all-inclusives, questionable.

Full access must go both ways. Sometimes this comes with a few hiccups and angry looks; sometimes it relates to having the right age, look, and talk. I[5] had spoken to Ms. Lambert, an outspoken schoolteacher working at one of the island's well-known vocational schools. She had lambasted the Sonesta resorts because she was not allowed to have dinner in the restaurant. The restaurant had been full and thus her party was told to wait for two hours. She had left angrily and then proceeded to criticize the establishment on Facebook for discriminating against locals and black and brown Caribbean newcomers. She got many likes. She also threatened to write an article in the newspaper and take her complaint to the popular radio disc jockeys. This was her country that she was willing to share with newcomers, but the latter should not overdo it. No one wanted this ruckus. Sint Maarten is a small place, and tourists sensing ethnic strife might stop coming.

Those managing the restaurant immediately contacted Ms. Lambert and apologized. Sonesta Great Bay was for locals, newcomers, and tourists alike. She knew it too, for we had yet to witness an establishment that refused to cater to the islanders. It made good business sense, for during the low season—the period from the end of May to the end of October, the period that coincides with hurricanes and summer heat—businesses depended on the money of the existing population.

Perhaps because we could pay and had access to media and the ear of people in high places, we entered the hotel without a problem. No security guard rushed to ask questions, nor did the front desk clerks. As one of us started to systematically engage the Sonesta Great Bay, he was greeted: "Good afternoon, Mr. Guadeloupe, how are you doing?"

From that day onward I made it my weekly habit, for four months, to sit in the lobby or restaurant and to engage tourists, staff, and Keith Graham. I did not perform any interviews, that method whereby the anthropologist is directly or indirectly seeking control of information, but continued to practice the art of becoming object, letting myself be seduced. For instance, since Mr. Graham and I were part of the St. Maarten Hospitality and Trade Association (SHTA), the major economic bloc and interlocutor on the island, I was privy to how he spontaneously reasoned, engaged others, and managed the Sonesta Great Bay. I also attended functions held at the establishment and experienced their entertainment evenings.

In the first instance the programming resembles the dime-a-dozen you find in all-inclusive hotels throughout the Caribbean. A little bit of zumba, beer pong, water aerobics, singers with DAT recordings, a karaoke night, and some local live entertainment. As always, however, the devil—the surprise, the unexpected within the horizons of the expected, what thrills and awakens—is in the details. What the entertainment evenings revealed, specifically those involving the live bands, was a blurring of the distinction between entertainers and audience. We were privy to a radical enactment of what ethnomusicologists term *musicking* (Small 1998). "To music is to take part in any capacity, in a musical performance, whether by performing, by listening, by rehearsing or practicing, by providing material for performance (what is called composing), or by dancing" (Small 1998, 9).

The band 3+1 consists of laid-back men in their early forties and fifties who have been doing music in hotels, restaurants, and other live venues, as they put it, "since Jesus was a child." Like a few of the staff of Sonesta, they have been with the hotel since before it was transformed into an all-inclusive. On the first evening we witnessed their performance, we were completely mesmerized. This had to do with the fact that Leroy, the lead singer of 3+1, would move throughout the hotel, from the patio to the restaurant and then upstairs to the lobby, and even close to where rooms were located, while performing. The musicians that accompanied him were nondescript. They hardly moved while playing their instruments—bass and lead guitar, drums, and keyboard—in a corner that was hardly visible. Yet, due to the right acoustics and engineering, their music occupied in various degrees of intensity (for instance, less loud close to the bedrooms) all the areas that the lead singer roamed.

The singer reminded me of the butterfly in the Catholic church. He displayed perfect syncopation between his voice and the movement of his body. I also had to think of a music video of Marvin Gaye on *Soul Train* performing his classic "Let's Get It On," which I had a habit of watching on YouTube.[6] The reason for this was that the band's warm-up song is an instrumental rendition of "Hold on I Am Coming," and Leroy sang Gaye's "Sexual Healing," along with many of the Motown evergreens between his renditions of popular soca and reggae songs. He switched accents with every song. Yet no matter what he sang, he remained effortlessly cool, like the soulful and ska crooners of yesteryear. I imaged Leroy as a synthesis between the butterfly and Marvin Gaye, causing me to revise my experience in the church. The dance song of the butterfly in the church took place during a full sermon. I began to appreciate the *Rhopalocera* as an avatar of Father Charles, an insectile variant of the charismatic priest, which was one with the place and the people, and therefore in a subtle way encouraged everyone to be part of the performance. Leroy was doing similar work as he made sure to constantly interpellate the tourists and the regular workers of the hotel, as an audience that was simultaneously part of his band.

He gave them a sense that they were the ones entertaining themselves. His movement throughout the hotel had purpose, strategically sharing the microphone with specific tourists, or inviting them to dance and gain an audience while also being part of the audience. What's more, thinking this through and beyond the performance, we began to realize that the entire staff of the hotel was actually doing a similar kind of performance. The guests felt as though they were hosting themselves in a kind of a way. During the carnival period, we witnessed how, while one of the persons working behind the buffet had "lost it" and was briefly becoming the center of attention by dancing with a guest, the tourist's friends served themselves. On another occasion there was much Cheech-and-Chong as one guest gave the bartender a chip from a casino located in Philipsburg as a tip. Like Leroy, this guest was joking with guests and staff, and he was up and down the hotel during the performance of 3+1, inviting us to go downstairs and dance along. The staff was in control, and had to do their work as the lines between tourists and workers remained; one group sweated for bucks and the other for fun, but they sought to make these clear-cut positions as imperceptible as possible. The head of the entertainment team, Devon, originally hailing from Jamaica where he was recruited from Sandals, explained that the objective was to make the tourists feel that Sonesta was their home away from home, like the rest of Sint Maarten. It meant that all the fancy gimmicks found at more exclusive all-inclusive hotels weren't regularly employed; instead, the technique of enhancing antiphony between tourist and worker was privileged. This mode of engagement, of being hospitable to tourists, began in the lobby.

I[7] have to admit that the lobby was my favorite spot. I could see everything and let the sounds speak to me. Everyone passed through here, and many a day people would sit and have a chat with me. As I listened and was touched by the rhythms and pitches of voices and related this to the expectations of sight, the all-inclusive challenged my previous imaginations. I became more aware of my prejudices concerning sound and face. Let me recount.

Having read so many articles on how the front desk and other representative functions in all-inclusive hotels are dominated by persons with what is considered more traditional European features, in terms of hair, skin, face, and bone, and, having spoken extensively with Ms. Lambert, who is well versed in Afrocentric rhetoric, I expected to encounter workers with a white European appearance as I had imagined those with a black African phenotype to be working in less accessible parts of the resort. In my less aware moments I divided the world into dark brown, light brown, and pink—or, more simplified, into black and white. Was this my effort to order the manifold of individual faces? The truism of the colonization of life by integral reality—that is, stereotypical symbols and binary codes— suddenly dawned on me (Baudrillard 2005; Gilroy 2004).

My ordering was based on the images that had once (and sometimes still) reached my eye/I through certain discourses. My surprise was not only a case of shortsightedness. It clearly pointed out the enslavement of sound to the sensual domination of an abstracted sense of vision (Howes 2010; Ingold 2003, 2015; Pink 2010). The many versions of English and Spanish I heard—Jamaican, Kittisian, Saban, New Yorkese, Londonese, local Sint Maartenese, Colombian, Dominican, and so on—I identified with these specific ethnicities. Hearing the front desk person, a dark-skinned woman with a weave, yanking and thereafter reverting to Jamaican, led me to connect the latter with the person's more authentic tongue. What odd abstractions I was performing.

It was barbarism. A truncated sense of the human, for if there was one thing that we both believed, wrote about, and taught at the university, it was that freedom is our species-specific integration into life (Guadeloupe 2009, 2010, building on Marx and Engels's philosophical manuscripts of 1844 [1988] and the varied critiques thereof by Baudrillard 2005, 2007; Ingold 2003; Jackson 1989; McKittrick 2015; Rorty 1990; Seidman 1989). We are, of course, socialized in particular ethical communities—in this case ethno-national groupings that privilege a particular tongue—but to equalize this to that pseudo-natural concept of the "authentic" was playing with fire, and could burn down the entire edifice of our avowed antiracist way of dwelling in life.

In primary schools on Sint Maarten, where I[8] spend most of my days, a continuous play with language and imagined identity pushes the every-day reality, and in similar ways I had to continuously remind myself not to fall into the authenticity trap. Doing research into the relations between sounds, images, and the imagination of children on the issues of belong-ing, I am often fooled by the ways I combine what I/eye sense with my own presuppositions. From my notebook I quote:

As we [me and four second graders] are talking, I ask them where their families are [from]. The boy whom I earlier described as Indian[9] tells me he has family in the U.S., Guyana, Suriname, and the Nether-lands. The girls, who I found harder to pinpoint, have family in the Netherlands and also in Haiti and Curaçao. Two of them were born in the U.S. Again, nothing is what it seems to me. Again, I am confronted with my preexisting notions of identity that I push into transactions on the island, which makes very little sense. It is like when Rudi, the dance teacher at Sister Borgia, told me that there is one little girl who he has a hard time communicating with because she only speaks Dutch. I pictured a white girl. But she was not. Obviously.

As I became self-aware (again), I decided to consciously practice the art of listening without prejudice, to return to becoming object. I then appre-ciated that the plethora of accents and tongues were styles individuals em-ployed that might be related to their belonging to specific ethnic groups, but this needn't be the case. I based this on the fact that I had been wit-ness to how Sint Maarteners were skilled in imitating each other's accents. Different sounds, languages, and meanings continuously pushed me into the pupils' histories and present realities. They asked me to speak Span-ish, Dutch, or French with them, and while they laughed at my mistakes they expected me to fully understand their fast-paced Dominican Spanish or passionate French. The speed of the languages they practiced at home pushed itself into the English they spoke in the classroom. That speech forced me to pay full attention and use all my interrelated senses, become object, to grasp the messages that they conveyed.[10]

On a daily basis, children mocked my linguistic abilities. One morning Dane was trying my sense of humor: "Teacher, I am white," he pronounced, while batting his big eyes at me and using an accent that was very unlike the one he uses to greet me in the morning. Dane is a very bright and cheerful boy who may claim a Spanish background when he feels like it. Immediately his two best friends, the tall Spanish boy Emanuel and the smaller sports talent Dave, who claims Jamaican ties, imitate him and tell me they are white men: "Look at us, teacher!" I listen to how they (pretend to) speak with a potato in their throats. They sound odd to me, nothing like I believe I sound. So I ask them if this is how I speak. "No, teacher, no, you ain't like that. We speak just like the white people." When I ask them what the difference is between me and a white person, they explained that I am not a tourist.

But as I move through the school, I am reminded that tourists should not solely be equated with pink-skinned visitors hailing from the North Atlantic. During the carnival period—from the middle of March to the beginning of May—one of the dark-skinned teachers from this public school, one I work closely with, occupies a room in Holland House, one of the best-known hotels on the island. Each year, her entire family stays there for three days to watch the parades and enjoy the peak of carnival as intensely as possible. She becomes a tourist. During this period, the Sonesta Great Bay is populated primarily by dark-skinned tourists hailing from the island itself or other Caribbean isles; they come to enjoy the festivities and to reconnect with family and friends. Often they have close relatives and friends who work on the island or at the hotel where they are staying. For example, one of the employees who works in the kitchen informed us that she gives gifts for her grandchildren to Arubans who stay at the Sonesta Great Bay during carnival.

This influx of Caribbean tourists is not a periodic affair, for throughout the year Sint Maarten receives tourists from the Caribbean who aren't "white." To this must be added the brown-skinned North American, European, and Asian visitors. "Tourist" as a term is an invitation to recognize opaque multiplicity rather than posit a known unitary identity.

The pupils I work with have this implicit knowledge too. From them I began to understand that tourists aren't always "white." When visiting the boardwalk with Emanuel and Dave during the carnival period, mingling with thousands of newly arrived day-trippers from the cruise ships, the boys saw another chance to play and took it. Taxi drivers asked us if we needed a ride and some easygoing beach boys wanted to sell us their umbrellas and sunbeds. "Teacha, we are tourists! We are Japanese now," Dave explained to me. To the taxi drivers they responded: "No, we don't need no taxi, we going swim." And after learning the price of the sunbeds they decided we could lie on the sand; the sunbeds were "way too expensive." During their play on the boardwalk, the boys became tourists without the "white" accents they had busied themselves with in the classroom weeks earlier. As Japanese tourists, Emanuel and Dave altered their style of walking and talking, but in ways entirely new to me. After all, we were Japanese tourists today and we were playing within an entirely different situation.

Due to the conviviality of the island, the myth of unitary identities and pure ethnic tongues was hard to uphold without crossing one's fingers. What one encounters on Sint Maarten is actually the beauty of the subtle play of languages and styles of life, whereby individuals express and deepen their individuality through the borrowing of words and accents and expressions from the Sint Maarten reality. Claudia, one of the ladies working at the front desk of the all-inclusive, someone whom I[11] had unthinkingly classified as a local Sint Maartener, puzzled me as she spoke New Yorkese as though she was born and raised there, and then turned out to be a child of Dominican newcomers. When she switched to Spanish I could hear Santo Domingo in her.

This all seemed far removed from butterflies. We began thinking that perhaps the metaphor wasn't really apt. It was then that we remembered Father Charles, a man who had never set foot in one of the island's all-inclusive hotels, but who had averred that on the island nothing could be all-inclusive. He had told one of us a story about a couple of young men who had entered the lobby of the Westin hotel bareback, with short pants, making lots of noise. They were proving a point. They wanted to go to the beach and were unhappy with that establishment's attempt, through fences and buildings and security guards, to make it impossible for nonvisitors to access the beach. When the security guard sought to turn them away, they told him to call the police and gave him the telephone number. They knew their rights: all beaches should be accessible to the people of the island. Fearing a scandal and knowing that Sint Maarten politicians were against any privatization of this common resource, the fences came down.

The butterflies respect no boundaries, Father Charles had said. He had also suggested that besides our nominalist bent, we think about metamorphosis and butterflies in world transformational forms. What exactly happened on Sint Maarten in the aftermath of Columbus's journey? Listening to the sound of the island, he had said: "They snatched our sound, we snatched theirs. Colonialism was about sound snatching, good doctor!"

Sound Snatcher—What Kind of Creature Is That!

One of the most memorable tourists I[12] met at Sonesta Great Bay was an elderly American gentleman called Richard. A recently widowed general practitioner from New York in his early sixties, Richard was trying to figure out what to do next. Visiting on a cruise ship with his wife a couple of years earlier had been pleasant, and a taxi driver had made them feel so welcome that he decided to come back to Sint Maarten. I would not have spoken to Richard, as he never sat in the lobby, were it not for the fact that he first spoke to me.

He was sitting at the bar of the Chesterfield restaurant, a twenty-minute walk from Sonesta Great Bay. He was with some Sint Maarten guys who usually hung out there. The latter are solidly middle-class, owning small businesses, so I knew they weren't the tourist workers he would meet at Great Bay. While I was exchanging chit-chat with them, he spontaneously said, "Hey, I know you, aren't you the guy who sits in the hotel typing? Using the free Wi-Fi, right?" After the necessary introductions, I asked him what he was doing here, and he went on to explain that he had struck up a conversation with one of the guys at a beach bar in the afternoon and was invited to come and hang out in the evening. It's easy to meet people here, he said. They speak English, it is safe, and it is not as if leaving the hotel is like landing in an exotic Third World place. So the sights and sounds are familiar, I asked, to which he replied: "exactly."

We came to appreciate this familiarity by walking the route that tourists like Richard take on their strolls to Philipsburg. The music from the lobby, which can be characterized as a potpourri of sounds with Caribbean-inflected Black Atlantic compositions front and center, subtlety emulated by the speakers in the lush plants strategically placed around the entrance.

When not paying full attention, the immediately aware part of one's self could easily walk past these without noticing the sounds welcoming and bidding farewell to tourists and all other passersby on their way down to Philipsburg, the island's capital. It was a preparation and continuation of music and sounds to come. The first stop down the hill for tourists could easily be the Walter Plantz Square, with its plethora of restaurants serving Caribbean dishes and its lavish water fountain leading to the white sandy beach. Regularly, national and international bands gave free performances at the square and DJs turned their tables every Friday night. During happy hour a designated DJ played a rich selection of soca, calypso, rhumba, salsa, reggaeton, and R&B, interlaced with Justin Bieber's latest hits, a French chanson, and Dutch hip-hop. Further down the road, tourists are treated to a Latino band spurring on younger and older couples to express themselves at the Kokonut bar. Then there is the burger bar, where they may meet tourists doing karaoke as they sing the evergreens that Leroy and 3+1 performed. Close to the heart of Philipsburg they hear Bob Marley's voice and that of other popular reggae artists encouraging them "not to worry about a thing," and, a bit further on, Metallica reminding them of a music form and identity that they do not expect to find in the Caribbean. All along the boardwalk the different styles would alternate and mix until they arrive at Chesterfield and then the harbor where the cruise ships dock.

Musically, Sint Maarten represents the French, Dutch, Spanish, and English Caribbean. In addition, as hinted at by Metallica, provisions are made for, so to speak, "niche sound markets." If a tourist would feel more at home at a classical concert, a choir evening, or jazz jam, s/he could visit these at different times in specialized cafés and venues. These niche markets also attracted some residents. Father Charles, for instance, was a great aficionado of classical music and even had his own twenty-four-hour classical radio station at one time. Sint Maarteners are aware of the richness of their tastes in music. They proudly proclaim that the troupes representing the island in the Caribbean carnival in Florida are discernible due to the fact that they dance to all music from the basin.

What was true for music was generally also true for their cosmopolitan orientation, which allowed tourists to have a sense of being at home away from home. That evening I sat with Richard for a while and realized how he connected with the guys as they spoke about Trump, Obama, local politics, the war on terror, the state of the economy, women, raising children, and the mythical old days when all was better than today. As most Sint Maarteners have access to more than fifty American TV channels in real time, and the middle class travel regularly to the United States, they can easily make the tourists feel at home. Genuine relations between tourists and Sint Maarteners are possible.

Reminiscing on this after I had left Richard, we began to ask ourselves what exactly would be unfamiliar to visiting tourists. What sights and sounds were here before the journey of Columbus? We realized, not much. Sint Maarten belonged to what is known as the old colonies, places where European colonialism lasted the longest and was most intense. The indigenous populations and their ways of life were virtually wiped out. Not only the people and culture but also most of the flora and fauna did not date back more than five hundred years. These were Creole societies (Brathwaite 2005; Hall 2010; Mintz 1996; Price and Price 1997).

Truthful and insightful as this explanation is, at its best empirically foregrounding the specificity of the Caribbean experience, the concept of Creole societies can breed the idea of exceptionality, as in "we are hybrids in a world of pure cultures." Or, "as Creoles we are out of place; our true motherlands are Africa, Asia, and Europe." This is why we agree that

> Creolization as an idea is not primarily the glorification of the composite nature of a people: indeed, no people have been spared the cross-cultural process . . . creolization demonstrates that henceforth it is no longer valid to glorify "unique" origins that the race safeguards and prolongs. . . . To assert that peoples are creolized, that creolization has value, is to deconstruct in this way the category of "creolized" that is considered a half way between two "pure" extremes. (Glissant 1989, 140–41)

And yet one cannot simply undo the historical, political, and social scientific understandings the concept of creolization has acquired. As far as we know, Europe is never referred to as a Creole continent; words bear traces. We needed to transpose the idea of global creolization into . . . into what?

The butterfly in the church returns to our minds and conversation. We find ourselves wondering about its metamorphosis. We cannot imagine it, but we hear the sound of it as a caterpillar eating leaves that shrink back from the carnage.

That night I[13] dream about a gigantic caterpillar in a garden of even more and bigger leaves. The caterpillar proceeds to munch on the leaves. Bleeding red blood, they shriek in horror and try to shake it off, to no avail. The caterpillar wins out. Leaves disappear and the sound of the caterpillar gorging grows louder and louder until, until, there is only an obese larva left. The battle between the caterpillar and the leaves continues in its stomach. The situation grows unstable. The caterpillar goes into chrysalis. I cannot see what is happening, but the result is a beautiful, rainbow-colored butterfly. It suddenly notices me and comes menacingly closer. I wake up.

I proceed to become object to my dream. I buy crayons that day and start to draw the butterfly. And the drawing becomes my frame, eventually *our* frame, with which to engage the world in the world. What if the planet after five hundred years of feasting—genocide, enslavement, capitalist exploitation, religious subjugation, and patriarchal violence—whereby the leaves only survived by becoming part of the process of chrysalis—is actually this butterfly!

Sint Maarten becomes a different place. It is simply one of the colors of the butterfly. The *Rhopalocera* is all there is. Therefore, this island cannot indeed be a strange land for Richard. The Sonesta Great Bay cannot keep the Richards that come to visit inside. And the management of the hotel is not trying to do so. The general manager, Keith Graham, likens the idea of a gated hotel fully cut off from the rest of society to madness, and an evil act. He had been to similar establishments in Jamaica and other Caribbean islands, and had spoken to several guests who had and simply hated it. He never ceased to convey to friend, foe, acquaintance, and stranger that he was comfortable on Sint Maarten, and felt that his guests should experience what he experienced too: life in a land where everyone can be.

Keith was born and raised in Hong Kong and moved to London to study in the country of his forefathers. In Hong Kong he was clearly one of the invaders, while in the United Kingdom his ways were too different from those of the natives whom he looked like. On Sint Maarten, however, he said he had a sense of belonging because no one could belong. His sons were born here, but they would never unconditionally be seen as Sint Maarteners. Even the locals like Ms. Lambert, he would say, could never take for granted that the newcomers would recognize them as the firstcomers. Political independence would not solve this. He and his sons would continue in a world in which everyone was on the move. A total renewal was in order. But he had no idea how such a new order would look! Perhaps, he reasoned, we had to endorse and keep promoting multiculturalism in all states. That was all he could think about. A perfect world he no longer believed in, yet he felt that Sint Maarten remained an unfinished project.

At first we did not fully catch the importance of Graham's statement that the island was an unfinished project. We did not connect it to what Father Charles had said about a world needing to become fully Catholic. Deep understanding of life, poetic truth, comes when it comes. We focused on Graham's statement of Sint Maarten being an open place and the implications of this statement for the all-inclusive character of the Sonesta Great Bay. We had verified Graham's practice of ordering and buying as much as possible from the small businesses on the island, of which many of the owners were local families like that of Ms. Lambert. As they ran the government, it was Graham's way of making sure that the civil service kept a direct stake in the industry. He was mindful of making sure that his personnel reflected the ethnic diversity of the island. The sights and sounds in the hotel were similar to those of the wider society.

So what was so all-inclusive about the all-inclusive Great Bay hotel? It had to do with dollars and cents. All-inclusives gave tourists the sense that they were getting the better of the hotel. They could eat and drink and be taken care of to their heart's desire. But they never did. Instead of gluttony and drunkenness, they showed moderation. There were exceptions, but that was a once-in-a-blue-moon situation. Graham argued that this moderation was partly caused by the way tourists policed each other. Mostly they also weren't accustomed to behaving worthlessly in their daily lives.

Then there was the extra perk that guests of the Sonesta Great Bay also had access to the amenities of its sister facility located in the lowlands. This resort is a twenty-minute drive away, and in between tourists are treated to a strip of nightclubs, fast-food chains, and upscale restaurants. And they took full advantage of it. The younger hotel guests that we met could not stop talking about the reggae nights at the Karakter restaurant located on the Simpson Bay beach, the salsa parties at the restaurant-dance club, the Harbour in Colebay, the wild clubbing at the nightclub Tantra a stone's throw away from the Sonesta Beach Resort. Closer to the Great Bay location, with Chesterfield being the last establishment before the cruise terminal, was the Philipsburg boardwalk with its water sports, locally owned restaurants, and varied soundtrack, as was explained above. Daily, thousands of cruise ship tourists can be found there, giving stay-over tourists the sense that they fall into a safe anonymity. The boardwalk in Philipsburg is where one encounters casinos, boutiques, jewelry stores, and grocery stores. Here tourists might also meet hucksters, hustlers, and other workers who assist them in finding their way to the brothels, gay clubs, or gain access to weed, knowing that the police are lenient in relation to the moderate use of that substance.

In such a situation, where the all-inclusive Sonesta Great Bay is part of the all-inclusive Sint Maarten, all sectors of Sint Maarten indeed have a stake in the tourist industry. And they seek to attract and invite the multiplicity of tourists to participate. An example is the carnival, where international artists and bands such Rick Ross, Kes the Band, and Carimi perform, and one finds various commodities in tailor-made form being advertised. During these performances we witnessed and were part of the Caribbean and the wider world of those with discretionary cash to buy the spoils of the world, dancing together and entering into communion . . . even if briefly. In no way does this amount to one happy island. The agonism that most definitely exists has to do with individuals and groups feeling that they should have a bigger piece of the pie. On Sint Maarten there is no all-in-all exclusion, with static and violent boundaries separating us and them, and Sonesta Great Bay exemplifies this.

So was this a happy ending?

Unfinished Project . . . Isn't That What a Chrysalis Is?

A sense of unfinishedness remained as we sat down and wrote down our findings and ponderings. Father Charles, Keith Graham, and those disgruntled Sint Maarteners—oldcomers and newcomers alike—sense that the island was indeed an unfinished project, which remained troubling to us. We went over our notes, becoming object to the draft, and then it hit us. The butterfly was still a chrysalis, and this essay was being written inside it—recall the dream of the *Rhopalocera* coming toward us! As part of the chrysalis, which we began to liken to a decolonial world still in the making, we can only offer a critique of existing solutions. Astute participants, who are doing this essay with us by reading it and taking it further, can distill hints at what not to keep doing. And perhaps what to do.

More Christian-oriented Sint Maarteners like Father Charles seek resolution in a global Christendom that we cannot fully endorse. Why privilege one faith over another? That is our first and lesser objection. A more substantial problematic is the issue of the stifling character of this monotheism and its way of dividing life into what is possible in this world (the secular realm) and a more ideal one to come that can only occur through divine extra-human intervention.

Now this whole secular/religious divide bears an uncanny resemblance to the human/citizen distinction. And with that, an amputated planetary multiculturalism was born that, even while recognizing diversity within nations, remains violent in its implications. The list of hauntings after Western colonialism with which we began this chapter bears witness to this social fact. The humanity of a human who is not a citizen of a particular nation-state is usually not recognized. The Ms. Lamberts of Sint Maarten and the wider world had no qualms with this. To eliminate excessive economic and political abuse they would reason that newcomers should acquire the right papers, or come with enough financial or educational means to take care of themselves. Just as Graham did. These Ms. Lamberts would continue arguing that pressure be put on those nation-states ruled by unjust politicians, where most of the poorer new Sint Maarteners migrate from.

Now, this solution seems miles away from that of Father Charles, but it isn't! Ms. Lambert, like Graham, reasoned that a decent world was a fool's dream. It had to do with the human element. For them, our human condition was one of brokenness and imperfection—the idea of sin, in different words. No all-inclusive could be reached, as some would remain outside the Catholic unity or outside the brotherhood of oldcomers in any geographical or man-made island in this modern world. What must we then do? Must we stop dreaming the fool's dream? Or was there a lesson in this story, in listening to the dance of the butterfly, listening to the pupils and listening to the people working in the Sonesta Great Bay lobby? A decent world would not consist of unity, of a unitary identity, whereby we are just to the We and careless about the non-We. Instead, it would be a meeting of open and mutually attracting unknowns where we consent

> [n]ot merely to the right to difference but, carrying this further, agree also to the right to opacity that is not enclosure within an impenetrable autarchy but subsistence within an irreducible singularity. Opacities can coexist and converge weaving fabrics. To understand these truly one must focus on the texture of the weave and not on the nature of its components. For the time being, perhaps, give up this old obsession with discovering what lies at the bottom of natures.

There would be something great and noble about initiating such a movement, referring not to Humanity but to the exultant divergence of humanities. Thought of self and thought of other here become obsolete in their duality. Every other is a citizen and no longer a barbarian. What is here is open, as much as this there. The right to opacity would not establish autism; it would be the real foundation of Relation, in freedoms. (Glissant 1997, 190)

To weave and to acknowledge the unexpected interlacing of others, isn't that what a caterpillar does? This is both a work of hands and a work of sound—forbidden touch. As we start and remain faithful to ways of listening whereby by becoming object we reweave the world, our sense of sense allows us to mutually and consciously inhabit and cohabit.

There are indeed corporeal and celestial poles of hearing—the one sensing, the other sensible—which, when they collide, generate the experience of sound. And that very sound, born of the fusion of the affective and the cosmic, where what is heard turns out to be our own hearing, also divides us such that—much as in a dream—we are simultaneously at home in our bodies and at large in the cosmos. (Ingold 2015, 108)

We would thus say that we must keep enticing others and ourselves to undo the certitudes and identities of today. Our becoming as objects can undo the walls and fenced-off islands we have come to take for granted, in the ways we perceive of and in a decolonial world. As part of the chrysalis, we cannot be divided from the leaves and the workers and the songs in the church, just as we cannot escape the touch of the sound of the Dominican Spanish mixed with New Yorkese, spoken by a new Sint Maartener or the American slang of a primary school boy. The butterfly does not stop at the border between north and south Saint Martin but flies and weaves where it needs to be heard. Thus, as part of the chrysalis, we continue the conversation with Father Charles, Ms. Lambert, Graham, Dane, and you, physically and by way of doing this essay. The butterfly is not our final stage.

NOTES

1. https://www.sonesta.com/sx/philipsburg/sonesta-great-bay-beach-resort-casino
-spa-st-maarten.

2. This I who was first mesmerized by the dance of the butterfly is Francio Guadeloupe, the first author of this piece. He was later joined by the second author of this piece, Jordi Halfman, who shared in making (sense of) these imaginations.

3. Moreover, for us sound as a separate and isolated sense is a vital illusion effectuated by techniques, technologies, and knowledge productions, for the most part developed and overemphasized in North Atlantic societies. This is an argument that exceeds the scope of this essay. Suffice it to state that we choose not to perpetuate that illusion but follow Jean Baudrillard's insights (1985), radicalizing Marshall McLuhan's far too positive assessment, on the role of media and technology on humankind. See also Baudrillard (1983), who preempts interpretations of technological reductionism, or an analysis that is thoroughly negative, in relation to techno-culture and media.

4. https://www.youtube.com/watch?v=ehsqHkxVlFI&feature=youtu.be.

5. Francio Guadeloupe.

6. https://www.youtube.com/watch?v=4Wu_45scHNo. Last viewed on January 13, 2017.

7. Francio Guadeloupe.

8. Jordi Halfman.

9. This is taken from my field notes. I described the boy based upon what I/eye was able to perceive before fully relating to him as object.

10. I make no claim to knowing the pupils or to presenting you with a representation of Sint Maarteners. Like the opaque multiplicity that connotes the category of tourists, so too those who reside on the island are not grasped, to use the terms of Glissant (1997, 190–92). The opacity of the others we encounter is safeguarded when one becomes object and partakes of a symbolic logic, complicating taken-for-granted identities while at one and the same time undoing without remainders marked as Truth (Baudrillard 2005, 77–78). The category of Sint Maartener can be written about while upholding people's rights to opacity, never letting them coincide with text or be clear referents.

11. Francio Guadeloupe.

12. Francio Guadeloupe.

13. Francio Guadeloupe.

5 · SOUND MANAGEMENT

Listening to Sandals Halcyon in Saint Lucia

JOCELYNE GUILBAULT

"A garden paradise by a tranquil sea," Sandals Halcyon Resort and Spa is an intimate, laid-back beach resort in Saint Lucia. If there were ever a resort that embraces the quintessential Caribbean, Sandals Halcyon Beach is surely it. See all that Saint Lucia has to offer from the eyes of our host, as her senses are pampered at the most intimate Sandals of all East Caribbean Islands. Join her in a journey to a world of enchanting temptations that immerse you in the hypnotic realm of the islands.

http://www.sandals.com/main/halcyon/ha-media/

Music is a very important component of that business, can't do without it. I can't imagine what the hotels would be like without music.

—*David Samuels, former entertainment manager at several Saint Lucian hotels*

Say the words "all-inclusive hotels" and "tourist vacation," and one is immediately up against three forms of harsh academic suspicion.[1] The first suspicion comes from the belief that, by definition, tourism is bad for local people, for local economies, and for local environments. Linked to an overt support for workers, the second suspicion stems from the fear of manipulation on the part of the hotel management. The third suspicion is raised by the negative connotations about tourists, their bourgeois laziness, frivolities, and even at times immorality.

This study is not about praising or demonizing managers, musicians, or vacationers. It is not about whether the activity of tourism is suspicious or marvelous. Nor is it an accounting of consumption or objectification. My purpose in studying the political economy of music and sound at an-inclusive hotel is to investigate the complexity of management's and musicians' agency in a site that is often dominated by too much attitude (particularly in music studies) and too little empirical research. It is about exploring how something called the "touristic experience" through music and sound is generated out of particular conjunctions that are always mediated. Here I am putting in conversation the managers' and musicians' predicaments and interrelatedness as a conjunction that reveals the mediating forces of history, politics, and economics.

While this chapter focuses on the experience of sounds of vacation, I do not equate "experience" with first-person accounts by tourists. Rather, I am concerned by *what informs the tourists' experience.* I speak of experience in terms of the music and sound policies hotel managers make and the labor musicians do under different, yet simultaneous, regimes of values and constraints. This study examines how these regimes are informed as much by economic and political forces at a macro level, as by the management and musicians' distinct understandings of hospitality, personal tastes, and personal convictions. Through the lens of labor, this study further accounts for the moral force of long-held traditions and the economic implications for gender politics in terms of music-related employment and types of employment. It is in these conjunctions that I am locating the *shaping* of tourists' experience. So for every sound at the all-inclusive hotel, I am hearing sociality, power, and history vis-à-vis agency, mediation, and conjunction. I am thinking about financial cost, calculation, and compromise. I am paying attention to the strategies musicians use to heighten the sensual pleasures of vacation. Listening to music and sound is thus my way to engage the political economy of tourism in its affecting and affective dimensions.

Sound and music inform tourists' experience at every juncture — not just in the immediacy of the on-site experience. Similarly, managers and musicians all bring different knowledges, musical tastes, and experiences shaped by a wide array of mediations past, present, and future, compressed or spread out over a number of years. How does hotel management plan to reach out to tourists and, in the encounter, use the sameness and difference of sonic experience to create soothing, energizing, and pleasurable feelings of vacation? What kind of entertainment infrastructure is put into place to provide music for the ear and for the body? What policies and politics govern the hiring of musicians? To what extent is aural architecture a preoccupation in hotel design and renovations plans? How is the use of sonic space in the resort commodified and made economically profitable?

To explore these questions, I chose to work at one of the Sandals all-inclusive hotels. Sandals not only owns thirty resorts in the Caribbean — the greatest number of all-inclusive hotels owned by one company. It has also acquired a worldwide reputation in the tourist industry and has been recognized as the "world's leading all-inclusive company"—a title earned by being the World Travel Awards winner twenty-four years in a row (as of March 2018). Sandals's hotel management can thus be regarded as having successfully set standards revealing business acumen as well as critical aesthetic and ethical values in the tourist industry.

Known as one of the destinations attracting the greatest number of returning guests, Sandals Halcyon in Saint Lucia is where I conducted my fieldwork. At 169 rooms, it is the smallest of the three all-inclusive hotels owned by Sandals in Saint Lucia. Its relatively small size (compared to the 331 rooms and 339 rooms of the two other Sandals Saint Lucia properties), location alongside a sandy beach, and landscaping including sinuous paths amid tropical flowers and trees, has led Sandals to brand this all-inclusive property as ideal for couples and honeymooners. As is usually the case, Gordon "Butch" Stewart, founder and chairman of Sandals, buys existing hotels to make them part of the Sandals family. Already well known for some twenty years, Halcyon Beach hotel in Saint Lucia became the Sandals Halcyon resort in 1994.

These details about the hotel—its size, history, and privileged clientele—assume a particular importance because, from the outset, they tangibly affect the music and sound heard in this particular vacation site. They mediate the guests' proximity to the music and sounds in their surroundings, the selected range of music, the volume at which music is played, the settings where the music is performed, the number of live performances scheduled during the week—all of which greatly contrast with all-inclusive hotels of 250-plus rooms designed for families, for example. Yet at the same time, Sandals Halcyon enacts the hospitality philosophy, governing principles, and aesthetics and ethical values that are asserted by the management as common to all Sandals hotels. While the tourists at Sandals Halcyon enjoy free access and free transportation to the two other Sandals locations during the day and evening, I concentrated on Sandals Halcyon to understand how this particular all-inclusive hotel works through music and sound to heighten its guests' experiences.

I conducted my research at this all-inclusive hotel in Saint Lucia with both a sense of familiarity and a feeling of estrangement. A sense of familiarity because I know Saint Lucia well, having done research on musical traditions there for nearly eight years, from the late 1970s into the 1980s. A sense of familiarity also because since then I have continued to do research on popular music in many other islands in the Caribbean. My feeling of estrangement stemmed from having little experience working in a corporate context.

In this research, I could not lose sight of the fact that interviewing hotel management and interviewing musicians does not entail the same thing. Speaking with hotel management means speaking to a voice that is positioned in a chain of complex hierarchy. It means speaking to somebody whose statements by definition likely reflect more the corporation's decisions than individual agency. Speaking to musicians, by contrast, means hearing about the musicians' history, knowledge, and work conditions. Whereas managers articulate their positions as corporate representatives, musicians articulate their life experience as artists. Managers and musicians are both workers, but their respective work gives way to discourses that I had to hear differently and write about differently. Some of these discourses relate more personal stories than others. Some of these discourses focus more on concerns about the hotel infrastructure than others. Correspondingly, the tone I use to explore all of these discourses reflects as much the distinct positioning these various workers occupy at the hotel as the distinct kinds of work they actually do at this site.

In the first edition of the journal *Tourist Studies*, published in 2001, editors Adrian Franklin and Mike Crang remark how in tourist studies "it is not just bodily pleasure that have [sic] often been downplayed but pleasure *tout court*. . . . We need to say tourism matters because it is enjoyable, not in spite of it. . . . A legacy of one-too-many jibes about fieldwork in exotic places and fears of being trivialized, have given a sometimes desperately earnest tone to tourist studies" (Franklin and Crang 2001, 14). Since that call, some tourism scholars have addressed pleasure, but mainly from psychology and gender perspectives. Very few studies have focused on bodily pleasure or simply pleasure in relation to music in the hotel or resort industry. The few exceptions that have done so focus mainly on music in relation to sex tourism and drug use in specific touristic sites.[2]

My interest here is not to focus on the tourists' experience of pleasure, but rather to address how, through music and sound, the hotel management and the musicians attempt to provide the resort's guests sensuous pleasures as well as the conditions to experience them. One of my key propositions is thus to link the political economy of music and sound to the political economy of hospitality. It is to show how musical entertainment and the curating of sounds are inextricably connected in all-inclusive hotels with a particular kind of hospitality: commercial hospitality (cf. King 1995). Commercial hospitality by definition provides its guests with a sense of wellness and care, but, in contrast to private hospitality, it is designed and offered for profit. As part of a capitalist enterprise, the analysis of commercial hospitality must thus be examined in terms of financial investment, hiring strategies for entertainment staff and musicians, and careful calibration of "emotional economies." To address how the all-inclusive hotels cater to what Matei Candea and Giovanni da Col (2012) call "emotional economies," I explore the kinds of activities and spaces that the hotel management creates to offer vacationers a wide range of emotional experiences, ranging from anticipation to amazement, from serenity to excitement.

In what follows, I examine how hospitality is conceived and how emotional economies are managed through music and sound. To do so, I focus on what it takes materially in terms of human resources to make music part of the business of an all-inclusive resort. I then explore how the all-inclusive hotel defines the concept of entertainment and what practices involving music and/or sound this concept sets into motion. In the last section, I pay close attention to how musicians working in an all-inclusive hotel define and perform hospitality in practice.

Sandals's Entertainment Personnel, Musicians, and Hiring Policies

One of my first inquiries concerned who provides the entertainment at Sandals Halcyon. What financial investment is devoted to entertainment? What is the politics of gender in such an establishment today? What criteria appear crucial to getting hired?

In some islands, the question of "who" provides the entertainment cannot be easily answered. It depends greatly on the political status of the island—independent versus French overseas department—which alone determines the employment visa requirement and thus greatly influences the management hiring policies for resort employees. Whereas in a French overseas department such as Guadeloupe, an all-inclusive resort can recruit workers from different parts of Europe without visas, the independent English-speaking islands such as Saint Lucia have such strict employment visa requirements that most employees working in the resorts are locals.[3] Apart from the hotel manager, who is from Jamaica,[4] all the other employees I met at Sandals Halcyon were thus Saint Lucians of African descent who, on the island, constitute the majority of the population.

At Sandals resorts, the substantial financial investment in entertainment is made clear by the elaborate hierarchy of positions in this department (it is indeed a whole department). In addition to the general manager who oversees the hiring of the employees and all of the activities occurring in the hotel, the entertainment personnel include a Sandals entertainment manager for the eastern Caribbean, an entertainment manager for each hotel (including, in our case, one for Sandals Halcyon), and "playmakers" (as these facilitators are called in local parlance), whose number varies according to the size of the hotel. At Sandals Halcyon, which is considered a small all-inclusive hotel, there are four. (A playmaker is someone hired to supervise and participate in cultural, sports, and gym activities to boost the guests' participation and social interactions.)

In the postcolonial analysis of labor, the issue of gender is unavoidable.[5] At Sandals Halcyon, I considered gender—in particular, women's positionalities—through the lens of labor. Women carry out three kinds of labor: service employees, management, and entertainers. In the service sector, the type of work assigned to women still follows traditional gendered roles: women deal with "domestic" tasks such as room cleaning, and men take care of things such as landscaping. In the entertainment sector, I also observed how the typical gendered positionalities remain intact: women are featured as dancers and as singers, with a notable exception that I will discuss below. The position of women in management could not, however, be as easily predicted.

While the hotel manager and the Sandals regional entertainment manager are both male, the entertainment manager at Sandals Halcyon is a woman, Charlyn Leonce-Charles—the first woman at the Sandals hotels in Saint Lucia to head this department. In her early thirties, she is a dynamic woman who combines a wealth of experience as a dancer, actress, tourist guide, playmaker, assistant cruise ship director, and head playmaker—experiences that prepared her well to occupy her current position. In charge of music management for the entire resort, she uses her social skills to assess the guests' musical interests and to hear their comments about the music programming at the hotel. From the time of my first meeting with her, I was struck by her knowledge of and passion for artistic expression and by her commitment to her job. If such positions were male-dominated in the past, this is no longer the case. Another woman now heads the entertainment department at one of the larger Sandals hotels in the country. The most visible and most present members of the entertainment personnel during the guests' activities are the playmakers, which at Sandals Halcyon include women as well as men. While the highest positions in this elaborate hierarchy continue to be occupied by men, Sandals is undoubtedly mindful of gender politics. But most likely, the owner of Sandals is also looking for the distinct skills, high performance standards, and personal appeal that each individual brings to the establishment.

But one of the strikingly common characteristics of the Sandals Halcyon's entertainment personnel is that they are all seasoned travelers. They have all traveled extensively, either to obtain a business degree in Canada, to acquire some artistic training in Jamaica and New York, or to work on cruise ships. Some others have traveled around the Caribbean to work and to perform. That the entertainment personnel are composed of travelers should not come as a surprise since West Indians are known to travel either to study or to work abroad. But not all Saint Lucians can afford to do so. Hence, could it be that one of the recruiting criteria to be part of the entertainment personnel at Sandals is to have extensive travel experience? In all cases, through their travel experience, the entertainment personnel at Sandals Halcyon possess an intimate knowledge of many different countries, cultures, and musics.

This world experience of the management and entertainment personnel is significant in the all-inclusive hotel context. It certainly refutes the idea that the history of encounters in and through sound in an all-inclusive hotel such as Sandals Halcyon can be conceived (if it were ever possible) as involving people who are total strangers to each other—the natives (including the hotel management and musicians) on one side and the resort's guests on the other—the sedentary "locals" whose identity, sense of place, and knowledge have been long portrayed as fixed and immutable, and the tourists who in contrast have been depicted as travelers and forever in quest of new knowledge (see Sheller 2003). Rather, the history of encounters in and through sound in a touristic site such as Sandals Halcyon must be viewed as encounters among cosmopolitans whose experiences may differ on numerous points and yet overlap in others.[6]

The history of encounters in touristic sites in the Caribbean indeed has typically involved "locals" with long vernacular cosmopolitan experiences, experiences that have been informed by being British colonial subjects for over a century and even after Independence, by living with the enduring legacies of many British institutions and cultural practices to the present day—cosmopolitan experiences that have been intensified by exposure to a wide range of musics and different ways of living and being in the world through mass media, cosmopolitan experiences that for many people had to do with having to live in diaspora in different parts of the world in search of better job opportunities and training. It can safely be argued that these histories of encounters for many Caribbean people have nurtured, to use Ulrich Beck's wording, "a cosmopolitan outlook" (Beck 2006, 21).[7]

Significantly, the managers and playmakers are the ones hired to directly intervene in the tourists' experiences of music and sound at Sandals resorts. The ways in which the staff's cosmopolitan experiences have shaped their knowledge and attraction to many musics, in no small measure, facilitate their work at the all-inclusive hotel. They can not only imagine but also relate to many of their guests' musical habitus and preferences. As managers and playmakers, the goal is then to use this knowledge to reach out to tourists, to meet their musical tastes, while also offering them new and stimulating sonic experiences. This entertainment personnel's cosmopolitan musical experience thus constitutes an asset in making decisions about as well as in making changes to the programming of live and piped-in music throughout the resort. They can quickly adjust their decisions about what music should be played in relation to the clientele they receive during any given week, knowing something about the dominant musics of their guests' country of origin, their ethnicity, their class, their age, and more.

The entertainment management is in a position of power. To give a few examples: Based on their aesthetic judgments informed partly by their musical experience and musical taste as well as their knowledge of the local music scene and their tourist clientele, the managers hire some musicians and not others. They establish the do's and the don'ts in relation to the selection of music. "No profanity, of course," I was told. "We don't encourage heavy metal or hardcore dub [dancehall]." "Even if it is clean, no dancehall. Calypso? I will play [on loudspeakers] some, but I won't play others." Is it because some musical styles and songs are considered too local, too bold, or too loud? Or is it because they are too "irreverent" and "uncompromising" to non-Caribbean ears or visitors of a certain class? The selection of music is a moral call as much as a business decision from the perspective of the administration: any music, sound, or lyrics that could potentially disturb or annoy the hotel's vacationers is avoided for fear of losing some of their clientele. Entertainment managers thus define through their musical selections the geo-moral space of the Sandals resort in terms of political economy.

From her office, the Sandals Halcyon's entertainment manager monitors the music throughout the resort. She showed me the sound equipment that allows her to do so: a Mackie twenty-four-track console to monitor live performance on the traditional stage in the main reception room, often operated by her sound engineer; a CD player, Denon DN-D-4000, to play music for that same room—music that she either selects herself or that is selected by one of her playmakers; and a control center, Denon FBX 900, which literally enables her to control the selection of the different sound tracks and the volume at which they are played in different spaces (the restaurants, the bar, the lobby, and so on) throughout the resort.[8]

As Sandals's entertainment manager for the eastern Caribbean, Trevor King explained, entertainment managers oversee the appropriateness of music for different times, different activities, and signature events such as the manager's cocktail party. They are also encouraged to create new music entertainment experiences, for example, by introducing a new show concept or a new staging for a show (described at greater length below). In short, they oversee the entire musical atmosphere of the resort—a form of skilling too little appreciated and too little examined in music and tourism studies.

The Hiring of Musicians

One of the most obvious impacts entertainment management has on tourists' experiences of vacation is the selection of musicians who perform at the resorts. The artists' musical abilities and knowledge of repertoire, not to mention social skills, all contribute to tourists' experiences of "fantasy, feeling, and fun"—thus making the selection of musicians of critical importance.[9]

As is typically the case throughout the Caribbean region, I noted that the musical acts at Sandals Halcyon were male dominated. Women were typically present, as in entertainment business more generally, as dancers (e.g., in a masquerade folkloric group) and as singers (e.g., in a jazz ensemble). However, I also encountered a surprise, a woman instrumentalist, Barbara Cadet. And perhaps even more surprising in the Caribbean context, she was playing the soprano saxophone, alone, accompanied by a recorded track coming out of the latest Bose equipment, which she controlled before and after each tune. Barbara Cadet mesmerized the guests as she combined outstanding musical skills on her instrument with a thorough knowledge of music technology, reputed in both cases to be the domain of men. I asked her how it feels performing alone as a woman and as an instrumentalist at Sandals Halcyon and at the many other hotels where she regularly works. She answered without hesitation: "I function as a man in a man's world. I am not a singer. I play the saxophone, and I am also a composer and a bandleader." My way of thinking about her positionality is to describe it as hypergender. By this I mean she not only engages a very traditionally male domain by playing the saxophone, using sound technology, and working as an entrepreneur and a manager—activities especially associated with male agency and success. She also simultaneously performs her distinctive femininity by her tone of voice, her presentation of appeal and affect, and fashionably feminine style of dress, long hair, and high heels. Barbara Cadet stands as a unique figure on the island. She is highly respected as a musician, not only at the hotel, but also among local musicians.

In addition to the powerful mediating factor of gender, the hotel's hiring practices for musicians (the term *musicians* here includes singers) have been structured and shaped by several other forces. These include transnational and local economics, state politics, and music industries, all of which have dramatically changed over the years, not only in Saint Lucia but across the entire Caribbean region. To situate all-inclusive hotels' hiring practices around musicians in the tourist sector today—not exclusive to Sandals, but also including those of Sandals—all the musicians I interviewed took a historical detour back to the 1970s. For example, Ronald "Boo" Hinkson, a guitarist, songwriter (including for Grammy nominees), arranger, and one of, if not "the," most respected and commercially successful musician in and outside Saint Lucia,[10] most tellingly explained current practices in terms of the changes that occurred in the hotel industry over the past forty years thus:

> In that era, there was no all-inclusive hotels. The hotels then provided music entertainment not only for its guests, but also for the local people. They hired the best musicians in the land. At the time, Tru-Tones [Hinkson's band] was a hit. We were going to hotels to perform like, say, the Fisherman's Wharf, and we would play every Saturday night, and people would flood the place to come to hear the Tru-Tones. People paid to come to hear us. Since Tru-Tones was re-

garded as the best in the country, all the tourists would congregate to hear us. In addition to that, the local people would come to hear us. (Hinkson, interview with the author, November 2017)

As Hinkson remarked, the hotels made money, and he made money. Since the Tru-Tones had a following, he was able to ask, in addition to the performance flat fee, half of the ticket receipts (for successful bands, it was common practice to negotiate a percentage of the door fees). And because the Tru-Tones attracted a large clientele, the hotel also made money on the entrance fees and the purchase of drinks at the bar. In that era, music entertainment was thus a source of revenue for the hotel. But with the advent of the all-inclusive concept, Hinkson explained, "entertainment now generally is no longer a source of revenue for the hotels. The tourists have paid everything before they come here. And the all-inclusives do not allow people to come to the hotels and pay to come in and buy drinks." As a result, for the all-inclusive hotels' administrators, music entertainment is regarded as an expense and accordingly is simply assessed as one of the "services" the hotel provides. Hence, depending on the hotels' anticipated expenditures, be they in relation to new projects or building renovations, the budget for music entertainment is reevaluated and adjusted, as is the case for some other departments, to help balance the overall operating budget of the hotel.

Viewed as an expense, the music entertainment budget in all-inclusive hotels is tightly regulated. With the closure by the late 1980s of most regular hotels and restaurants that once provided live music, the all-inclusive hotels since the early 1990s represent the most important source of employment for musicians on most islands, including Saint Lucia. In this context, local musicians now have little bargaining power to negotiate salaries. The predicament in which musicians find themselves, however, cannot be viewed as having been "caused" exclusively by the all-inclusive hotel concept or the powerful company of Sandals in the islands.

Several other mediations have contributed to local musicians' state of precarity. The poor economy of Saint Lucia since the late 1980s has led not only to the closure of several establishments providing live entertainment, but also to a severe unemployment rate for the population at large—evaluated at almost 20 percent in 2017.[11] The banana industry, which provided the main source of economic revenues in the country up to the early 1990s, experienced a serious downfall following the European Union's gradual dismantling of the preferential trade barriers initially put in place to protect Britain's former colonies. The clothes factories that used to employ many women closed down to move to places where outsourcing is cheaper. The free trade agreement signed in 2008, which now prevents the Saint Lucia government from charging import taxes at previous rates, has significantly decreased the government's revenues and left little budget for once-supported art initiatives.[12]

The musicians' state of precarity in Saint Lucia is not only related to the poor economic situation of the nation-state or the Caribbean at large. It is also related to the profound shift in the music industry. Recordings no longer sell.[13] In addition to the increasing difficulty of finding a day job to supplement the revenues earned from performances, local musicians can thus no longer count on revenues from CDS. Even though modest for most, these revenues nonetheless helped some musicians pay a few bills.

Paradoxically, and still unrelated to the "all-inclusive" concept, Saint Lucian musicians' state of precarity is also related to things that, according to many musicians, have not changed and should change. They are referring to local radio programming. In spite of the twenty-plus radio stations in Saint Lucia, musicians still complain that there is little airplay of Saint Lucian music. This situation, I was told in several interviews, is not only because of globalization. It is deeply linked to the colonial legacy and enduring contracted mentality, to use the words of a prominent musician, that "the outside [by definition] is better." The result of little airplay for Saint Lucian musicians means not only a lack of exposure, but also an absence of royalties. Hence only a very small percentage of the royalties collected by the Eastern Caribbean Collective Organization for Music Rights (ECCO) go to Saint Lucian musicians.

For most musicians in Saint Lucia, all-inclusive hotels represent their main source of employment. With the rising costs of living, transportation, equipment, and instrument repair, many musicians are nonetheless willing to play for less money than they earned in the 1970s and 1980s. There is no musicians' union, and musicians need to work to survive. The competition among musicians is severe, and hence the all-inclusive hotels can hire musicians for short-term contracts, at relatively low fees, and in the company's best interests.

As a result, many Saint Lucian musicians choose to work on cruise ships to make a better living. The pay is usually better than in all-inclusive hotels, and many musicians I interviewed reported that the experience on cruise ships is very formative. Curtis Mondesir, a pianist who now works six nights a week at one of the restaurants at Sandals Halcyon, performed as a band member on cruise ships for eleven years. The story he tells powerfully recalls what I have heard from other Saint Lucian musicians about their cruise ship experience — the learning, the challenge, the laughter, but also the desire to come back home and stay at home after a few years back and forth at sea. For Mondesir, that experience began in 1994 with a contract of six months. As he recounts,

> The ship asks for a certain repertoire. So I had to learn about a hundred songs. We played a set of popular calypsos because we had a Caribbean night where you teach Caribbean dances. And then we had the 1950s and '60s night where you had to learn the Elvis and all this kind of '60s band stuff, so we had this as well. We also had a country night, at the time a bunch of black guys playing country. [!] That was so funny. And then they added a Latin night. So we had to learn Latin music now. We did stuff like Ricky Martin, that was a very popular music back then, and songs like "La Bamba." We also played disco music with Kool & the Gang, for example. People danced a lot on this kind of music. We did all kinds of music on the ships. We did Madonna's "Like a Virgin," "La Isla Bonita." We did some Michael Jackson too: "Thriller," "Beat It," "Billie Jean," "Man in the Mirror." So we did that kind of repertoire back then. At that time, I never had played with two keyboards. And you had to play one up, and one down, and [at the same time] a special style [genre of music]. So I had to learn this. But when you are up for a challenge, you learn. Playing different kinds of music, listening to a lot of musicians, this is where I grabbed my style. . . . I quit the ship in 2006 because my girlfriend was pregnant. I decided to quit the ship because I wanted a family life. (Mondesir, interview with the author, December 2015)

This story is important because it shows how the cruise ship is deeply connected to tourists' experience at the all-inclusive hotels. Many of the musicians performing at the all-inclusive hotels have in fact developed their knowledge of a wide range of repertoire on the ships. This learning experience helps them to be particularly well prepared and at ease to respond to the guests' eclectic musical tastes and demands. The musicians' hectic schedule of six-month contracts at sea also helps the all-inclusive in yet another way. As Trevor King, the entertainment manager for Sandals resorts in the eastern Caribbean, explained, Sandals often hires cruise ship musicians when they return home in between their six-month contracts—even if it is only for a short period of time—because they provide a refreshing difference in both sounds and looks. For the musicians, these gigs help round out their salaries. For the hotel, these musicians' performances help break any potential monotony for the hotel personnel as well as their guests.

The all-inclusive concept structuring Sandals's hiring practices for musicians cannot be examined in isolation from the hotel management and the entertainment management's own policies and politics, the nation-state's economics (the severe rate of unemployment), state politics (free trade agreements), transnational policies (the European Union's intervention in regard to the banana market), and transnational commercial practices (closure of clothes factories in favor of cheaper outsourcing and cruise ships). In their combination, these forces deeply mediate which musicians are hired to play in the all-inclusive hotels and for how long, where they acquire their training, and which repertoire they perform for the guests' aesthetic and kinesthetic pleasure.

On the Concept of Entertainment at an All-Inclusive Hotel

The concept of entertainment is not self-evident. It must be linked to the context in which entertainment takes place—in our case, sites of vacation—and it must be linked also to what is distinct to this context, the politics of hospitality that governs and distinguishes all-inclusive hotels and the activities at these sites. What can be learned about the political economy of music and sound by looking at how the concept of entertainment is understood at the Sandals Halcyon? To what extent is the concept of entertainment the defining feature of what hospitality means at this hotel? What follows begins to answer these questions.

In many areas of tourism, as Franklin and Crang note, it is assumed that "tourists are seeking to be *doing something* in the places they visit rather than being endlessly spectatorially passive" (2001, 13; emphasis in the original). Accordingly, one of the first definitions of the concept of "entertainment" at Sandals Halcyon refers not only to music, but also to a wide range of activities including beach volleyball, pool volleyball, gym assistance, tennis, water regatta, bocce ball, and a giant outdoor replica of a chess board. While they do not involve live music performance, many of these activities are resolutely imagined by the Sandals hotel management as indissociable from music accompaniment. As these activities take place during the day, they significantly inform the music one can hear from breakfast to the end of the afternoon in the resort. The choice of music or the listening to ambient sounds one comes to expect at the all-inclusive hotel becomes deeply linked not only to specific activities, but also to the specific times at which these activities take place. Entertainment accompanied by music offers a wide range of rhythms and moods to the vacation site.

Business scholar S. Maitel (2002) summarizes the contemporary orientation in marketing by this motto: "Don't sell commodities, sell experiences." What Maitel does not mention is how the selling of experience does not mean by default only "new" experience. In this regard, I agree with cultural studies scholar Tim Edensor, that "tourism is [usually] represented as removed from the quotidian, as a common-sense understanding, but also as a theoretical way of marking tourism as a separate scholarly field of enquiry." As he argues, "Although suffused with notions of escape from normativity, tourists carry quotidian habits and responses with them; they are part of their baggage. Tourism thus involves unreflexive, habitual and practical enactions which reflect common-sense understandings of how to be a tourist" (Edensor 2001, 60–61), or at least, it could be added, of how to be a tourist away from routine but never without routine.

The Sandals Halcyon management clearly bears these insights in mind when planning the resort activities for both day and evening. Many of these activities, which include power walking, volleyball, yoga, and so on, are not new to many of the resort's guests. They are part of their daily or weekly activities, their routines at "home." And one of the intended or imagined joys of vacation is indeed to have the time to do a good workout without feeling the pressure of having to quickly return to a daily job. For other guests, the meaning of vacation is to enjoy being a "tourist," and thus to take part in activities which they never have the time or inclination to engage in at home. Either way, the activities offered during the day at the all-inclusive are not, in and of themselves, out of the ordinary. The fact that most of these activities are accompanied by music is not new or different either. What is important to examine here is how, for example, in addition to relying on common sense to entertain people of different ages and different degrees of physical fitness, the sport and dance instructor uses his athletic and artistic skills and his knowledge of people from different parts of the world to select the rhythms and moods of the music accompanying each activity.

Meet Jermaine Alexander, a multitalented artist and athlete who has worked full-time at Sandals Halcyon since 2014 and whose profile well reflects the sought-after qualities of a playmaker at the Sandals corporation. He is a professional dancer and choreographer who studied dance in Guadeloupe. Upon his return to Saint Lucia, he created his own Miracle Dance Company and also worked as a contract dancer. In addition to giving personal dance classes, he also plays the bongo drums. Prior to working full-time at Sandals Halcyon, Alexander performed in several resorts, including the three Sandals hotels in Saint Lucia. He is thus an experienced performer, choreographer, and teacher. Having been actively involved in sports throughout his life, he serves as a coach for many sport activities in the resort. He is in charge of power walking, aqua-fitness, dance lessons, leg-butt-tum (leg, buttock, and tummy) exercises, Pilates, yoga, kickboxing, and gym assistance (private guided exercises).

Soon after he ended his aqua class on a Tuesday morning, I met him to ask how he chooses the music to accompany all of these activities. "It depends on a number of specific factors," he replied. "For the power walk? No musical accompaniment. Just nature. Because this place here is not as big as other properties, I do my power walk on the beach where you really push hard, and so we just hear the water, nature, and in the morning, you can hear the birds singing. You're in Saint Lucia, what else could you ask for!"

To create the hype when he conducts aqua-fitness classes around 10:30 AM, Alexander follows DJs' common strategies: he looks for music that is popular and that people can relate to. But in selecting the music, and most specifically the tempo of the music, he takes into account several factors, like the fitness, age, and abilities or disabilities of the clients who signed up for the activity. Near the large swimming pool, there is a stage equipped with speakers located at each end of the ceiling and also a table on the side where Alexander sets his computer with his sequenced music selections. However, as he indicates, "I may have prepared some music of 160-plus beats a minute, but when I look at who is in the class, I have to tone it down. We do have elderly people who are not as active as the younger generation. So you can't use the same music as you would for younger people." For older people, I asked? "I go a little slow. I take songs with a slow tempo and then gradually build into it." For younger people, Alexander plays a mixture of music "like funk and [I] look for what's new. And then something with Wyclef Jean, a little Bob Marley, and later Damien Marley, and some power soca [fast tempo and energizing rhythms]—music from all over the Caribbean." But, as he explains, his choice of music does not depend only on the people in the water, but also on those within earshot. The aqua-fitness class takes place in an outside pool—the Sunset pool near the bar, the pool table, and the main restaurant of the hotel. So he always plans a mix, not to overwhelm anyone with only one type of music. He thus plays some of the latest American top-forty songs or newly acclaimed songs from the Caribbean followed by old hits from the 1960s to cater to the musical taste of everyone around.

Alexander's selection of music for dance classes is also based on distinct patterns, but this time in relation to another consideration: the newlyweds versus the older couples. Alexander teaches salsa, soca, zouk, and even country. When he has newlyweds among those who signed up for the class, as he puts it, "I would teach them the *kolé*. The kolé, which is associated with zouk, refers to dance movements that are performed by a couple in very close proximity to each other.

In other cases, the activity itself imposes its own predilection for particular kinds of music. For the Pilates or yoga class, Alexander systematically chooses music with a slow to medium tempo, soft sounding instrumentation, and fluid melodies such as in smooth jazz. As he remarked, in all cases he selects the rhythms and moods of the music accompanying each activity with one preoccupation in mind: *hospitality*. Following the general guidelines of Sandals all-inclusive hotels, hospitality for Alexander's daily activities means treating guests in a friendly and generous way in a place that is out of place, with the emphasis on the gentle ease of activity and musical options without any pressure.

Not all sport activities require the presence of a playmaker. For pool volleyball, for instance, there is no instructor. The music is then selected by the entertainment manager and played on the loudspeakers. It typically features fast-tempo songs with dynamic melodies and strong voices. Amid the screams and shouts, laughter and loud exchanges among the players, Caribbean soca is often the music of choice. At the outside spa where people enjoy a massage away from the more crowded areas, no music is played. As one massage therapist explained to me, "this is the time to listen. There are already so many sounds around to fill your head."

Similar to Alexander's comments about the power walk on the beach, this therapist is equally convinced—or at least, wants to convince me— that the sounds of nature and avian life (surf, wind, and birds) are unquestionably part of the sensual pleasures the resort offers to its guests. For anyone who listens, these sounds contact people and, as the entertainment manager Leonce-Charles put it, "they send you in another zone." Alexander and the massage therapist thus invite their guests to listen, as they both unequivocally conceive these environmental sounds as heightening the experience of vacation. In political economy terms, these sounds are presented as commodities, as the bonuses that come with being at this all-inclusive hotel.

The Sandals Halcyon management is clearly aiming to provide a wide range of physical activities filled with music and sound—activities that for some of their guests are part of their daily routines wherever they are, and that for others constitute exploratory ways of "feeling" in vacation. This is one of the definitions of Sandals Halcyon's entertainment and ways of imparting a sense of hospitality to the hotel's vacationers.

A second concept of entertainment stems from the management aiming to cater to guests whose definition of vacation is to be able to have a quiet time and space—meaning a time and space with a minimum of human interference and a minimum of this subjective thing called "noise"—a luxury notion in the Caribbean and a reality that few people residing in the islands are in a position to experience.

When I reached the south side of the resort, I was struck by the change of ambiance. To accommodate tourists who look for tranquility during their vacation, there is no music diffused on speakers, not at the Paradise restaurant or at the Paradise pool (the other pool on the resort). Here the guests speak softly. One can only faintly detect the sound of the waves hitting the shore. The many trees and bushes surrounding this side of the resort efficiently mute or soften most ambient sounds. I say "most" ambient sounds because even with the thickest bushes around, in the Caribbean the talkative robin red-breast can still wake people up in the wee hours of the morning, the doves' soft calls can still produce an unwanted lull in late afternoon, and the tree frogs with their high-pitched ostinato patterns mixed in hocket style with the male crickets' chirping can also keep people alert when darkness settles in.[14]

The absence of music and keeping human voices at minimum volume in this part of the resort while there is music in other parts signals that tourists have the luxury of being able to be of two minds: (1) to turn off and chill, and (2) to participate in activities.

At Sandals Halcyon, a third definition of the concept of entertainment is articulated through the creative use of space in the resort. The goal? to play on the senses of seeing and hearing different things depending on where the guests are hosted; to capitalize on different sounds in different sections of the resort as commodities. To use cultural theorist Tim Edensor's metaphor, tourist space is "staged" (2001). In contrast to Edensor's focus on the tourists' "performance" in such spaces, I explored here how entertainment managers select and stage performance spaces. The theater metaphors of stage and performance used by Edensor are particularly apt in addressing how the hotel management stages tourist space to direct the guests' attention to this location and not others, to incite them to listen to these sounds and not others. Interestingly, these theater metaphors may actually be more than metaphors, as they refer to the kind of experience that Sandals seems to privilege in their choice of entertainment managers. Indeed, both the entertainment manager for the eastern Caribbean Sandals resorts and the entertainment manager at Sandals Halcyon I interviewed began to work at Sandals after years of experience in theater and acting.

In my meeting with Trevor King, I asked him when stand-alone performers became prominent in their entertainment programming. His answer did not allude to the fact that thanks to new sound technology such as sampling and backup tracks, single performers can sound as though they are performing with a full band and thus replace bands and save money. His answer instead focused on how Sandals's trademark is to constantly innovate. Stand-alone performers became prominent, he explained,

> when we became diverse at Sandals in terms of taking our entertainment out of the traditional stage settings and putting them in different little quaint and nice pockets of the property like under a tree, like by the waterfalls, or in the gazebo. These places do not call for this big twelve-man or five-man band. You are more into intimate settings where one person could still create that, you know . . . ["vibe" connected with live music]. (King, interview with the author, December 2015)

The staging of tourist space at Sandals Halcyon not only takes different shapes, but also creates different acoustic possibilities and sonic mixtures. One evening at Sandals Halcyon, Telvin John, a stand-alone singer with an amazing vocal range, performed on an open-air platform facing the Sunset pool. Passing over the water, the sound traveled far and resonated through the night air. Guests came and sat on lounge chairs and regular chairs around the pool to listen. From where I sat, I could still hear faintly to my right the striking sounds of the cues hitting the balls on the pool table. But the singer's voice and his playback track accompaniment dominated the open-air space. At times, leaving his equipment on stage and coming close to the guests while singing, John impressed me with a surreal-sounding presence, near and far, expansive, even though he was performing alone.

On another occasion, I had to leave the gazebo where I was taking notes, as a wedding was going to take place there two hours later. I watched a worker set up a speaker where a stand-alone musician was going to perform during the ceremony. As the gazebo was set on high ground near the sea, the music this time was going to be accompanied by the sounds of the crashing waves hitting the shore and by the whisper of the wind serving as an obligato to the sonic medley that afternoon.

Speaking with Sandals Halcyon's entertainment manager, I learned about another strategy used to stage tourist space, this time in some uncanny places—in the bushes outside a restaurant, and along the sidewalk leading to the beach. I learned about the "rock" speaker. A "rock" speaker is a speaker covered with fabric resembling green moss, a camouflage that helps make it blend in among bushes. Softly playing the same soundtrack provided in the lobby in counterpoint with the environmental sounds, the "rock" speaker plays the role of cultural intermediary between a listener and the multitude of sounds of nonhuman species and physical surroundings, between a listener and the undesired sounds produced by other humans. The "rock" speaker stages the tourist space as a reassuring and friendly place.

Even if this expression was not used in the interviews I conducted, the Sandals Halcyon management counts on the "aural architecture" of its indoor public spaces and on its selected open-air musical stages to sonically provide an overall feeling of warmth, connectedness, and intimacy for its guests.[15] Sandals's managers are keenly aware that a room that is acoustically dry or produces too much reverb can affect how long guests may want to stay in that room. The renovated buildings in this regard clearly demonstrate that much architectural care has been given to the rooms' acoustics. The gym fitness room, for instance, is conceived to be well lit but not overwhelmingly hot thanks to the meticulous placement of the skylights at different angles in the ceiling. The six speakers are placed in ceiling positions, tilted downward toward the areas where the guests work out. The central ventilation column reaches across the room and does not cross the acoustic pathway of the ceiling speakers. Sound is both emitted to specific areas as well as dispersed evenly throughout the room. One hears the rhythmic synchrony of guests on machines with the tempo and the accent structure of the piped-in music.

At Sandals Halcyon, there is a tacit management theory that understands hearing and listening as controllable or partially controllable through the staging of tourist space and the music programming by the staff.

A fourth prevalent understanding of entertainment at the all-inclusive hotel is informed by people's incessant desire today to expand their sensual pleasures. As anthropologist Brian Moeran puts it, "Tourism becomes more sensually diverse" (Moeran 1983, 96, quoted in Franklin and Crang 2001, 13). This is particularly true for food and for the construction of social imaginaries through food. Over the past few years, Sandals has expanded the number of specialty restaurants at its resorts. Sandals Halcyon Beach alone counts four restaurants: Mario's, Kimonos and Soy, the French Brasserie by the bay side, and Kelley's Dockside out on a pier. Interestingly, one rule now applies to all Sandals restaurants: the food specialty dictates the music that will be played in the restaurant. Sandals thus conceives space, time, and culinary taste and music as an experiential totality. As entertainment manager Leonce-Charles explained, "if you decide to eat French cuisine, you will not want to hear hip-hop. We want to set up an ambience in the restaurant. So if it is a French restaurant, we provide French music. If you go to the Japanese restaurant, same thing. It's kind of . . . 'Oh! I am in Japan now'" (Leonce-Charles, interview with the author, November 2015).

At least two points can be made about this new approach to music management. The first point is that sports and dance are not the only physical activities mediating the music selection at the resort. Food also does. The interrelation of food, beverage, and music, however, is nothing new. In the Caribbean, in particular, it is proverbial that "if you have food, you have to have music. And if you have music, you have to have food." It is thus not surprising to learn from Leonce-Charles that the food and beverage department works in close collaboration with the entertainment department. What is new, at least in Saint Lucia and many other Caribbean islands, is the new conception of the political economy of music in relation to food. The selection of food in articulation with the selection of music is now put to work to reinforce a sense of national identity and space as *brand* in the resort context.

The second point that can be made has to do with how this branding of different foods, sounds, and social imaginaries of place in the resort positions Sandals Halcyon not only as a local site in Saint Lucia—and by extension, in the Caribbean—but also as emblematic of a cosmopolitan outlook and participation in "worldly" practices of marketing and consumption. In this perspective, Caribbean food and music are presented as "delicacies" equal to, and no more exotic than, Italian, French, Japanese, and "continental" ones. In all cases, the neatly divided repertoire of music according to "national/regional" food specialty at dinner time aims to structure the tourists' aesthetic expectations, desires, and experiences during their vacation.

A fifth concept of entertainment at play at Sandals Halcyon is entirely based on music. As is the case for all Sandals resorts, every evening is "themed," to use the hotel management's expression. Here is a sample of one of the weeks' music programming in December 2015: Monday is a Caribbean night and thus features live performance of Saint Lucia/Caribbean "traditional" music. Tuesday is organized to celebrate the returnees. The dinner served in their honor is accompanied by a jazz trio. Wednesday evening is dedicated to the honeymooners, with an expressive stand-alone singer. Thursday is a casino night enlivened by American top-forty music diffused on loudspeakers around the room. Whereas Friday night features a band's live performance of reggae, Saturday is animated by a karaoke sing-along or a stand-alone singer performance. Sunday is "an evening of tranquility," often showcasing Saint Lucia's only female stand-alone saxophonist and acclaimed performer, arranger, and producer, Barbara Cadet, whom I discussed earlier. This programming can change depending on the season, the number of guests present for each event, their age, and their nationality, among other factors.

Each night's entertainment is not only based on a set of expectations nurtured long before the tourists arrive at their vacation destination, but also creates them or, at the very least, reinforces them. For the Caribbean night on Monday, out of all the possible choices of "traditional" music in Saint Lucia or the Caribbean at large, the music that is selected for the show is the masquerade—a music that features drumming, driving rhythms, carnival characters, colorful costumes, and energetic dance movements widely associated with African traditions—plus at times the famous limbo and fire eaters, also accompanied by drumming. The Caribbean night thus serves as a confirmation to the tourists that the exotic Caribbean presented online to promote Caribbean vacation packages actually does exist, even if it is only performed in a particular version conceived for them for that night at the all-inclusive hotel.

At the heart of this concept of entertainment through music is the sense, from the management's perspective, that there has to be a delicate balance between music that is familiar and music that brings a feeling of discovery. Interestingly, except for Monday (which is dedicated to local music), the music performed on all the other days of the week, except Friday, is selected to make the guests feel at home — literally. The music performed live by the jazz trio or stand-alone performers, as well as the karaoke night, is based on songs from different eras as well as different countries, but mainly if not exclusively from England and the United States, where most of the guests are from. The majority of these songs are typically considered "standards" or "classics," songs that have had a wide appeal and have circulated widely. On one Tuesday night, for example, Barbara Cadet played Sting's "Desert Rose," Elton John's "Your Song," Stevie Wonder's "Rainbow in the Sky" and "Isn't She Lovely," and the Carpenters' famous song, "They Long to Be (Close to You)." She also performed oldies, such as "Fever" and "Georgia." However, as is the case for all the other musicians and singers performing at the resort, she also regularly plays contemporary hits, for example, by John Legend, Beyoncé, and Michael Bublé, to reach younger guests. On that Tuesday night, she played, among others, "Quando, Quando" by the Black Eyed Peas. The Thursday karaoke night also features Euro-American mainstream songs, as karaoke by definition relies on songs that people already know. While some guests may know a few Caribbean songs, the majority do not.[16] Most of the songs the guests choose to sing on karaoke night thus belong to their "home" and own repertoires.

The reggae night on Friday contrasts significantly from all the other nights. It is a night of popular music exclusively from the Caribbean. While reggae is the music of choice, other musics such as zouk (from Martinique and Guadeloupe) and soca (mainly from Trinidad, but also from Saint Lucia and other islands) are at times included. The Saint Lucian reggae band, Xtent, composed of four musicians and a singer, often hired to play on the Friday nights at Sandals Halcyon, builds its repertoire almost exclusively on songs presumably well-known outside of the Caribbean. By the time I arrived on one Friday night, the band was performing one of Bob Marley's enduring hits, "I Wanna Love You." After playing other favorites from Marley's repertoire, the band switched to a faster tempo and performed Arrow's famous soca song, "Hot, Hot, Hot." By then, the band focused on getting the listeners to come to the dance floor. They performed versions of soca songs including typical dance instructions, such as asking the audience to "wave your hand," "jump, jump, jump," or "go down low."

The themed nights, like the daily activities, emphatically demonstrate how musical entertainment is designed to offer the hotel's vacationers a good time. For Sandals hotel management, this means offering the guests musical variety within zones of comfort, a good dose of familiar music interspersed with what for many guests are lesser-known music and dance styles from the Caribbean. This cultivation of a sense of "home" away from home articulates an aesthetics that thrives on the production of sameness and difference always in the process of defining each other in "highly changeable 'border zone relations'" (Guilbault 1993).

Musicians' Performance of Hospitality

Music is all about hospitality.

—*Emmerson Nurse, Saint Lucian jazz pianist*

The relation between entertainment and hospitality in the all-inclusive hotels cannot be overemphasized. In one of my meetings with him at a café, I asked Curtis Mondesir, the regular pianist at Sandals Halcyon, how musicians manage hospitality relations at the hotel. "Look up the word 'entertainment' in the dictionary. You'll see," he said. I looked. In Webster's dictionary, "Entertainment: (a) amusement; (b) hospitality given or received." In the Collins dictionary: "Entertainment is shows, performances . . . that people watch for pleasure." I continued my search and looked up the word "hospitality" in the Oxford dictionary: "the friendly and generous reception and entertainment of guests, visitors or strangers." Echoing Emmerson Nurse, cited in the above epigraph, for Curtis Mondesir entertainment *is about hospitality*: "You must have a repertoire for the clientele to keep them entertained and have them come back"—that is, a wide range of repertoire that can connect with the vacationers' different age groups, the countries where they are from, and the various stages informing their couple relations, from honeymooners to old couple relationships.

This strong link between entertainment and hospitality for musicians playing at all-inclusive hotels is not simply a matter of instinct. It is also connected with the issue of employment. The musicians' performances are constantly rated in a questionnaire emailed to all the guests three days after they return home. Their employment thus depends on whether, from the perspective of both the management and the tourists, they successfully join entertainment with hospitality, provide musical pleasure, create fun and excitement, and heighten the feeling of vacation and comfort for all those present.

In the all-inclusive hotels, the musicians are asked to work in what business scholars B. J. Pine and J. H. Gilmore (1999) call "the experience economy." In other words, musicians are hired to provide experiences that are memorable, new, emotional, and interactive. To understand the strategies they use to accomplish this feat, I turned to pianist, composer, and arranger Richard Payne (also director of the Saint Lucia School of Music), who has been playing for more than twenty years on the hotel circuit, including at all the Sandals all-inclusive resorts in Saint Lucia. Here is a summary of his musical thinking when he performs for vacationers: Payne selects his repertoire to provide a comfort zone, an emotional space that recalls and simultaneously recasts the favorite tunes and habitus of the guests on vacation. His approach well summarizes the main principles of the entertainment economy that, in my listening, seemed to prevail at Sandals Halcyon: the music should require little or no effort for the listener, and the musical performances should be based on sonic familiarity with a gentle introduction of local newness as a place/context marker.

To impart such an experience to the hotel guests, Payne plays some standards such as "Smoke Gets in Your Eyes" by Jerome Kern[17] or "A Time for Love" by Johnny Mandel[18] and songs by John Legend, *but* with some Caribbean flavor or twist. He plays Bob Marley's "Who the Cap Fit," but in a very jazz-oriented style because, he explained, "I think that the guests want to hear something new. You have to take the guests from what they are familiar with, and bring them slowly into your world — not bombard them with stuff they haven't heard before."

In contrast to the pianists, who typically feel free in the restaurants or in the hotel lobby to introduce varied versions of the hit songs they are playing, band members hired to perform on the themed nights rarely deviate from the style of music that has been advertised for the night. On the reggae-themed night, for instance, the bands play well-known reggae songs quite close to the original version the guests would have heard. Here the idea is to sound "real" Caribbean, to "be" the Caribbean the guests have heard. The contrast between the pianists' and the bands' approach to entertainment and hospitality highlights Candea and da Col's (2012, S8) argument that it is crucial to take into account "the scale, the contingency, and the specificity of each hospitality event—in other words, the 'happenstance' of hospitality." The management's requirements and the tourists' expectations for musicians playing in a restaurant or lobby versus musicians performing an advertised style of music at a show on stage greatly influence how musicians sonically manage hospitality relations.

The "traditional" Caribbean musics and dances that the guests imagine, but have not necessarily heard on recordings or seen live, paradoxically leave the musicians performing on the Caribbean-themed night more at liberty to choose how and through what music they want to produce a memorable experience for the guests. As anthropologist Jane Desmond discerningly writes, "tourism is not just an aggregate of commercial activities; it is also an ideological framing of history, nature and tradition; a framing that has the power to reshape culture and nature to its own needs" (Desmond 1999, xiv, quoted in Franklin and Crang 2001, 17). The same could be said about the performance of "traditional" music. The performance of traditional music is not just part of the entertainment at all-inclusive resorts; it is also an ideological framing of history and what "tradition" means for the local artists—a framing that has the power to redefine local culture in relation to their own knowledge and experience, but, it should be emphasized, in ways that do not challenge the tourist listener's standpoint.

The ideological framing of history and what "tradition" means for many artists—albeit not for all—has changed dramatically over the years. In the 1970s and up to the late 1980s, musicians from rural areas were brought to the hotels to perform music recognized as "traditional" in the country. There was no question then about whether what they played was traditional music or not. The musics these musicians performed were considered part of a long heritage. However, as cultural theorist Raymond Williams argues, "Tradition is always more than an inert historicized segment . . . it is not just 'a tradition' but a *selective tradition*: an *intentionally* selective version of a shaping past and a pre-shaped present, which is then powerfully operative in the process of social and cultural definition and identification" (Williams 1977, 115). The "traditional" music the musicians from the rural areas performed in the hotels was indeed selective in at least two ways: it featured some musics and not others that also have had a long past in Saint Lucia. It did not include, for example, any music from the East Indian population, which, admittedly, is small, but nonetheless part of Saint Lucia. It also featured only some versions, not all versions, of how the given traditional music is played in the country. At any rate, many musicians from the country's capital I spoke to admit that the traditional music performed by musicians from the rural areas for a long time has been viewed, and in many cases continues to be viewed, as "fixed" and "rigid," in part due to "the [allegedly] limited knowledge of the rural musicians who have not been exposed to other similar musics outside the country." Today, at least for some musicians in Saint Lucia, the meaning of "tradition" has been redefined.

On one Caribbean themed night, I came to Sandals Halcyon to listen to the Lapo Kabwit, a group known for its performance of traditional music. The entertainment manager had mentioned to me that the group was going to perform masquerade music (music performed during carnival). I was most interested to attend this performance because I had studied this music locally during my research in the early 1980s. As the group entered the stage, I noted that the penny whistle and the snare drum "typically" (I thought!) accompanying the masquerade were missing. Even after listening attentively to the performance, I could not recognize the main rhythmic pattern the musicians were playing. None of the three drummers did any singing, even if only briefly, as was the case in the 1980s. I had to recognize that my knowledge of masquerade was based on—or better put, limited to—the region where I had worked as a doctoral student. I wondered whether the performance of Lapo Kabwit that night was another Saint Lucian version of masquerade. I was intrigued and went to meet the musicians after the show.

I learned that all three musicians come from around Castries, the capital. All have traveled extensively. Two of them worked on cruise ships. They have all attended many drumming workshops in various parts of the Caribbean, and in one case also in Senegal. One of the group members explained, "What we played there is not the strict masquerade. It is a mix of Haitian rhythm and Trinidadian rhythm. You could say, it is a masquerade 'intent'" (Jason Alcide, interview with the author, November 2015). Here "tradition" was not limited to Saint Lucian rhythms. Rather, it embraced the African diasporic space and its multitude of rhythmic patterns and versions of particular musical genres. On that night at Sandals Halcyon, the Lapo Kabwit offered the guests an experience of hyperreality, a version of tradition simultaneously expanded and contracted, an experience of masquerade that was not unreal, but more real than real—an experience that demonstrated the expansive agency of musicians to *present* tradition as opposed to *re-present* it.[19]

Former entertainment manager David Samuels mentioned how in the 1970s and early 1980s, young up-and-coming musicians playing instruments other than those associated with traditional music were not interested in, to use his own wording, "folk" music. However, over the past ten years the musicians' mentality has changed. Some of the musicians I met playing at Sandals Halcyon and at other resorts echoed Payne's musical philosophy: "What we try to do today—and I feel very passionate about it—is to insert local elements into what we play." In Trevor King's wording, "a lot of musicians take the folk, re-create it, and modernize it. Like Barbara Cadet, for example. She has an entire CD [in a style] which she did not have before, called *Indigenously Yours*." One could also cite Richard Payne's CD, *Blue Mango*, and a growing number of similar projects that take well-known "traditional" songs and transform them with new instrumentation, arrangements, and musical styles.[20] World music influence? Greater confidence to perform difference? Or is it that local musicians perceive the tourists' musical tastes as changing, as now embracing a synthesis considered central to "the aesthetics of the global imagination" today?[21] A growing, albeit still small, number of musicians have now begun to integrate some of these compositions into their performances at the all-inclusive hotels. From an entertainment manager's perspective, these new initiatives are most welcome. As King put it, "the tourists are hungry for the creative element."

Hospitality through Listening to Audiences

The musicians' own ways of thinking musically about how to perform hospitality in an all-inclusive hotel constituted only one part of the story they shared with me. The musicians I interviewed all emphasized that one specific act of musical performance that shapes and enhances the tourists' experience of vacation is first and foremost "to be in tune" with the guests. Here is how they put it: "You must read the audience and get the sense of their taste and adjust accordingly"; "I see my role as enhancing the guests' experience and understanding what could make them uncomfortable"; "I judge my 'effectiveness' by the comments and the clap"; "After doing this over many years, you get a sense, almost like a sixth sense, of who might really be listening to what you're doing"; "Sometimes whatever you play, it is not working. So you have to ask yourself, what would sound nice to them?" I heard these descriptions as references to the affective labor that musicians perform in touristic sites. Affect in this case can be understood as the desired or created connection between the worker/musician and his or her audience.

In addition to listening to their audiences' reactions, musicians have developed several strategies to create audiences' responses. The singers of both Xtent and Prodigy Band (also regularly featured at Sandals Halcyon) employ stage talk, addressing the guests directly to introduce what they will play or to ask them questions. At other times, musicians call on the guests to play a part in their performance, like "Everybody, give a little snap where you are. I want to know that you enjoy the music," as was the case, for example, when Telvin John began singing "Stand by Me" by Ben E. King. As a stand-alone musician playing at several all-inclusive resorts, saxophonist Barbara Cadet explained that her way to communicate with the hotel guests, particularly in enclosed rooms, "is to play very softly to draw the listener to you." "In contrast," she added, "in an open-air environment, it is to play forcefully." For the pianist playing at one of the restaurants, engaging the guests musically also often entails engaging them socially. As Curtis Mondesir put it, "No matter how good you are and what you play, you have to have that social thing. And if you put that social part in there, people may like your music just because of you. If somebody has a problem with the room, this is not my department, but I kind of fix it."

In other cases, musicians count on the exuberant effects of loudness and the power of time to create a synergy with and among the hotel's guests. As the evening progresses, some bands play the music louder as a way to encourage the guests to come to the dance floor instead of continuing to talk. At times, when the guests are visibly enjoying themselves, the musicians simply keep on playing. They lengthen the performance of the songs they are singing or begin performing a medley. Even if they are hired to play from 9 PM to 11 PM, they continue to play overtime (even for no extra pay) not to break the dance mood they have created and leave the guests stranded in the midst of having a good time. Enabling the guests to enjoy themselves is the goal, but ensuring that their experience is memorable may be even more important in making them want to come back. The hotel guests are the reason the musicians found employment. But the hotel musicians' performance cannot be reduced to mere calculations. To use Catherine Allerton's description of the transformative sounds of Manggarai hospitality reported by Candea and da Col, "the vital yet *ephemeral* 'buzz' or 'effervescence'" the hotel musicians create is contagious and constitutes one of the rewards of performing for others (Candea and da Col 2012, S11).

Concluding Remarks

One of the aims of this chapter has been to show how music and sound are central to the business of all-inclusive hotels, and vital to the tourists' experience of vacation. Examining the elaborate infrastructure of the entertainment personnel and the hotel's hiring policies has revealed how music and sound are the source of considerable financial investment and at the heart of political (in the large sense of the term) decisions. Addressing how tourist space is staged throughout the resort has demonstrated how environmental and avian sounds are exploited as commodities the resort offers. Focusing on entertainment managers, playmakers, and most particularly musicians has highlighted not only their artistic skills, but also their labor as workers in charge of providing the "affective ambience" in the resort (Candea and da Col 2012, S11).

This chapter has argued that music and sound are central to the emotional economies of hospitality in all-inclusive hotels. Jazz pianist Emmerson Nurse goes further and speaks of music as "the lifeblood of hotels." The hotel management at Sandals Halcyon unquestionably recognizes how music and sound in the all-inclusive resort mediates sociality, provides sensual pleasures, and elicits senses of fantasy, feeling, and fun—experiences that cannot be measured in number or calculated by statistics, and yet that have an immense impact on the well-being of the personnel and tourists alike. But musicians and managers know this. Much work still needs to be done to account for the political economy of music and sound in all-inclusive hotels and its capital role in the Caribbean tourism industry.

ACKNOWLEDGMENTS

My heartfelt thanks go first and foremost to Christopher Elliott, general manager of Sandals Halcyon in Saint Lucia, for having allowed me to do research in the resort and for his generosity and openness. I am also grateful to many members of the staff who have shared their knowledge about how the entertainment department works in Sandals resorts. I am also deeply indebted to the musicians and other local experts in the field of entertainment and Saint Lucian political and economic history for sharing their experiences and insights on the interrelationship of music and tourism in the country. I also want to thank Yves Renard, Pat Payne, Janice Suite, and Margaret Mitchell for their invaluable help, warmth, and friendship.

NOTES

1. On the concept of "all-inclusive," see Issa and Jayawardena (2003).

2. See, for example, Lamen (2014) and Uriely and Belhassen (2005).

3. I thank Yves Renard for this helpful reminder.

4. The Jamaican founder and chairman of Sandals Resorts, Gordon "Butch" Stewart, has tended to hire his hotel general managers from Jamaica.

5. The issue of gender in relation to labor, and most particularly in relation to sexism and sexualism, has drawn much attention. See Allen (2011), Curtis (2009), Ellis (1986), Gosine (2009), Gregory (2003), Heron and Nicholson (2006), Kempadoo (2004), Mohammed (2002), Mohammed and Shepherd (1988), Padilla (2007), Reddock (1988, 1994, 2004), and Sheller (2012), to name only a few.

6. On this point, see Rommen's chapter in this volume.

7. Beck defines the "cosmopolitan outlook" thus: "The (forced) mixing of cultures is not anything new in world history. . . . What is new is not forced mixing but awareness of it, its self-conscious political affirmation, its reflection and recognition before a global public via the mass media, in the news and in the global social movements of blacks, women and minorities, and in the current vogue for such venerable concepts as 'diaspora' in the cultural sciences. It is at once social and social scientific reflexivity that makes the 'cosmopolitan outlook' the key concept and topic of the reflexive second modernity."

8. I was fascinated to learn that it is a DJ from Jamaica, DJ Brian, who selects the music for each restaurant specialty, which adds one more layer in the configuration of the sonic mediations coming into play in the tourists' experience of vacation at dinner. While this DJ provides a wide repertoire of music for each restaurant, it is Charlyn who, on the ground at Sandals Halcyon, decides which tracks work best in each case.

9. I am quoting here the subtitle of Alistair Williams's (2006) important article, "Tourism and Hospitality Marketing: Fantasy, Feeling, and Fun."

10. The other Saint Lucia musician who is as much respected and hailed by many musicians I encountered over the past three decades as the best jazz saxophonist in the whole region is Luther François.

11. From CSO St. Lucia, http://192.147.231.244:9090/stats/index.php/statistics /labour/, accessed March 19, 2018. At the time of this writing, the Saint Lucian government had not yet released its statistics for the last quarter of 2017.

12. I thank Yves Renard for sharing these insights with me. For more information on the economic partnership between the CARIFORUM states and the European Community, see the foreign trade information system provided by the Organization of American States (OAS): http://www.sice.oas.org/Trade/CAR_EU_EPA_e/careu_in_e.ASP.

13. On the shift of the music industry, see Rogers (2013).

14. Ironically, at the back of this resort section lies the main public road, which, at peak traffic hours, buzzes with car engines above and beyond anyone's decision to have a quiet time.

15. For further elaboration on aural architecture, see Blesser and Salter (2007).

16. Moreover, since the karaoke night depends solely on what is available online (which is projected on a large screen and accompanied by the music diffused on the room's speakers), the guests typically choose songs, old or new, that are well represented on karaoke websites. While a growing number of songs from the Caribbean are available in karaoke versions, many hit songs from many parts of the region are not.

17. "Smoke Gets in Your Eyes" was written in 1933, later recorded as a cover version by the Platters in 1958.

18. "A Time for Love" has been often associated with the widely circulated 1968 cover version by jazz pianist Bill Evans, which, Payne remarked, he "absolutely loves." It is important to note that the repertoire musicians play for tourists is oftentimes composed of songs that have nostalgic and great aesthetic value not only for the tourists, but also for the musicians, who have also grown up with them. Musical repertoire enacts particularly vividly how the so-called "global" is enmeshed with the local.

19. On hyperreality, see Baudrillard (1993). See also Williams (2006) in relation to tourism and marketing.

20. I was truly delighted to hear new versions of "Mangotin Lababad ka Bwilé," also variously called "Ziwa" and "Zaywan," on two wonderful CDs produced over the past few years. One version can be found on Barbara Cadet's CD, *Indigenously Yours*, and another version on Richard Payne's *Blue Mango*. This is a song I had recorded in Piaye, Saint Lucia, in the early 1980s, that featured Leonard John. This recording became part of a CD titled *Musical Traditions of St. Lucia, West Indies*, published by Smithsonian Folkways in 1993 (SF 40416).

21. I am quoting here the title of Veit Erlmann's (1996) inspiring article, "The Aesthetics of the Global Imagination."

EPILOGUE · THE POLITICAL ECONOMY
OF MUSIC AND SOUND

PERCY C. HINTZEN

Capitalism, from its inception, has, by necessity, always been a global project, with the Caribbean plantation and the institution of slavery at the center of its formative impetus (cf. Williams 1994). But there have been fundamental transformations in its iterations over time, in phases marked
by changes in its social and technical conditions of production. The all-
inclusive is an instantiation of the current phase of political economy, characterized by a transformation of the system of global capital away from
"countries and regions . . . linked to each other via trade and financial flows
in an integrated international market, to a *global economy* in which nations
are linked to each other more organically through the transnationalization
of production processes, of finance, and of the circuits of capital accumulation" (Robinson 2014, 2). What is critically important for the analysis of
and engagement with both the all-inclusive and its constituent soundscape
is the fractal-like structure of this global economy, where its general system
of organization is reproduced in all of its constituent parts and at all levels.
In other words, its structure is reproduced both in the technical and social
order of the all-inclusive and in the latter's constituent soundscape, both of
which are the objects of the ethnographic analyses of this volume.

Thus, like the global economy itself, what is characteristic of the all-
inclusive and of its soundscapes are their relative disarticulation from the
national moorings that characterized the prior phase of a world economy.
Important in this regard is the perpetual quest of global capital for the concentration of earnings in the enterprise itself rather than dispersed and
externalized through national and international processes.[1] This results
in significant reductions in earnings that come with the high transaction
costs of dependence on territories under national authority, jurisdiction,
and control and where the capitalist firm is subjected to fees, charges, regu-

lations, taxation regimes, conditions of production, market imperfections, transportation costs, infrastructural conditions, rents, corruption, and so on. In the international competitive environment that characterizes this phase of global capital, the firm is forced to rely on the effectiveness of national efforts if it is to secure a comparative advantage over its competitors. The all-inclusive resolves many of these problems by placing almost the totality of the tourist experience under the control of owners involved in transnational processes.

Given the fractal-like structural order of the global economy, national regimes of authority and their national apparatuses, the nationally based private sector, professionals, and segmented labor in both the formal and informal sectors are compelled to participate in these transnational processes on terms that are highly favorable to the concentration of earnings in the all-inclusive as a transnational actor. Such participation is impelled by the "functional integration" and the "extensive geographic pattern" of the internationally dispersed activities in which transnational capital is involved (Robinson 2014, 14). The resort studied by Camal, for example, was located in the French Antilles, was owned by a Chinese investment firm, and had offices in both Europe and North America. Participation in the global economy allows capitalist firms like all-inclusive companies to expand their global reach while taking advantage of processes occurring within the boundaries of a national authority in ways that lower their transaction costs significantly. It provides the conditions for flexibility and fluidity in decision making as to the location of productive operations, marketing activities, and sales. So, for the all-inclusive, the tourist experience, as its product, is separated from the geographic locus of its sales and financial transactions, and from its marketing activities. Transnational capitalists are able to use this portability to dictate and determine costs and who should bear them.

As we observe in its employment of musicians, the all-inclusive is able to externalize its costs through subcontracting on the basis of zero-hours contracts without guarantees of work, where musicians are compelled to work whenever and as many hours as the company dictates, and where they are paid only for the numbers of hours that they actually work. These workers are provided with no benefits and are employed only when the need arises. Nationally based providers of services (such as labor), inputs, infrastructure, facilities, and so on are forced into a dependent relationship with transnational firms because of the imperative of securing transfers of income from the global economy. This, as referenced by Camal, has led Polly Pattullo to describe one of the all-inclusive companies in the Caribbean as operating under the illusion of a "self-supporting little empire in the sun . . . tucked away and a law unto itself" (Pattullo 1996, 74).

But this description elides the indispensability of the emplaced territory upon which the all-inclusive depends and its reliance upon national jurisdictions over which it dictates the terms of its relationship. Refusal by national entities to engage in these transnational processes on the terms specified by the transnational firm comes with the near certainty of being cast off as unusable. At the national level, it produces capital flight and leads to an inability to attract foreign direct investment. This new form of dependency has produced a new pattern of direct engagement by capitalist investors in the governing of "usable" local communities, national territories, and workers in the Global South.[2] They "hop over" unusable areas while reducing their commitment to the agendas of governing regimes. This has reduced access by these regimes to transfers from the global system and has compromised and diminished their capacities to exercise control over unusable areas and people, leading to their relative abandonment (Ferguson 2006, 38–42). Those who are abandoned are forced to seek out new strategies of engagement with global capital.

These are all features of the all-inclusives. They occupy a sliver of local territory over which they have exclusive control on terms that they dictate. They use natural and artificial means to erect barriers, including "walls of sound," between themselves and the rest of the country, choosing to retain and reorganize only the things (and people) that fit the narrative out of which their hyperreality is constituted. And they camouflage local presences in ways that shape them to these narratives. In Camal's chapter, the local workforce is disciplined into silence as exotic local presences. They provide "local color" (only a touch) for the tourist experience, reminding the tourists that they are actually on a tropical island vacation.

The all-inclusive is just one step removed from the cruise ship industry in its disarticulation from national spaces and emplaced national entities. In the latter, the near totality of the tourist experience occurs onboard ships owned exclusively by the transnational capitalist class. All-inclusives share with cruise ship companies the capacity to dictate the terms of engagement with national authorities and emplaced national entities. Such terms are determined (dictated) almost entirely at the discretion of the transnational corporations that own them (cf. Sprague 2015, chapter 2).

How are soundscapes involved in this fractal reproduction, and why is sound such a critical, even indispensable element in the tourist experience? In the introduction, Guilbault and Rommen point to sound as a "sonic marker" that can be marshaled, corralled, amplified upon, minimized, and otherwise manipulated. Sound is also portable and transmissible, which, when combined with its "affective power," make it indispensable to a tourist industry whose primary function, according to Guilbault in her chapter on Saint Lucia, is the satisfaction of multivalent desires for "feelings of vacation." Because affective commodification is the pillar around which the political economy of the tourist industry is organized, sound provides the nexus for mobilization of affect and sentiment. Affective marketing is the central constitutive element of the tourist industry. And soundscapes are the most critical elements in producing what Guilbault refers to as "feelings of vacation" experienced as the heightened sensual pleasure derived from the mobilization of affect.

The tourist industry is engaged in the sale of pleasure for profit. It mobilizes the desire for joy and pleasure. The very point of Guilbault and Rommen's introductory chapter is to demonstrate the essential connection between the affective marketing of the tourist industry and place-making through sound. Musicians are engaged in the affective labor of place-making that is sensually and cognitively powerful. They are located at the critical center of strategies to enhance sensual pleasure. As labor, they create the conditions for the commodification of "sonic space" by the all-inclusive. Sound is an instrumentality of hospitality. Musicians are conscripted into roles of "reception and entertainment of guests, visitors or strangers" through their friendly and generous performances aimed at producing affective states of joy and pleasure.[3] What distinguishes the tourist industry from all others is its association with place, or with places away from home; hence the importance of sound in place-making. It can create the experience of "touring." Sound feeds the desire to experience the "elsewhere" with which it is associated. And it marks and confirms the experiences of "being there," which elicits the "feelings of vacation."

Like every other aspect of the tourist industry, the "sounds of vacation" play a role in the managed production of "fantasy." They contribute to the hyperreality of the tourist experience. Music performance, as labor, raises a challenge to that version of Marxist thinking that relegates production to its material engagements. Musicians are involved in the immaterialities of affect, both as product and as the motive force behind their attraction for and involvement with music. For them, as Jocelyne Guilbault and Roy Cape have argued in a biography of a Trinidadian bandleader, it is a "labor of love" (Guilbault and Cape 2014). Immaterial labor and its immaterial product, as the objects of regimes of discipline and control, are critical to the accumulation of profit in the tourist industry. This is particularly the case for hospitality as the labor through which fantasy's illusions are produced.

The capacity of the all-inclusive to produce fantasy and the hyperreal was made possible by changes occurring in the social and technical conditions of production at the heart of structural changes in the global capitalist economy. Sound is highly imbricated with these changes. Technological advancements associated with the transnationalization of the global economy are reflected in new forms of sound technologies that have facilitated transnational circulation of sonic markers of place and their cosmopolitanization. When the tourist resorts were integrally tied to the marketing of national territories, national entities were in a much better position to define the national space, as Rommen argues in his ethnography of the Bahamas.

They were also able to ensure that the pleasurable experiences of "being there" for the visitor occurred outside of the resort and in locally owned establishments, including hotels and guest houses protected from international competition. The "feelings of vacation" were produced out of the experience of "being" in the emplaced realities of the national territory. Music, as a cognitive marker of national territory, provided income-earning opportunities to local producers and managers under conditions where limitations in communication, transportation, and information technology made necessary a need to "be there." The production and circulation of "sounds of vacation" were more or less confined to the local territory because of these technological limitations.

Technological changes associated with transformation to a global economy have been accompanied by a process of cosmopolitanization of representations of place mediated across time and space in the conjunctures of transnational flows. By this, I mean that historical understandings that exist in different territorialized spaces have been brought together in global circuits, through technology, to produce new cosmopolitanized understandings of place. In the tourist industry, these understandings have been foisted upon national official bodies and local labor in their efforts to cater to these "cosmopolitan" forms that appear as cognitive maps in the imaginations of visitors. These increasingly standardized cosmopolitan imaginaries are reproduced through decisions made by entertainment managers in the all-inclusive industry about what is represented and their forms and content. Such representations are no longer and not necessarily connected to the territorial location of the resort. The cruise ship serves as a perfect example of the delinking that occurs between the regions and territories that are referents for regimes of representation and the location in which they occur. The experience of place can occur anywhere.

In the all-inclusive, representations of the local are converted into cosmopolitanized and standardized universal forms that have little relationship to the local popular. Given who the tourists are and where they come from, these markers of place, as Susan Harewood points out in her chapter, are mediated by pedagogies that are highly imbricated in colonial imaginations. This is not to deny that, for the Caribbean, place and its musical and sonic markers have always been overdetermined by these colonial imaginaries. This was true even when the "national brand" was the product of local agency in the initial phases of tourist marketing. What technology has done, however, is to standardize and universalize these imageries in universal circuits, including in their recirculation back to the places for which they serve as markers. In making this point, Harewood refers to the "island sounds" produced by West Indian performers in the "calypso craze" of the 1950s. Their accommodation in North America and Europe related directly to the role they played in confirming colonial imagination. The lyrics and rhythms of songs like "Yellow Bird" and "Banana Boat Song" have now become enduring cosmopolitanized and standardized musical markers of the islands in transnational processes. Changes in technology have facilitated such transformations and have allowed their reproduction anywhere and everywhere in "hyperreal" spaces.

This volume's focus on sound and music may be equally important for revealing, through the concreteness of ethnography, the fundamental ways in which technology and the mobilization of affect and sentiment are employed by global capital for the concentration of earnings in the capitalist enterprise. Their fluidity, transmissibility, transportability, and amenability to management are evident in productions and reproductions of place in the all-inclusive. No more is there a need for a congruence of sound and place. Repertoires of sound and music in the all-inclusive are designed to create different experiences of being in multiple national and regional spaces disarticulated from territory. The various nightly "themes" at Sandals in Saint Lucia, discussed in Guilbault's chapter, are exemplary and worth repeating. Monday is "Caribbean night," featuring selected and highly transformed performances of Saint Lucia's "traditional" music. These represent the musicians' "intent" to reproduce the "local" in ways that are informed by cosmopolitan understandings transmitted in transnational circuits. The musicians are selected based on their capabilities and capacities to reproduce these understandings. Their performances, in Guilbault's words, contributed to the "experience of hyperreality." The music repertoires on Tuesday, Wednesday, and Saturday were primarily standards from Great Britain and England, featuring a "jazz trio" or "stand-alone" singers. Thursday was "casino night," featuring "Euro-American mainstream" songs. Friday was the night for "popular music" from all parts of the Caribbean that was familiar to the audience, explaining its designation as "reggae night." Sunday's evening of "tranquility" was animated by a female saxophonist performing a mix of "standards" that include contemporary hits. Because of the disarticulation of the all-inclusive from the national territory, the desire of the clientele is not to "experience the island" but to be secluded in "zones of comfort" where they participate in the "familiar," interspersed with "lesser-known music and dance styles from the Caribbean," no doubt as markers of being in "the islands," but not specifically in the particular territory in which the all-inclusive is located.

Such disarticulation is a universal phenomenon, not confined to the national economies of the Caribbean. The economic precarity that it produces, evident in the lives of the music producers in the volume, are the universal effects of this new global economy. These effects are manifest in every local and national community and in the conditions of everyone who provides material and immaterial labor in its transnational processes. The reliance on hyperreality and fantasy for the mobilization of sentiment is a universal phenomenon in this new phase of global capital. Nowhere is this more visible than in Las Vegas and in the themed parks of Disney and Universal Parks and Resorts, where visitors can, in one or a few days in a single geographic location, experience being in multiple places in multiple times. Their experiences are produced by managers who exercise authorial power and by professional and technical workers responsible for their design and planning. The capabilities provided by technology to reproduce place and time, either real or imagined, bring more efficiencies into the marketing and production of the tourist experience and make this experience much more susceptible to corporate fashioning. They also allow representations of place to be much more congruent with the imaginations of their clients. The corporate authors of experience are able to employ what Arjun Appadurai identifies as "technoscapes" and "mediascapes" produced out of the deterritorializing and disjunctive forces of global capital to create "multiple imagined worlds" constituted out of "historically situated imaginations of persons and groups spread around the world" in rapidly shifting "ethnoscapes" (Appadurai 1990).[4]

Appadurai's definition of "mediascapes" is worth noting because of its uncanny relevance for understanding tourist experiences. They are "image-centered, narrative-based accounts of strips of reality and what they offer to those who experience and transform them" (Appadurai 1990, 299). They shape the experiences of vacation, as products of "private or state interests." For the all-inclusive, state interests are defined and determined by the private corporation. All this becomes evident in the experience of sound, which has become the almost exclusive product of managers, through their power to define the form and content of the musical performance. In the process, national entities have lost what little power they had to shape the proto-narratives of their own national spaces in keeping with their own accumulative interests and in influencing the "desire for movement" by the tourist. Representations of the nation are now mediated by colonial imaginaries used by corporate marketers in ways that "help to constitute narratives of the 'other' and proto-narratives of possible lives, fantasies which could become prolegomena to the desire for acquisition and movement" (Appadurai 1990, 299). In the Caribbean, the results are felt in the dramatic losses of tourist revenues by national political economies. Nostalgic accounts of the earlier "nationalist phase" by music performers and producers, especially in the chapters on Saint Lucia and the Bahamas, reveal the pain and violence of the loss of power, however compromised, over the production of these representations.

Expectations of the Caribbean experience are now shaped by global mediascapes rendered much more appealing because they are consistent with the mediated and overdetermined understandings of North Americans and Europeans, who constitute the large majority of the clients of the all-inclusive. Tourists' experiences cater to their conditioned desires. The congruence between these mediascapes and the production of such experiences, through the cognitive shaping of their expectations, act to prevent what Camal identifies as the arrhythmia of exposure to the pathologies and suffering manifest in the quotidian realities of life in localized places. However, Guadeloupe and Halfman, in their chapter on Sint Maarten, see possibilities for decolonization in such exposures, because they allow for forms of conviviality and commingling that can reveal the mutuality of the cosmopolitanized orientations of the tourist and local populations.

But there is much more to arrhythmia than this. Local sounds and the realities of human existence are ever-present in the experiences of the tourists, notwithstanding efforts to keep them in the background or to drown them out altogether. They create, in the words of Harewood, insurgent noises that disturb. The labor that provides the material base of existence cannot be separated from the hyperreality and fantasy of the vacation experience. The very presence of those who provide the material conditions upon which experience rests threatens to reveal as fetish the affect and sentiment marketed by the tourist industry, which are at the very root of tourism's exchange value.

This tension permeates every single one of the ethnographies. Why is it, for example, that visitors to Sint Maarten would choose one of the only two all-inclusives on the island when much of their experience occurs off its premises and in local spaces? Because, according to the authors, and this is very telling, "all-inclusives gave tourists the sense that they were getting the better of the hotel." They turn economic theory on its head through a distortion that rejects the notion of scarcity, replacing it with the myth of unlimited means available for the satisfaction of unlimited desires (as ends).[5] This hides the limitations placed on consumption by the capacities (means) of the resort itself. The all-inclusive is able to deploy its corporate power to dictate and determine the nature and limits of the "unlimited" choices being offered, while marketing to the tourist the possibility of consumption beyond human limits. In order to discipline consumption expectations, visitors are "preprogrammed" to contain their choices within these limits. They are conditioned to accept what the all-inclusive is prepared to offer. They come with prior knowledge of the repertoire of consumptive activities offered, be it entertainment, food, accommodations, or physical ecology. All is not included. And the resort is able to use logistical calculus (logistics), made possible by advances in computer technology, to predict individual patterns of consumption and desires in ways that allow efficient coordination of facilities, supplies, and programming that enhance profit maximization.

But technology, the mobilization of sentiment, and the marketing of affect can only go so far. Camal points to the "oxymoronic" combination of labor structures and the marketing of leisure in the all-inclusive. As an "es-

cape from labor," the vacation demands that the work involved in the production of its material conditions be "kept invisible." But the imperative of
labor refuses such escape. Industrial time imposes itself upon the tourist
experience in many ways, from the chiming of the clock at the heritage site
in Barbados that intrudes in the tourist experience, to the regimentation
of the guests into "factory-like rhythms" in Camal's ethnographic account,
to the physical presences of staff doing the chores of reproduction (such
as cooking, cleaning, housekeeping, facilities maintenance, security, etc.)
who are always intruding in the spaces of leisure.

The all-inclusive studied by Camal in the French Antilles attempts to
relegate local, exclusively dark-skinned, labor involved in material productions to the background by imposing codes of silence in their interactions
with guests, and stereotypical representations of Creole exoticism in dress
codes that serve as exotic "echoes of slavery." The labor of those involved
in the intimacies of "hospitality" is hidden and disguised as play. The immaterial goods that they produce are at the critical center of the "selling of
happiness." Hospitality work requires intimate involvement in the eurythmia of fun, pleasure, and joy of the tourist experience. This demands that
those who perform it be disciplined and managed in ways that deny their
representation and recognition as labor. But they experience the "pathologies and suffering" of superexploited labor. The workday of the predominantly white European "organizers" of hospitality in Camal's account can
extend to more than sixteen hours of hard, grueling, and repetitive labor.
They, along with the local musicians who are the focus of all the ethnographies, and everyone engaged in "hospitality" in the all-inclusives: all see
themselves as workers.

Musicians in the all-inclusive serve as ideal types for workers in the
new global economy. As Guilbault argues, their role is to produce "experiences that are memorable, new, emotional, and interactive." This is not
much different from the producers of the computer software that is the
hallmark of the new global economy. To ensure their survival, musicians in
the all-inclusive engage in forms of labor flexibilization that have become
the modus operandi of the new global economy.[6] They deliver a repertoire
of cosmopolitanized music genres that demand, according to Guilbault in
her chapter on Saint Lucia, "intimate knowledge of many different countries, cultures, and musics." They have "to be in tune with the guests" and
to have developed the ability to read their mood. As a survival strategy, they
are forced to earn their incomes by working in different segmented labor

markets, including work on cruise ships. For the most part, the all-inclusive is a secondary labor market for them, characterized by casual and informal labor. So many are forced to rely on the primary labor market in the formal sector to ensure their economic security. Others are forced to perform gigs in multiple venues, as is demonstrated by Rommen in his chapter on the Bahamas in this volume. And most are hired as subcontractors, requiring them to bear the cost of the performance by providing their own equipment, clothing, and so on. And they are regimented and disciplined by managers employing technologies of surveillance to monitor, manage, and control all aspects of their music presentations. In the Bahamas, continued employment turns on positive reviews posted on TripAdvisor (self-described as the world's largest travel site) by guests. In Saint Lucia, their performances are rated in questionnaires filled out by visitors after their departure.

The repetition of ethnographic detail in this epilogue is purposeful. Michel-Rolph Trouillot speaks about the importance of ethnographic examination of the "banality of daily life." He was referring specifically to a means for describing the "effects" of political economy (what he terms *state effects*) when the latter is divorced from national authority and from the territorial sites over which such authority is exercised. He sees this disarticulation as particularly characteristic of the current phase of globalization with which this volume is engaged (Trouillot 2001). What the ethnographies in this volume reveal, with their specific focus on sound and on the all-inclusive, is a fundamental relationship between the mobilization of affect and sentiment on the one hand, and fetish and exchange value on the other. This relationship has always been present as a fundamental feature of capitalism, and has been essential for the accumulation of profit.

The all-inclusive and the soundscape upon which it depends for the production of pleasure is revelatory as an ideal example of the institutional arrangement through which, in the current phase of global capital, revenues become concentrated in the capitalist enterprise. Contained in these ethnographies are examples of the crisis of our postmodern existence and its relationship to the commodification of desire. Visitors are searching for a past and for an order of meaning that are reproduced and rememorialized in the mediated hyperreality of the tourist experience marketed by the all-inclusive. The experience of the "islands," disarticulated from the local reality, is a hyperreal simulacrum of the racialized and color/class order of the plantation. And this becomes evident in every one of the ethnographies in the volume. But these experiences are polysemous. They can offer a primitive exotic escape from the "hurly-burly of modern life and labor" and a return to "European idleness." This is Harewood'a conclusion, derived from her ethnographic account of a heritage-themed all-inclusive in Barbados. Technology and logistics create hyperrealities that "quell colonial anxieties" and absolve the visitors from colonial violence. They offer a prophylactic shield from the "threatening noises" of colonial legacy.

There is, in all of this, the reaffirmation of status and class positions made uncertain by postmodernity. Camal points to the inherent contradiction in forms of leisure delivered through the "factory-like rhythms." But this underscores the polysemy of the "vacation." The desire that is being satisfied is for the habitus of the space of experience "where upper-middle-class (mostly European) professionals go to meet each other." Here, the desire for leisure as an escape from the labor structures of modernity becomes subservient to status reaffirmation. This also explains the attraction of the local clientele to the all-inclusive. The Breezes chain, for example, exploits the desires of members of the local middle and upper classes for reaffirmation of their class positions and of their cosmopolitanism that "access for purchase" provides. But, as Rommen argues, this "economics of exclusivity" allows entrance to "only a certain type of local who is . . . able to afford this luxury." Locals are accommodated because, as a special class, their cosmopolitan sensibilities do not disturb the habitus of their equally exclusive foreign visitors.

But there are other ways in which local presences, as customers, serve the accumulative interests of the all-inclusive. In Sint Maarten, where the "entire island is an all-inclusive" and where cosmopolitan conviviality is for sale, locals are welcomed in the two all-inclusive resorts. Everyone on the island is recruited into the project of selling the tourist experience and for the labor of hospitality. Through public narratives of their cosmopolitanism, locals are disciplined and regulated into roles of unpaid labor, even when they are customers of the tourist industry.

The editors' charge in the writing of this epilogue is to analyze the ways in which the contributions to this volume bring new understandings (among other things) to the politics of hospitality and management "in the context of the postcolonial Caribbean nation-states." I think that the volume goes much farther than this. It is an exegesis of what Michel Foucault proposes as the connection among technology, control of the body, and power in what he terms *bio-power*.[7] Such connection is even more of a feature of late capitalism where technological capacities for control are enormously enhanced. Technology allows for more effective and efficient conscription of everyone, even as consumers, into the capitalist project. The all-inclusive employs the sensual power of desire and pleasure to harness energies to the task of accumulation.

What this volume reveals is "exactly how this form of power is made to work on the local level" (Dreyfus and Rabinow 1983, 8). It demonstrates, through ethnographies of sound, how desire itself is disciplined, regulated, and managed by the capitalist enterprise for the concentration of accumulation. But always, there is the arrhythmia of the presences of those who produce the material and immaterial conditions upon which the enterprise rests, and who are suffering under the increasing pathologies of superexploitation. And there are the noises in the background of those who are excluded from a tourist industry that "constitutes an outsized portion of the Caribbean economy," in the words of Guilbault and Rommen in the introduction. It is an industry that employs over two million people in the Caribbean, and that brings in over \$31 billion in foreign exchange earnings.

The lesson for the region is writ large in the consequences of the fractal-like structure of the global economy, of which the all-inclusive is but one significant example. Disarticulation, revenue concentration, the diminution of national authority, and the superexploitation of labor are revealed in the politics of hospitality and in the management of the all-inclusive, if politics is understood to be the contentious relations in arenas of struggle. And these relations are replicated everywhere in the global political economy. The lesson of this volume is not confined merely to the postcolonial context of Caribbean nation-states. It is revelatory of transnational processes that affect everyone, everywhere.

NOTES

1. Here I am making a distinction between international processes where the primary actors are national entities, and transnational processes where the primary actors are engaged in a global economy that is disarticulated from national processes (Robinson 2014, 14).

2. This process is discussed extensively by Ferguson (2006, 38–42).

3. The definition of hospitality is taken from the Collins dictionary and cited by Guilbault in her chapter on Sandals in this volume.

4. See Appadurai (1990, 297–99), who defines "ethnoscapes" as "the landscape of persons who constitute the shifting world," and technoscapes as "the global configu-

ration, also ever fluid, of technology . . . that now moves at high speeds across various kinds of previously impervious boundaries."

5. Here I am referring to Lionel Robbins's definition, which has become "an article of faith" among its practitioners, that economics is "a science which studies human behavior as a relationship between ends and scarce means which have alternative uses" (Robbins 1932, 15).

6. David Harvey discusses this at length in his work on late capitalism (1989). See also the work of Aihwah Ong on the relationship among flexibility, transnational processes, and the disarticulation of sovereign territory and capitalist production (1999).

7. See the discussion of Foucault by Dreyfus and Rabinow (1983).

References

Abreu, Christina. 2015. *Rhythms of Race: Cuban Musicians and the Making of Latino New York City and Miami, 1940–1960*. Chapel Hill: University of North Carolina Press.

Agamben, Giorgio. 1998. *Homo Sacer: Sovereign Power and Bare Life*. Stanford, CA: Stanford University Press.

Allen, Jafari S. 2011. *Venceremos? The Erotics of Black Self-Making in Cuba*. Durham, NC: Duke University Press.

Alleyne, Mike. 1994. "Positive Vibration? Capitalist Textual Hegemony and Bob Marley." *Caribbean Studies* 27, no. 3–4: 224–41.

Alleyne, Mike. 1998. "'Babylon Makes the Rules': The Politics of Reggae Crossover." *Social and Economic Studies* 47, no. 1: 65–77.

Alleyne, Mike. 2000. "White Reggae: Cultural Dilution in the Record Industry." *Popular Music and Society* 24, no. 1: 15–30.

Amirou, Rachid. 2012. *L'imaginaire touristique*. Paris: CNRS Editions.

Anonymous. 2013. "Changing of the Sentry." In *Bridgetown and Its Garrison Map and City Guide*, edited by Hermina Charlery, 10–11. Barbados: Cube.

Appadurai, Arjun, ed. 1986. *The Social Life of Things: Commodities in Cultural Perspective*. Cambridge: Cambridge University Press.

Appadurai, Arjun. 1990. "Disjuncture and Difference in the Global Cultural Economy." *Public Culture* 2, no. 2: 295–310.

Ateljevic, Irena, Keith Hollinshead, and Nazia Ali. 2009. "Worldmakings of Tourism." *Tourism Geographies* 11, no. 4: 427–43.

Attali, Jacques. [1977] 1985. *Noise: The Political Economy of Music*. Translated by Brian Massumi. Minneapolis: University of Minnesota Press.

Augé, Marc. 1995. *Non-Places: Introduction to an Anthropology of Supermodernity*. Translated by John Howe. London: Verso.

Austerlitz, Paul. 1997. *Merengue: Dominican Music and Dominican Identity*. Philadelphia: Temple University Press.

Bahamas Hotel and Tourism Association. 2012. *BHTA Retrospective*. Nassau: BHTA.

Bakhtin, Mikhail. 1981. *The Dialogic Imagination: Four Essays*. Translated by Caryl Emerson and Michael Holquist. Austin: University of Texas Press.

Banerjee, Onil, Martin Cicowiez, et al. 2015. "A Quantitative Framework for Assessing

Public Investment in Tourism—An Application to Haiti." *Tourism Management* 51: 157–73.

Barbados Garrison Historical Consortium. 2016. *The Historic Garrison Tour.*

Barbados Museum. 2013. "Zouave Uniform." http://www.barbmuse.org.bb/web /?portfolio=zouave-uniform.

Basu, Ranjeeta, and Mtafiti Imara. 2014. "From the Perspective of Musicians in Goa: How Has Tourism Changed Music Culture?" *Journal of Tourism and Hospitality Management* 2, no. 9: 343–56.

Baudrillard, Jean. 1983. *In the Shadow of the Silent Majorities or the End of the Social.* New York: Semiotext(e).

Baudrillard, Jean. 1985. "The Masses: The Implosion of the Social in the Media." *New Literary History* 16, no. 3: 577–89.

Baudrillard, Jean. 1993. *The Transparency of Evil: Essays on Extreme Phenomena.* London: Verso.

Baudrillard, Jean. 2005. *The Intelligence of Evil or the Lucidity Pact.* New York: Berg.

Baudrillard, Jean. 2007. *Forget Foucault.* Cambridge: Semiotext(e) Foreign Agents.

Baumann, Max Peter, and Linda Fujie, eds. 1999. "Music, Travel, and Tourism." *World of Music* 41, no. 3.

Baver, Sherrie L., and Barbara Deutsch Lynch. 2006. *Beyond Sun and Sand: Caribbean Environmentalisms.* New Brunswick, NJ: Rutgers University Press.

Beck, Ulrich. 2006. *Cosmopolitan Vision.* Translated by Ciaran Cronin. Malden, MA: Polity.

Becker, Howard S., and Alain Pessin. 2006. "A Dialogue on the Ideas of 'World' and 'Field.'" *Sociological Forum* 21, no. 2: 275–86.

Beckles, Hilary. 1999. *The Development of West Indies Cricket, Vol. 1: The Age of Nationalism.* London: Pluto.

Beckles, Hilary. 2000. *The Development of West Indies Cricket, Vol. 2: The Age of Globalization.* London: Pluto.

Beckles, Hilary. 2013. *Britain's Black Debt: Reparations for Slavery and Native Genocide.* Kingston, Jamaica: University of the West Indies Press.

Bell, David. 2001. *Pleasure Zones: Bodies, Cities, Spaces.* Syracuse, NY: Syracuse University Press.

"Bell Chime." 2010. *Encyclopedia Britannica.* Article published May 20.

Beckerman, Joel, with Tyler Gray. 2014. *Sonic Boom: How Sound Transforms the Way We Think, Feel, and Buy.* New York: Man Made Music.

Benítez-Rojo, Antonio. 1996. *The Repeating Island: The Caribbean and the Postmodern Perspective.* Durham, NC: Duke University Press.

Benjamin, Walter. 1968. *Illuminations: Essays and Reflections.* Translated by H. Zohn. New York: Schocken.

Berrian, Brenda. 2000. *Awakening Spaces: French Caribbean Popular Songs, Music, and Culture.* Chicago: University of Chicago Press.

Best, Curwen. 2000. "Popular/Folk/Creative Arts and the Nation." In *The Empowering Impulse: The Nationalist Tradition of Barbados,* edited by Glenford Howe and Don D. Marshall, 232–55. Mona, Jamaica: Canoe Press UWI.

Best, Curwen. 2001. *Roots to Popular Culture: Barbadian Aesthetics, Kamau Brathwaite, to Hardcore Styles*. London: Macmillan Caribbean.

Best, Curwen. 2003. "Reading Graffiti in the Caribbean Context." *Journal of Popular Culture* 36, no. 4: 828–52.

Biemann, Asher, ed. 2002. *The Martin Buber Reader: Essential Writings*. New York: Palgrave Macmillan.

Bilby, Kenneth. 2008. *True-Born Maroons*. Gainesville: University Press of Florida.

Blesser, Barry, and Linda-Ruth Salter. 2007. *Spaces Speak, Are You Listening? Experiencing Aural Architecture*. Cambridge, MA: MIT Press.

Born, Georgina. 2013. *Music, Sound and Space: Transformations of Public and Private Enterprise*. Cambridge: Cambridge University Press.

Botterill, David. 2001. "The Epistemology of a Set of Tourism Studies." *Leisure Studies* 20, no. 3: 199–214.

Bourdieu, Pierre. 1987. *Distinction: A Social Critique of the Judgement of Taste*. Translated by Richard Nice. Cambridge, MA: Harvard University Press.

Bourdieu, Pierre. 1993. *The Field of Cultural Production: Essays on Art and Literature*. New York: Columbia University Press.

Brathwaite, Kamau. 2005. *The Development of Creole Society in Jamaica, 1770–1820*. Kingston, Jamaica: Ian Randle.

Brown, Wendy. 2003. "Neo-Liberalism and the End of Liberal Democracy." *Theory and Event* 7, no. 1. https://muse.jhu.edu/article/48659.

Bruner, Edward M. 1995. "The Ethnographer/Tourist in Indonesia." In *International Tourism: Identity and Change*, edited by Marie-Françoise Lanfant and Edward M. Bruner, 224–41. London: SAGE.

Bruner, Gordon C. 1990. "Music, Mood, and Marketing." *Journal of Marketing* 54, no. 4: 94–104.

Buber, Martin. 1998. *Ik en Jij*. Utrecht: Bijleveld.

Bull, Michael, and Les Back. 2003. *The Auditory Culture Reader*. New York: Berg.

Burgie, Irving. 2006. *Day-O!!! The Autobiography of Irving Burgie*. Brooklyn, NY: Caribe.

Burrowes, Marcia P. A. 2000. "History and Cultural Identity: Barbadian Space and the Legacy of Empire." PhD dissertation, University of Warwick.

Butler, Mark. 2014. *Playing with a Thing That Runs: Technology, Improvisation, and Composition in DJ and Laptop Performance*. New York: Oxford University Press.

Butler, Toby. 2006. "A Walk of Art: The Potential of the Sound Walk as Practice in Cultural Geography." *Social and Cultural Geography* 7, no. 6: 889–908.

Buzinde, Christine N., and Carla Almeida Santos. 2008. "Representations of Slavery." *Annals of Tourism Research* 35, no. 2: 460–88.

Buzinde, Christine N., Carla Almeida Santos, and Stephen L. J. Smith. 2006. "Ethnic Representations: Destination Imagery." *Annals of Tourism Research* 33, no. 3: 707–28.

Buzinde, Christine N., and Iyunolu F. Osagie. 2011. "Slavery Heritage Representations, Cultural Citizenship, and Judicial Politics in America." *Historical Geography* 39: 41–64.

Byron, Reginald, ed. 1995. *Music, Culture, and Experience: Selected Papers of John Blacking*. Chicago: University of Chicago Press.

Camal, Jerome. 2014. "DestiNation: The Festival Gwoka, Tourism, and Anti-Colonialism." In *Sea, Sun, and Sound: Music and Tourism in the Circum-Caribbean*, edited by Timothy Rommen and Daniel T. Neely, 213–37. New York: Oxford University Press.

Camal, Jerome. 2016. "Putting the Drum in Conundrum: Guadeloupean Gwoka, Intangible Cultural Heritage, and Postnationalism." *International Journal of Heritage Studies* 22, no. 5: 395–410.

Candea, Matei, and Giovanni da Col. 2012. "The Return to Hospitality." *Journal of the Royal Anthropology Institute* 18, no. 1: S1–S19.

Cashman, David. 2013. "Popular Music Venues on Cruise Ships as Touristic Spaces of Engagement." *International Journal of Event Management Research* 7, no. 1–2: 26–46.

Cashman, David. 2014. "Corporately Imposed Music Cultures: An Ethnography of Cruise Ship Showbands." *Ethnomusicology Review* 19: 23–48.

Cavarero, Adriana. 2011. *Horrorism: Naming Contemporary Violence*. New York: Columbia University Press.

Chambers, Donna, and Christine Buzinde. 2015. "Tourism and Decolonization: Locating Research and Self." *Annals of Tourism Research* 51: 1–16.

Chamoiseau, Patrick. 1994. *Texaco*. Paris: Gallimard.

Chapple, Steve, and Reebee Garofalo. 1977. *Rock 'n' Roll Is Here to Pay: The History and Politics of the Music Industry*. Chicago: Nelson-Hall.

Charles, Owen. 1992. "Building a Relationship between Government and Tourism." *Tourism Management* 13, no. 4: 358–62.

Chion, Michel. [1982] 1999. *The Voice in Cinema*. Translated by Claudia Gobman. New York: Columbia University Press.

Cleare, Angela. 2007. *History of Tourism in the Bahamas*. Bloomington, IN: Xlibris.

Clifford, James. 1988. *The Predicament of Culture: Twentieth-Century Ethnography, Literature, and Art*. Cambridge, MA: Harvard University Press.

Coderre, Laurence. 2015. "Socialist Commodities: Consuming Yangbanxi in the Cultural Revolution." PhD dissertation, University of California, Berkeley.

Cohen, Colleen Ballerino. 2010. *Take Me to My Paradise: Tourism and Nationalism in the British Virgin Islands*. New Brunswick, NJ: Rutgers University Press.

Cohen, Sara. 2007. *Decline, Renewal and the City in Popular Music Culture: Beyond the Beatles*. Aldershot: Ashgate.

Cohen, Sara, Robert Knifton, et al., eds. 2013. *Sites of Popular Music Heritage: Memories, Histories, Places*. New York: Routledge.

Connell, John, and Chris Gibson. 2003. *Sound Tracks: Popular Music, Identity, and Place*. New York: Routledge.

Constant-Martin, Denis. 1993. "'Musique et politique': Entretien avec Denis Constant-Martin par Alain Darré." *L'Aquarium: Bulletin de liaison et d'information du Centre de Recherches Administratives et Politiques Université Rennes* 1, no. 11–12.

Cooley, Timothy J. 2005. *Making Music in the Polish Tatras: Tourists, Ethnographers, and Mountain Musicians*. Bloomington: Indiana University Press.

Cooper, Carolyn. [1993] 1995. *Noises in the Blood: Orality, Gender, and the "Vulgar" Body of Jamaican Popular Culture*. Durham, NC: Duke University Press.

Cooper, Carolyn. 2004. *Sound Clash: Jamaican Dancehall Culture at Large*. New York: Palgrave Macmillan.

Corbin, Alain. 1998. *Village Bells: The Culture of the Senses in the Nineteenth-Century French Countryside*. Translated by Martin Thom. New York: Columbia University Press.

Couldry, Nick. 2009. "Rethinking the Politics of Voice." *Continuum: Journal of Media and Cultural Studies* 23, no. 4: 579–82.

Cowley, John. 1996. *Carnival, Canboulay and Calypso: Traditions in the Making*. Cambridge: Cambridge University Press.

Craig, Maxine Leeds. 2013. *Sorry I Don't Dance: Why Men Refuse to Move*. New York: Oxford University Press.

Crang, Mike. 2011. "Tourist: Moving Places, Becoming Tourist, Becoming Ethnographer." In *Geographies of Mobilities: Practices, Spaces, Subjects*, edited by Tim Cresswell and Peter Merriman, 205–24. Farnham, UK: Ashgate.

Craton, Michael. 2002. *Pindling: The Life and Times of the First Prime Minister of the Bahamas*. London: Macmillan Caribbean.

Craton, Michael, and Gail Saunders. 1998. *Islanders in the Stream: A History of the Bahamian People*. Athens: University of Georgia Press.

Crichlow, Michaeline, and Patricia Northover. 2009. *Globalization and the Post-Creole Imagination: Notes on Fleeing the Plantation*. Durham, NC: Duke University Press.

Crick, Anne P., and Archibald Campbell. 2007. "McDonaldization, Mass Customization and Customization: An Analysis of Jamaica's All-Inclusive Hotel Sector." IDEAZ 6: 22–41.

Crick, Malcolm. 1989. "Representations of International Tourism in the Social Sciences: Sun, Sex, Sights, Savings, and Servility." *Annual Review of Anthropology* 18: 307–44.

Crick, Malcolm. 1995. "The Anthropologist as Tourist: An Identity in Question." In *International Tourism: Identity and Change*, edited by Marie-Françoise Lanfant and Edward M. Bruner, 205–23. London: SAGE.

Crouch, David, Rhona Jackson, and Felix Thompson. 2005. *The Media and the Tourist Imagination: Converging Cultures*. New York: Routledge.

Crowley, Daniel J. 1959. "Toward a Definition of Calypso (Part II)." *Ethnomusicology* 3, no. 3: 117–24.

Curtis, Debra. 2009. *Pleasure and Perils: Girls' Sexuality in a Caribbean Consumer Culture*. New Brunswick, NJ: Rutgers University Press.

Dash, J. Michael. 1998. *The Other America: Caribbean Literature in a New World Context*. Charlottesville: University Press of Virginia.

Daye, Marcella, Donna Chambers, and Sherma Roberts. 2008. *New Perspectives in Caribbean Tourism*. New York: Routledge.

De Jong, Lammert, and Dirk Kruijt. 2005. *Extended Statehood in the Caribbean: Paradoxes of Quasi Colonialism, Local Autonomy, and Extended Statehood in the USA, French, Dutch, and British Caribbean*. Amsterdam: Rozenberg.

Deleuze, Gilles, and Félix Guattari. 1987. *A Thousand Plateaus: Capitalism and Schizophrenia*. Minneapolis: University of Minnesota Press.

Derrida, Jacques. 1999a. "Hospitality, Justice and Responsibility: A Dialogue with Jacques Derrida." In *Questioning Ethics: Contemporary Debates in Philosophy*, edited by R. Kearney and M. Dooley, 65–83. New York: Routledge.

Derrida, Jacques. 1999b. *Adieu to Emmanual Levinas*. Palo Alto, CA: Stanford University Press.

Derrida, Jacques. 2000. *Of Hospitality*. Translated by R. Bowlby. Palo Alto, CA: Stanford University Press.

Derrida, Jacques. 2001. *On Cosmopolitanism and Forgiveness*. London: Psychology Press.

Desmond, Jane. [1991] 1999. *Staging Tourism: Bodies on Display from Waikiki to Sea World*. Chicago: University of Chicago Press.

Desroches, Monique, Marie-Hélène Pichette, Claude Dauphin, and Gordon E. Smith, eds. 2011. *Territoires musicaux mis en scène*. Montreal: Les Presses de l'Université de Montréal.

DeVeaux, Scott K. 1997. *The Birth of Bebop: A Social and Musical History*. Berkeley: University of California Press.

Díaz, Junot. 2013. *This Is How You Lose Her*. New York: Riverhead.

Dicks, Bella. 2004. *Culture on Display: The Production of Contemporary Visitability*. New York: Oxford University Press.

Downes, Aviston. 2005. "From Boys to Men: Colonial Education, Cricket and Masculinity in the Caribbean." *International Journal of the History of Sport* 22, no. 1: 3–21.

Dreyfus, Hubert, and Paul Rabinow. 1983. *Michel Foucault: Beyond Structuralism and Hermeneutics*, 2nd ed. Chicago: University of Chicago Press.

Dudley, Shannon. 2007. *Music from Behind the Bridge: Steelband Aesthetics and Politics in Trinidad and Tobago*. New York: Oxford University Press.

Dyde, Brian. 1997. *The Empty Sleeve: The Story of the West India Regiment of the British Army*. St. John's, Antigua: Hansib.

Dyer, Richard. 1992. *Only Entertainment*. New York: Routledge.

Edensor, Tim. 2001. "Performing Tourism, Staging Tourism: (Re)Producing Tourist Space and Practice." *Tourist Studies* 1, no. 1: 59–81.

Eldridge, Michael. 2002. "There Goes the Transnational Neighborhood: Calypso Buys a Bungalow." *Callaloo* 25, no. 2: 620–38.

Elkins, W. F. 1970. "A Source of Black Nationalism in the Caribbean: The Revolt of the British West Indies Regiment at Taranto, Italy." *Source and Society* 34, no. 1: 99–103.

Ellis, A. B. 1885. *History of the First West India Regiment*. London: Chapman and Hall.

Ellis, Pat, ed. 1986. *Women of the Caribbean*. London: Zed.

Erikson, Daniel P., and Joyce Lawrence. 2008. "Beyond Tourism: The Future of the Service Industry in the Caribbean." In *Caribbean Paper No. 3*. Waterloo, Ontario: Caribbean Policy Research Institute (CaPRI) and Centre for International Governance.

Erlmann, Veit. 1996. "The Aesthetics of the Global Imagination: Reflections on World Music in the 1990s." *Public Culture* 8, no. 3: 467–87.

Erlmann, Veit, ed. 2004. *Hearing Cultures: Essays on Sound, Listening, and Modernity*. New York: Berg.

Essah, Patience. 2001. "Slavery, Heritage and Tourism in Ghana." *International Journal of Hospitality and Tourism Administration* 2, no. 3–4: 31–49.

Fanon, Frantz. 1971. *Peau Noire, Masques Blancs*. Paris: Points Essais.

Fanon, Frantz. 2005. *The Wretched of the Earth*. New York: Grove.

Fanon, Frantz. 2008. *Black Skin, White Masks*. New York: Grove.

Feld, Steven. 1988. "Notes on World Beat." *Public Culture Bulletin* 1, no. 1: 31–37.

Feld, Steven. 1996. "Waterfall of Song: An Acoustemology of Place Resounding in Bosavi, Papua New Guinea." In *Senses of Place*, edited by Steven Feld and Keith H. Basso, 91–135. Santa Fe, NM: School of American Research Press.

Feld, Steven. 2012. "The Acoustic Turn." In *Sound and Sentiment*, by Steven Feld, xxiii–xxviii. Durham, NC: Duke University Press.

Feld, Steven. 2015. "Acoustemology." In *Keywords in Sound*, edited by David Novak and Matt Sakakeeny, 12–21. Durham, NC: Duke University Press.

Feld, Steven, and Donald Brenneis. 2004. "Doing Anthropology in Sound." *American Ethnologist* 31, no. 4: 461–74.

Feld, Steven, Aaron A. Fox, Thomas Porcello, and David Samuels. 2004. "Vocal Anthropology: From the Music of Language to the Language of Song." In *A Companion to Linguistic Anthropology*, edited by Alessandro Duranti, 321–45. Oxford: Blackwell.

Feldman, Joseph P. 2011. "Producing and Consuming 'Unspoilt' Tobago: Paradise Discourse and Cultural Tourism in the Caribbean." *Journal of Latin American and Caribbean Anthropology* 16, no. 1: 41–66.

Ferguson, James. 1988. "Cultural Exchange: New Developments in the Anthropology of Commodities." Review of *The Social Life of Things: Commodities in Cultural Perspective* by Arjun Appadurai. *Cultural Anthropology* 3, no. 4: 488–513.

Ferguson, James. 2006. *Global Shadows: Africa in the Neocolonial World Order*. Durham, NC: Duke University Press.

Finkelstein, Sidney. 1947. *Art and Society*. New York: International Publishers.

Finkelstein, Sidney. 1960. *Composer and Nation: The Folk Heritage of Music*. New York: International Publishers.

Finney, Ben R., and Karen Ann Watson, eds. 1977. *A New Kind of Sugar: Tourism in the Pacific*. Santa Cruz, CA: Center for South Pacific Studies.

Franklin, Adrian, and Mike Crang. 2001. "The Trouble with Tourism and Travel Theory." *Tourist Studies* 1, no. 1: 5–22.

Frith, Simon. 1978. *The Sociology of Rock*. London: Constable.

Frith, Simon. 1996. "Music and Identity." In *Questions of Cultural Identity*, edited by Stuart Hall and Paul DuGuy, 108–27. Thousand Oaks, CA: SAGE.

Frith, Simon. 2004. "What Is Bad Music?" In *Bad Music: The Music We Love to Hate*, edited by Christopher Washburne and Maiken Derno, 15–36. New York: Routledge.

Garlin, Francine, and Katherine Owen. 2006. "Setting the Tone with the Tune: A Meta-Analytic Review of the Effects of Background Music in Retail Settings." *Journal of Business Research* 59, no. 6: 755–64.

Gibson, Chris. 2009. "Geographies of Tourism: (Un)Ethical Encounters." *Progress in Human Geography* 34, no. 4: 521–27.

Gibson, Chris, and John Connell. 2005. *Music and Tourism: On the Road Again*. Clevedon, UK: Channelview.

Gill, Rosalind, and Andy Pratt. 2008. "In the Social Factory? Immaterial Labour, Precariousness, and Cultural Work." *Theory, Culture and Society* 25, no. 7–8: 1–30.

Gilroy, Paul. 2004. *After Empire: Multiculture or Postcolonial Melancholia*. New York: Routledge.

Gilroy, Paul. 2005. *Postcolonial Melancholia*. New York: Columbia University Press.

Glissant, Édouard. 1989. *Caribbean Discourse*. Charlottesville: University Press of Virginia.

Glissant, Édouard. 1997. *Poetics of Relation*. Ann Arbor: University of Michigan Press.

Gmelch, George. 2003. *Behind the Smile: The Working Lives of Caribbean Tourism*. Bloomington: Indiana University Press.

Goffman, Erving. 1981. *Forms of Talk*. Philadelphia: University of Pennsylvania Press.

Gopinath, Sumanth, and Jason Stanyek, eds. 2014. *Oxford Handbook of Mobile Music Studies*, vols. 1 and 2. New York: Oxford University Press.

Gosine, Andil, ed. 2009. "Special Issue: Sexual Desires, Rights, and Regulation." *Caribbean Review of Gender Studies* 3.

Goveia, Elsa. 1970. *The West Indian Slave Laws of the 18th Century*. Barbados: Caribbean Universities Press.

Graeber, David. 2001. *Toward an Anthropological Theory of Value: The False Coin of Our Own Dreams*. New York: Palgrave.

Grant, Colin. 2009. "Caribbean Voices Parts 1 & 2" [audio podcast]. BBC World Service Documentaries.

Greene, Oliver. 2017. *The Garifuna Music Reader*. San Diego, CA: Cognella Academic Publishing.

Greene, Paul, and Thomas Porcello, eds. 2004. *Wired for Sound: Engineering and Technologies in Sonic Cultures*. Middletown, CT: Wesleyan University Press.

Gregory, Steven. 2003. "Men in Paradise: Sex Tourism and the Political Economy of Masculinity." In *Race, Nature and the Politics of Difference*, edited by Donald S. Moore and Anand Pandian, 323–55. Durham, NC: Duke University Press.

Gregory, Steven. 2007. *The Devil behind the Mirror: Globalization and Politics in the Dominican Republic*. Berkeley: University of California Press.

Guadeloupe, Francio. 2009. *Chanting Down the New Jerusalem: Calypso, Christianity, and Capitalism in the Caribbean*. Berkeley: University of California Press.

Guadeloupe, Francio. 2010. *Adieu aan de Nikkers, Koelies en Makambas: Een Pleidooi voor de Deconstructie van Raciaal Denken Binnen de Nederlandse Caraïbistiek*. Nijmegen: CIDIN, Radboud Universiteit Nijmegen.

Guilbault, Jocelyne. 1993. "On Redefining the 'Local' through World Music." *World of Music* 35, no. 2: 33–47.

Guilbault, Jocelyne. 2005. "Audible Entanglements: Nation and Diasporas in Trinidad's Calypso Music Scene." *Small Axe: A Caribbean Journal of Criticism* 9, no. 1: 40–63.

Guilbault, Jocelyne. 2007. *Governing Sounds: The Cultural Politics of Trinidad's Carnival Musics*. Chicago: University of Chicago Press.

Guilbault, Jocelyne. 2017. "The Politics of Musical Bonding: New Prospects for Cosmopolitan Music Studies." In *Ethnomusicology or Transcultural Musicology? Perspectives on a 21st Century Comparative Musicology*, edited by Francesco Giannattasio and Giovanni Giuriati, 100–125. Udine: Nota Edizioni.

Guilbault, Jocelyne, with Gage Averill, Edouard Benoit, and Gregory Rabess. 1993. *Zouk: World Music in the West Indies*. Chicago: University of Chicago Press.

Guilbault, Jocelyne, and Roy Cape. 2014. *Roy Cape: A Life on the Calypso and Soca Bandstand*. Durham, NC: Duke University Press.

Hall, Stuart. 2010. "Creolite and the Process of Creolization." In *The Creolization Reader: Studies in Mixed Identities and Cultures*, edited by Robin Cohen and Paola Toninato, 26–38. New York: Routledge.

Hall, Stuart, and Alan O'Shea. 2013. "Common-Sense Neoliberalism." *Soundings* 55: 9–25.

Handler, Jerome. 1984. "Freedmen and Slaves in the Barbados Militia." *Journal of Caribbean History* 19: 1–25.

Hanslick, Eduard. 1891. *The Beautiful in Music: A Contribution to the Revisal of Musical Aesthetics*. London: Novello, Ewer.

Hardt, Michael. 1999. "Affective Labor," *boundary 2* 26, no. 2: 89–100.

Hardt, Michael, and Antonio Negri. 2005. *Multitude: War and Democracy in the Age of Empire*. New York: Penguin.

Harvey, David. 1989. *The Condition of Postmodernity*. Oxford: Basil Blackwell.

Hearne, John. 1967. "What the Barbadian Means to Me." *New World Quarterly* 3, no. 1–2: 6–9.

Hebdige, Dick. 1987. *Cut 'n' Mix: Culture, Identity and Caribbean Music*. London: Methuen.

Hellier-Tinoco, Ruth. 2011. *Embodying Mexico: Tourism, Nationalism, and Performance*. New York: Oxford University Press.

Hennion, Antoine. 2003. "Music and Mediation." In *The Cultural Study of Music: A Critical Introduction*, edited by M. Clayton, T. Herbert, and R. Middleton, 80–91. New York: Routledge.

Henriques, Julian. 2011. *Sonic Bodies: Reggae Sound Systems, Performance Techniques, and Ways of Knowing*. New York: Continuum.

Henry, Paget. 2000. *Caliban's Reason: Introducing Afro-Caribbean Philosophy*. New York: Routledge.

Heron, Taitu, and Hilary Nicholson, eds. 2006. "Unraveling Gender Development and Civil Society in the Caribbean." *Caribbean Quarterly* 52, no. 2–3.

Herweg, Ashley P., and Godfrey W. Herweg. 1997. *Radio's Niche Marketing Revolution: FutureSell*. Oxford: Focal.

Hill, Donald. 1993. *Calypso Calaloo: Early Carnival Music in Trinidad*. Gainesville: University Press of Florida.

Hill, Edwin C. 2013. *Black Soundscapes, White Stages: The Meaning of Francophone Sounds in the Black Atlantic*. Baltimore: Johns Hopkins University Press.

Hintzen, Percy C. 1997. "Reproducing Domination Identity and Legitimacy Constructs in the West Indies." *Social Identities* 3, no. 1: 47–76.

Hintzen, Percy C. 2005. "Nationalism and the Invention of Development: Modernity and the Cultural Politics of Resistance." *Social and Economic Studies* 54, no. 3: 66–96.

Holder, Jean S. 2013. *Caribbean Tourism*. St. Augustine, Trinidad: Canoe Press UWI.

Hollinshead, Keith. 2002. "Tourism and the Making of the World: The Dynamics of Our Contemporary Tribal Lives." *FIU Honors Excellence Occasional Paper* 1, no. 2: 1–37.

Hollinshead, Keith. 2004. "Tourism and New Sense: Worldmaking and the Enunciative Value of Tourism." In *Tourism and Postcolonialism: Contested Discourses, Identities and Representations*, edited by C. Michael Hall and Hazel Tucker, 25–42. New York: Routledge.

Hollinshead, Keith. 2009. "The 'Worldmaking' Prodigy of Tourism: The Reach and Power of Tourism in the Dynamics of Change and Transformation." *Tourism Analysis* 14, no. 1: 139–52.

Holt, Fabian. 2007. *Genre in Popular Music*. Chicago: University of Chicago Press.

Howe, Glenford D. 2001. "De(Re)Constructing Identities: World War I and the Growth of Barbadian/West Indian Nationalism." In *The Empowering Impulse: The Nationalist Tradition of Barbados*, edited by Glenford D. Howe and Don D. Marshall, 103–32. Kingston, Jamaica: Canoe Press UWI.

Howes, David. 2010. "Response to Sarah Pink." *Social Anthropology* 18, no. 3: 333–40.

Hutchinson, Sydney. 2016. *Tigers of a Different Stripe: Performing Gender in Dominican Music*. Chicago: University of Chicago Press.

Idhe, Don. 1976. *Listening and Voice: A Phenomenology of Sound*. Albany: State University of New York Press.

Ingold, Tim. 2003. *The Perception of the Environment: Essays on Livelihood, Dwelling and Skill*. New York: Routledge.

Ingold, Tim. 2007. *Lines: A Brief History*. New York: Routledge.

Ingold, Tim. 2011. *Being Alive: Essays on Movement, Knowledge and Description*. New York: Routledge.

Ingold, Tim. 2015. *The Life of Lines*. New York: Routledge.

Inniss, Tara. 2012. "Heritage and Communities in a Small Island Developing State: Historic Bridgetown and Its Garrison Barbados." In *World Heritage, Benefits beyond Borders*, edited by Amareswar Galla, 69–81. Cambridge: Cambridge University Press.

Issa, John J., and Chandana Jayawardena. 2003. "The 'All-Inclusive' Concept in the Caribbean." *International Journal of Contemporary Hospitality Management* 15, no. 3: 167–71.

Jackson, Daniel. 2003. *Sonic Branding: An Introduction*. New York: Palgrave Macmillan.

Jackson, Michael. 1989. *Paths Toward a Clearing: Radical Empiricism and Ethnographic Inquiry*. Bloomington: Indiana University Press.

James, C. L. R. [1963] 2005. *Beyond a Boundary*. London: Yellow Jersey.

Järviluoma, Helmi. 2013. "Re-Sounding Pleasure in Soundscape Studies." *Wi: Journal of Mobile Media* 7, no. 1. http://wi.mobilities.ca/media/wi_07_01_2013_jarviluoma.pdf.

Jaworski, Adam, and Crispin Thurlow. 2010. "Silence Is Golden: The 'Anti-Communicational' Linguascaping of Super-Elite Mobility." In *Advances in Sociolin-*

guistics: *Semiotic Landscapes: Language, Image, Space*, edited by Adam Jaworski and Crispin Thurlow, 187–218. London: Continuum.

Jeon, Jin Yong, Joo Young Hong, and Pyoung Lik Lee. 2013. "Soundwalk Approach to Identify Urban Soundscapes Individually." *Journal of the Acoustical Society of America* 134, no. 1.

Johnson, Violet Showers. 2006. *The Other Black Bostonians: West Indians in Boston, 1900–1950.* Bloomington: Indiana University Press.

Johnston, Lynda. 2001. "(Other) Bodies and Tourism Studies." *Annals of Tourism Research* 28, no. 1: 180–201.

Kahn, Douglas. 2001. *Noise, Water, Meat: A History of Sound in the Arts.* Cambridge, MA: MIT Press.

Kasinitz, Philip. 1992. *Caribbean New York: Black Immigrants and the Politics of Race.* Ithaca, NY: Cornell University Press.

Kassabian, Anahid. 2013. *Ubiquitous Listening: Affect, Attention, and Distributed Subjectivity.* Berkeley: University of California Press.

Kaul, Adam R. 2009. *Turning the Tune: Traditional Music, Tourism, and Social Change in an Irish Village.* New York: Berghahn.

Keeling, Kara, and Josh Kun. 2011. "Introduction: Listening to American Studies." *American Quarterly* 63, no. 3: 445–59.

Keil, Charles, and Steven Feld. 1994. *Music Grooves: Essays and Dialogues.* Chicago: University of Chicago Press.

Kelley, Norman, ed. 2002. R&B *Rhythm and Business: The Political Economy of Black Music.* New York: Akashic.

Kempadoo, Kamala. 2004. *Sexing the Caribbean: Gender, Race, and Sexual Labor.* New York: Routledge.

Khan, Aisha. 2013. "Horizons of Caribbean Studies: An Afterword-Overture." In *Caribbean Cultural Thought: From Plantation to Diaspora*, edited by Yanique Hume and Aaron Kamugisha, 617–23. Kingston, Jamaica: Ian Randle.

Kincaid, Jamaica. [1988] 2000. *A Small Place.* New York: Farrar, Straus and Giroux.

King, Carol A. 1995. "What Is Hospitality." *International Journal of Hospitality Management* 14, no. 3–4: 219–34.

Kingsbury, Paul. 2011. "Sociospatial Sublimation: The Human Resources of Love in Sandals Resorts International, Jamaica." *Annals of the Association of American Geographers* 101, no. 3: 650–69.

Kirshenblatt-Gimblett, Barbara. 1995. "Theorizing Heritage." *Ethnomusicology* 39, no. 3: 367–80.

Kirshenblatt-Gimblett, Barbara. 2006. "World Heritage and Cultural Economics." In *Museum Frictions: Public Cultures/Global Transformations*, edited by Corinne A. Kratz, Ivan Karp, et al., 161–202. Durham, NC: Duke University Press.

Korstanje, Maximiliano. 2007. "The Origin and Meaning of Tourism: Etymological Study." *e-Review of Tourism Research* 5, no. 5: 100–108.

Krüger, Simone, and Ruxandra Trandafoiu. 2013. *The Globalization of Musics in Transit: Music, Migration, and Tourism.* New York: Routledge.

Lamen, Darien. 2014. "Sound Tracks of a Tropical Sexscape: Tropicalizing Northeast-ern Brazil, Channeling Transnational Desires." In *Sun, Sea, and Sound: Music and Tourism in the Circum-Caribbean*, edited by Timothy Rommen and Daniel T. Neely, 267–88. New York: Oxford University Press.

Largey, Michael. 2006. *Vodou Nation: Haitian Art Music and Cultural Nationalism*. Chicago: University of Chicago Press.

Lash, Scott, and John Urry. [1994] 1999. *Economies of Signs and Space*. London: SAGE.

Lashua, Brett, Karl Spracklen, and Phil Long. 2014. "Introduction to the Special Issue: Music and Tourism." *Tourism Studies* 14, no. 1: 3–9.

Lee, Benjamin, and Edward LiPuma. 2002. "Cultures of Circulation: The Imaginations of Modernity." *Public Culture* 14, no. 1: 191–213.

Lefebvre, Henri. [1974] 1992. *The Production of Space*. New York: Wiley-Blackwell.

Lefebvre, Henri. 2004. *Rhythmanalysis: Space, Time and Everyday Life*. Translated by Stuart Eden and Gerald Moore. London: Continuum.

Lévi-Strauss, Claude. 1971. *Tristes Tropiques*. Translated by John Russell. New York: Atheneum.

Lewin, Olive. 1989. "Banana Boat Song Forever?" In *Come Mek Me Hol' Yu Han': The Impact of Tourism on Traditional Music*, by the International Colloquium on Traditional Music, 1–6. Kingston: Jamaica Memory Bank.

Lewis, Linden. 2001. "The Contestation of Race in Barbadian Society and the Camouflage of Conservativism." In *New Caribbean Thought: A Reader*, edited by Brian Meeks and Folke Lindahl, 144–95. Mona, Jamaica: University of the West Indies Press.

Liu, Juanita. 2005. "Tourism and the Value of Culture in Regions." *Annals of Regional Science* 39, no. 1: 1–9.

Löfgren, Orvar. 2004. "The Global Beach." In *Tourists and Tourism: A Reader*, edited by Sharon Bohn Gmelch, 35–54. Long Grove, IL: Waveland.

Long, Philip. 2014. "Popular Music, Psychogeography, Place Identity and Tourism: The Case of Sheffield." *Tourist Studies* 14, no. 1: 48–65.

Lovelace, Earl. 1998. "The Emancipation-Jouvay Tradition and the Almost Loss of Pan." *Drama Review* 42, no. 3: 54–60.

Lowinger, Rosa, and Ofelia Fox. 2005. *Tropicana Nights: The Life and Times of the Legendary Cuban Nightclub*. Orlando: Harcourt.

Lysloff, Rene, and Leslie Gay, eds. 2003. *Music and Technoculture*. Middletown, CT: Wesleyan University Press.

MacCannell, Dean. 1973. "Staged Authenticity: Arrangements of Social Space in Tourist Settings." *American Journal of Sociology* 79, no. 3: 589–603.

MacCannell, Dean. 2008. "Why It Never Really Was about Authenticity." *Society* 45, no. 4: 334–37.

MacCannell, Dean. [1976] 2013. *The Tourist: A New Theory of the Leisure Class*. Berkeley: University of California Press.

Maitel, S. 2002. "Don't Sell Commodities, Sell Experiences." *New Corporate University Review*, May.

Malinowski, Bronisław. 2013. *Argonauts of the Western Pacific*. Long Grove, IL: Waveland.

Manuel, Peter. 1995. *Caribbean Currents: Caribbean Music from Rumba to Reggae*. Philadelphia: Temple University Press.

Manuel, Peter. 2000. *East Indian Music in the West Indies: Tan-Singing, Chutney, and the Making of Indo-Caribbean Culture*. Philadelphia: Temple University Press.

March, Roger, and Ian Wilkinson. 2009. "Conceptual Tools for Evaluating Tourism Partnerships." *Tourism Management* 30, no. 3: 455–62.

Marx, Karl, and Friedrich Engels. 1988. *The Economic and Philosophic Manuscripts of 1844 and the Communist Manifesto*. Translated by Martin Milligan. Amherst, MA: Prometheus.

Massey, Doreen. 2005. *For Space*. New York: SAGE.

McBride, Sean, and International Commission for the Study of Communication Problems. 1980. *Many Voices One World: Towards a New, More Just, and More Efficient World Information and Communication Order*. Lanham, MD. Rowan and Littlefield.

McCabe, Scott. 2005. "Who Is a Tourist? A Critical Review." *Tourist Studies* 5, no. 1: 85–106.

McGeary, Johanna, and Cathy Booth. 1993. "Cuba Alone." *Time*, December 6. Available online at http://www.time.com/time/magazine/article/0,9171,979762,00.html

McKittrick, Katherine, ed. 2015. *Sylvia Wynter: On Being Human as Praxis*. Durham, NC: Duke University Press.

Meier, Leslie. 2017. *Popular Music as Promotion: Music and Branding in the Digital Age*. Malden, MA: Polity.

Meintjes, Louise. 2017. *Dust of the Zulu: Ngoma Aesthetics after Apartheid*. Durham, NC: Duke University Press.

Meredith, Sharon. 2014. *Tuk Music Tradition in Barbados*. New York: Routledge.

Merleau-Ponty, Maurice. 1970. *Themes from the Lectures at the Collège de France, 1952–1960*. Translated by John O'Neill. Evanston, IL: Northwestern University Press.

Miller, Daniel, ed. 1998. *Material Cultures: Why Some Things Matter*. Chicago: University of Chicago Press.

Miller, Daniel. 2005. *Materiality*. Durham, NC: Duke University Press.

Miller, Rebecca. 2008. *Carriacou String Band Serenade: Performing Identity in the Eastern Caribbean*. Middletown, CT: Wesleyan University Press.

Milliman, Ronald. 1986. "The Influence of Background Music on Behavior of Restaurant Patrons." *Journal of Consumer Research* 13, no. 2: 286–89.

Minca, Claudio. 2010. "The Island: Work, Tourism and the Biopolitical." *Tourist Studies* 9, no. 2: 88–108.

Ministry of Community Development and Culture. 2010. *Historic Bridgetown and Its Garrison Nomination as a World Heritage Site Nomination Document*. whc.unesco.org /document/152514.

Mintz, Sidney. 1996. "Enduring Substances, Trying Theories: The Caribbean Region as Oikoumene." *Journal of the Royal Anthropological Institute* 2, no. 2: 289–311.

Moeran, Brian. 1983. "The Language of Japanese Tourism." *Annals of Tourism Research* 10, no. 1: 93–108.

Mohammed, Patricia, ed. 2002. *Gendered Realities: Essays in Caribbean Feminist Thought*. Kingston, Jamaica: University of the West Indies Press.

Mohammed, Patricia, and Catherine Shepherd, eds. 1988. *Gender in Caribbean Development*. St. Augustine, Trinidad: University of the West Indies Press.

Moore, Robin. 1997. *Nationalizing Blackness: Afrocubanismo and Artistic Revolution in Havana, 1920–1940*. Pittsburgh: University of Pittsburgh Press.

Mowatt, Rasul A., and Charles H. Chancellor. 2011. "Visiting Death and Life: Dark Tourism and Slave Castles." *Annals of Tourism Research* 38, no. 4: 1410–34.

Munro, Martin. 2010. *Different Drummers: Rhythm and Race in the Americas*. Berkeley: University of California Press.

Myers, Fred, ed. 2001. *The Empire of Things: Regimes of Value and Material Culture*. Santa Fe, NM: School of American Research Press.

Nancy, Jean-Luc. 2000. *Being Singular Plural*. Stanford, CA: Stanford University Press.

Neely, Daniel T. 2007. "Calling All Singers, Musicians and Speechmakers: Mento Aesthetics and Jamaica's Early Recording Industry." *Caribbean Quarterly* 53, no. 4: 1–15, 110.

Novak, David. 2013. *Japanoise: Music at the Edge of Circulation*. Durham, NC: Duke University Press.

Novak, David. 2015. "Noise." In *Keywords in Sound*, edited by David Novak and Matt Sakakeeny, 125–38. Durham, NC: Duke University Press.

Novak, David, and Matt Sakakeeny, eds. 2015. *Keywords in Sound*. Durham, NC: Duke University Press.

Ochoa Gautier, Ana María. 2014. *Aurality: Listening and Knowledge in Nineteenth-Century Colombia*. Durham, NC: Duke University Press.

Ong, Aihwah. 1999. *Flexible Citizenship: The Cultural Logics of Transnationality*. Durham, NC: Duke University Press.

Oostindie, Gert. 1998. *Het Paradijs Overzee: De Nederlandse Caraïben en Nederland*, 2nd ed. Amsterdam: B. Bakker.

Oostindie, Gert. 2006a. "Dependence and Autonomy in Sub-National Island Jurisdictions: The Case of the Kingdom of the Netherlands." *Round Table* 95, no. 386: 609–26.

Oostindie, Gert. 2006b. "The Study of Ethnicity in the Dutch Caribbean." *Latin American and Caribbean Ethnic Studies* 1, no 2: 215–30.

Osagie, Iyunolu, and Christine N. Buzinde. 2011. "Culture and Postcolonial Resistance: Antigua in Kincaid's *A Small Place*." *Annals of Tourism Research* 38, no. 1: 210–30.

Pacini Hernandez, Deborah. 1995. *Bachata: A Social History of a Dominican Popular Music*. Philadelphia: Temple University Press.

Padilla, Mark. 2007. *Caribbean Pleasure Industry: Tourism, Sexuality, and AIDS in the Dominican Republic*. Chicago: University of Chicago Press.

Palmer, Catherine. 1994. "Tourism and Colonialism: The Experience of the Bahamas." *Annals of Tourism Research* 21, no. 4: 792–811.

Pasler, Jann. 2008. "The Political Economy of Composition in the American University, 1965–1985." In *Writing through Music: Essays on Music, Culture, and Politics*, 318–62. New York: Oxford University Press.

Pattullo, Polly. [1996] 2005. *Last Resorts: The Cost of Tourism in the Caribbean*. London: Latin American Bureau.

Pearce, Philip L. 2007. "Persisting with Authenticity: Gleaning Contemporary Insights for Future Tourism Studies." *Tourism Recreation Research* 32, no. 2: 86–89.

Pérez, Lisandro. 1986. "Cubans in the United States." *Annals of the American Academy of Political and Social Science* 487, no. 1: 126–37.

Perraud, Marc. 2007. *Les Musicos: Enquête sur des musiciens ordinaires.* Paris: La Decouverte.

Pijl, Yvon van der, and Francio Guadeloupe. 2015. "Imagining the Nation in the Classroom: Belonging and Nationhood in the Dutch Caribbean." *European Review of Latin American and Caribbean Studies* no. 98: 87–98.

Pinch, Trevor, and Karin Bijsterveld, eds. 2012. *The Oxford Handbook of Sound Studies.* New York: Oxford University Press.

Pine, B. J., and J. H. Gilmore. 1999. *The Experience Economy.* Boston: Harvard Business School Press.

Pink, Sarah. 2010. "The Future of Sensory Anthropology/The Anthropology of the Senses." *Social Anthropology* 18, no. 3: 331–38.

Pratt, Mary Louise. 1992. *Imperial Eyes: Travel Writing and Transculturation.* New York: Routledge.

Price, Richard, and Sally Price. 1997. "Shadowboxing in the Mangrove." *Cultural Anthropology* 12, no. 1: 3–36.

Puri, Shalini. 2004. *The Caribbean Postcolonial: Social Equality, Post-Nationalism, and Cultural Hybridity.* New York: Palgrave Macmillan.

Putnam, Lara. 2013. *Radical Moves: Caribbean Migrants and the Politics of Race in the Jazz Age.* Chapel Hill: University of North Carolina Press.

Quiñones, Marta García, Anahid Kassabian, and Elena Boschi, eds. 2013. *Ubiquitous Musics: The Everyday Sounds That We Don't Always Notice.* Surrey, UK: Ashgate.

Qureshi, Regula, ed. 2002. *Music and Marx: Ideas, Practice, Politics.* New York: Routledge.

Rabinow, Paul. 2007. *Marking Time: On the Anthropology of the Contemporary.* Princeton, NJ: Princeton University Press.

Radano, Ronald M. 2000. "Hot Fantasies: American Modernism and the Idea of Black Rhythm." In *Music and the Racial Imagination*, edited by Ronald M. Radano and Philip V. Bohlman, 459–80. Chicago: University of Chicago Press.

Radano, Ronald M. 2016. "Black Music Labor and the Animated Properties of Slave Sound." *boundary 2* 43, no. 1: 173–208.

Radano, Ronald M., and Philip V. Bohlman, eds. 2000. *Music and the Racial Imagination.* Chicago: University of Chicago Press.

Radano, Ronald M., and Tejumola Olaniyan, eds. 2016. *Audible Empire: Music, Global Politics, Critique.* Durham, NC: Duke University Press.

Ramnarine, Tina. 2001. *Creating Their Own Space: The Development of Indian-Caribbean Musical Tradition.* Kingston, Jamaica: University of the West Indies Press.

Ramsey, Kate. 2011. *The Spirits and the Law: Vodou and Power in Haiti.* Chicago: University of Chicago Press.

Reddock, Rhoda E. 1988. *Elma Francois, the NWCSA and the Workers' Struggle for Change in the Caribbean.* London: New Beacon.

Reddock, Rhoda E. 1994. *Women, Labour and Politics in Trinidad and Tobago: A History*. London: Zed.

Reddock, Rhoda E., ed. 2004. *Interrogating Caribbean Masculinities: Theoretical and Empirical Analyses*. St. Augustine, Trinidad: University of the West Indies Press.

Rhodes, Gary D. 2001. *White Zombie: Anatomy of a Horror Film*. Jefferson, NC: McFarland.

Robbins, Lionel. 1932. *An Essay on the Nature and Significance of Economic Science*. London: Macmillan.

Roberts, Les. 2014. "Marketing Musicscapes, or the Political Economy of Contagious Magic." *Tourist Studies* 14, no. 1: 10–29.

Robinson, William I. 2014. *Global Capitalism and the Crisis of Humanity*. Cambridge: Cambridge University Press.

Rogers, Jim. 2013. *The Death and Life of the Music Industry in the Digital Age*. London: Bloomsbury.

Rohlehr, Gordon. 1990. *Calypso and Society in Pre-Independence Trinidad*. Port-of-Spain, Trinidad: Author.

Rojek, Chris, and John Urry, eds. 1997. *Touring Cultures: Transformations of Travel and Theory*. New York: Routledge.

Rolle, Sophia. 2015. "The Bahamas: Individual Island Branding for Competitiveness in Archipelago Tourism." In *Archipelago Tourism: Policies and Practices*, edited by Godfrey Baldacchino, 163–179. New York: Routledge.

Rommen, Timothy. 2007a. "'Localize It': Rock, Cosmopolitanism, and the Nation in Trinidad." *Ethnomusicology* 51, no. 3: 371–401.

Rommen, Timothy. 2007b. *Mek Some Noise: Gospel Music and the Ethics of Style in Trinidad*. Berkeley: University of California Press.

Rommen, Timothy. 2011. *Funky Nassau: Roots, Routes, and Representation in Bahamian Popular Music*. Berkeley: University of California Press.

Rommen, Timothy. 2015. "Créolité, (Im)Mobility, and Music in Dominica." *Journal of Musicology* 32, no. 4: 558–91.

Rommen, Timothy, and Daniel T. Neely, eds. 2014. *Sun, Sea, and Sound: Music and Tourism in the Circum-Caribbean*. New York: Oxford University Press.

Rorty, Richard. 1990. *Objectivity, Relativism and Truth: Philosophical Papers I*. Cambridge: Cambridge University Press.

Salazar, Noel B. 2012. *Envisioning Eden: Mobilizing Imaginaries in Tourism and Beyond*. New York: Berghahn.

Samuels, David W., Louise Meintjes, Ana María Ochoa Gautier, and Thomas Porcello. 2010. "Soundscapes: Toward a Sounded Anthropology." *Annual Review of Anthropology* 39: 329–45.

Schwartz, Rosalie. 1997. *Pleasure Island: Tourism and Temptation in Cuba*. Lincoln: University of Nebraska Press.

Scott, David. 1999. *Refashioning Futures: Criticism after Postcoloniality*. Princeton, NJ: Princeton University Press.

Scott, Joan W. 1991. "The Evidence of Experience." *Critical Inquiry* 17, no. 4: 773–97.

Seidman, Steven. 1989. *Jürgen Habermas on Society and Politics: A Reader*. Boston: Beacon.

Semidor, Catherine. 2006. "Listening to a City with the Soundwalk Method." *Acta Acustica United with Acustica* 92, no. 6: 959–64.

Sharpley, Richard. 2004. "Island in the Sun: Cyprus." In *Tourism Mobilities: Places to Play, Places in Play*, edited by Mimi Sheller and John Urry, 21–30. New York: Routledge.

Sheller, Mimi. 2003. *Consuming the Caribbean: From Arawaks to Zombies*. New York: Routledge.

Sheller, Mimi. 2009. "Infrastructures of the Imagined Island: Software, Mobilities, and the Architecture of Caribbean Paradise." *Environment and Planning A* 41, no. 6: 1386–1403.

Sheller, Mimi. 2012. *Citizenship from Below: Erotic Agency and Caribbean Freedom*. Durham, NC: Duke University Press.

Sheller, Mimi. 2014. "Cruising Cultures: Post-War Tourism and the Circulation of Caribbean Musical Performances, Recordings, and Representations." In *Sun, Sea, and Sound: Music and Tourism in the Circum-Caribbean*, edited by Timothy Rommen and Daniel T. Neely, 73–100. New York: Oxford University Press.

Shepherd, Verene. 2010. "Slavery, Shame and Pride: Debates over the Marking of the Bicentennial of the Abolition of the British Trans-Atlantic Trade in Africans in 2007." *Caribbean Quarterly* 56, no. 1–2: 1–21.

Shohat, Ella, and Robert Stam. 2014. *Unthinking Eurocentrism: Multiculturalism and the Media*. Abingdon, UK: Taylor and Francis.

Shusterman, Richard. 2003. "Entertainment: A Question of Aesthetics." *British Journal of Aesthetics* 43, no. 3: 289–307.

Siegel, Peter E., and Elizabeth Righter, eds. 2011. *Protecting Heritage in the Caribbean*. Tuscaloosa: University of Alabama Press.

Small, Christopher. 1998. *Musicking: The Meaning of Performing and Listening*. Middletown, CT: Wesleyan University Press.

Smith, Mark M. 1997. *Mastered by the Clock: Time, Slavery, and Freedom in the American South*. Chapel Hill: University of North Carolina Press.

Smith, Richard. 2014. "Loss and Longing: Emotional Responses to West Indian Soldiers during the First World War." *Round Table. The Commonwealth Journal of International Affairs* 103, no. 2: 243–52.

Smythe, Dallas W. 1977. "Communications: Blindspot of Western Marxism." *Canadian Journal of Political and Social Theory* 1, no. 3: 1–27.

Solomon, Maynard, ed. [1973] 1979. *Marxism and Art*. Detroit: Wayne State University Press.

Sprague, Jeb H. 2018. "Global Capitalism in the Caribbean." NACLA *Report on the Americas* 50, no. 2: 139–47.

Steinberg, Marc. 2012. *Anime's Media Mix: Franchising Toys and Characters in Japan*. Minneapolis: University of Minnesota Press.

Sterne, Jonathan. 1997. "Sounds Like the Mall of America: Programmed Music and the Architectonics of Commercial Space." *Ethnomusicology* 41, no. 1: 22–50.

Sterne, Jonathan. 2012. *The Sound Studies Reader*. New York: Routledge.

Sterne, Jonathan. 2013. "The Non-Aggressive Music Deterrent." In *Ubiquitous Musics:*

The Everyday Sounds That We Don't Always Notice, edited by Marta García Quiñones, Anahid Kassabian, and Elena Boschi, 121–37. Surrey, UK: Ashgate.

Sterne, Jonathan. 2015. "Hearing." In *Keywords in Sound*, edited by David Novak and Matt Sakakeeny, 65–77. Durham, NC: Duke University Press.

Sterne, Jonathan, and Emily Raine. 2006. "Command Tones: Digitization and Sounded Time." *First Monday* 7.

Stokes, Martin, ed. 1994. *Ethnicity, Identity, and Music: The Musical Construction of Place.* Oxford: Berg.

Stokes, Martin. 2002. "Marx, Money, and Musicians. In *Music and Marx: Ideas, Practice, Politics*, edited by Regula Qureshi, 139–66. New York: Routledge.

Stokes, Martin. 2007. "On Musical Cosmopolitanism." Paper No. 3. Macalester International Roundtable.

Stolzoff, Norman C. 2000. *Wake the Town and Tell the People: Dancehall Culture in Jamaica.* Durham, NC: Duke University Press.

Strachan, Ian Gregory. 2003. *Paradise and Plantation: Tourism and Culture in the Anglophone Caribbean.* Charlottesville: University of Virginia Press.

Symonette, George. 1955. Liner notes to *Bahamian Troubadour.* ALP-10. Miami: Art Records.

Tatar, Elizabeth. 1987. *Strains of Change: The Impact of Tourism on Hawaiian Music.* Honolulu: Bishop Museum Press.

Taylor, Timothy D. 1997. *Global Pop: World Music, World Markets.* New York: Routledge.

Taylor, Timothy D. 2001. *Strange Sounds: Music, Technology and Culture.* New York: Routledge.

Taylor, Timothy D. 2012. *The Sounds of Capitalism: Advertising, Music, and the Conquest of Culture.* Chicago: University of Chicago Press.

Taylor, Timothy D. 2014. "Fields, Genres, Brands." *Culture, Theory and Critique* 55, no. 2: 159–74.

Taylor, Timothy D., Mark Katz, and Tony Grajeda, eds. 2012. *Music, Sound and Technology in America: A Documentary History of Early Phonograph, Cinema, and Radio.* Durham, NC: Duke University Press.

Théberge, Paul. 1997. *Any Sound You Can Imagine: Making Music/Consuming Technology.* Middletown, CT: Wesleyan University Press.

Théberge, Paul, Kyle Devine, and Tom Everrett, eds. 2015. *Living Stereo: Histories and Cultures of Multichannel Sound.* New York: Bloomsbury.

Thomas, Deborah A. 2004. *Modern Blackness: Nationalism, Globalization, and the Politics of Culture in Jamaica.* Durham, NC: Duke University Press.

Thompson, Krista. 2006. *An Eye for the Tropics: Tourism, Photography, and Framing the Caribbean Picturesque.* Durham, NC: Duke University Press.

Toop, David. 2001. *Ocean of Sound: Aether Talk, Ambient Sound, and Imaginary Worlds.* London: Serpent's Tail.

Törnqvist, Maria. 2015. *Tourism and the Globalization of Emotions: The Intimate Economy of Tango.* New York: Routledge.

Trouillot, Michel-Rolph. 2001. "The Anthropology of the State in the Age of Globalization." *Current Anthropology* 42: 125–38.

Trouillot, Michel-Rolph. 2002. "Culture on the Edges: Caribbean Creolization in Historical Context." In *From the Margins: Historical Anthropology and Its Futures*, edited by Brian Keith Axel, 189–210. Durham, NC: Duke University Press.

Tsing, Anna. 2005. *Friction: An Ethnography of Global Connection.* Princeton, NJ: Princeton University Press.

Tucker, Hazel, and Elizabeth Carnegie. 2014. "World Heritage and the Contradictions of 'Universal Value.'" *Annals of Tourism Research* 47: 63–76.

Urban, Greg, and Kyung-Nan Koh. 2013. "Ethnographic Research on Modern Business Corporations." *Annual Review of Anthropology* 42: 139–58.

Uriely, Natan, and Yaniv Belhassen. 2005. "Drugs and Tourists' Experiences." *Journal of Travel Research* 43, no. 3: 238–46.

Urry, John. 2007. *Mobilities.* New York: Polity Press.

Urry, John, and Jonas Larsen. 2011. *The Tourist Gaze 3.0.* Los Angeles: SAGE.

Urry, John, and Mimi Sheller, eds. 2004. *Tourism Mobilities: Places to Play, Places in Play.* New York: Routledge.

Veal, Michael. 2007. *Dub: Soundscapes and Shattered Songs in Jamaican Reggae.* Middleton, CT: Wesleyan University Press.

Voegelin, Salome. 2010. *Listening to Noise and Silence: Towards a Philosophy of Sound Art.* New York: Continuum.

Walcott, Derek. 1992. *The Antilles: Fragments of Epic Memory: The Nobel Lecture.* New York: Farrar, Straus and Giroux.

Walcott, Derek. 1998. *What the Twilight Says: Essays.* New York: Farrar, Straus and Giroux.

Walcott, Stefan. 2014. "A Song, Two Rhythms and Rihanna: Musical Sounds, Meaning and Power in Four Genre Worlds." PhD dissertation, University of the West Indies, Cave Hill, St. Michael, Barbados.

Washburne, Christopher. 2008. *Sounding Salsa: Performing Latin Music in New York City.* Philadelphia: Temple University Press.

Washburne, Christopher, and Maiken Derno, eds. 2004. *Bad Music: The Music We Love to Hate.* New York: Routledge.

Waterman, Christopher. 1990. *Jùjú: A Social History and Ethnography of an African Popular Music.* Chicago: University of Chicago Press.

Waterton, Emma, and Steve Watson. 2014. *The Semiotics of Heritage Tourism.* Bristol: Channel View.

Weidman, Amanda. 2015. "Voice." In *Keywords in Sound*, edited by David Novak and Matt Sakakeeny, 232–45. Durham, NC: Duke University Press.

Williams, Alistair. 2006. "Tourism and Hospitality Marketing: Fantasy, Feeling, and Fun." *International Journal of Contemporary Hospitality Management* 18, no. 6: 482–95.

Williams, Eric. [1944] 1994. *Capitalism and Slavery.* Chapel Hill: University of North Carolina Press.

Williams, Raymond. 1977. *Marxism and Literature.* New York: Oxford University Press.

Williams, Stephanie. 1986. "Yellow Bird—Ai Zuzuwah: Stagnation or Growth?" In *Come Mek Me Hol' Yu Han': The Impact of Tourism on Traditional Music*, by the International Colloquium on Traditional Music, 17–28. Kingston, Jamaica: Jamaica Memory Bank.

Wright, Steve. 2005. "Reality Check: Are We Living in an Immaterial World?" *Mute* 2, no. 1: n.p.

Yelvington, Kevin A., Jason L. Simms, and Elizabeth Murray. 2012. "Wine Tourism in the Temecula Valley: Neoliberal Development Policies and Their Contradictions." *Anthropology in Action* 19, no. 3: 49–65.

Contributors

JEROME CAMAL is Associate Professor of Anthropology at the University of Wisconsin–Madison. His research seeks to better understand French Antillean postcoloniality through the study of sounds, music, and dance. Specifically, Camal has spent about ten years exploring the political import of *gwoka*, Guadeloupe's drumming tradition. He is currently at work on a book manuscript tentatively titled *Contested Aurality: Guadeloupean Gwoka and Postcolonial Politics*. Camal earned his PhD at Washington University in Saint Louis. Prior to joining the UW, he was a Mellon postdoctoral fellow in the humanities at the University of California, Los Angeles.

STEVEN FELD is Senior Scholar at the School for Advanced Research, Santa Fe, New Mexico, and Distinguished Professor Emeritus of Anthropology and Music at the University of New Mexico. His books include *Sound and Sentiment*, *Jazz Cosmopolitanism in Accra*, *Senses of Place* (with Keith Basso), and *Music Grooves* (with Charles Keil). His CDs include *Voices of the Rainforest*, *The Time of Bells 1-5*, *Por Por: Honk Horn Music of Ghana*, and *Bufo Variations* (with NII Otoo Annan). His films include *Hallelujah*, *Accra Trane Station*, *Por Por Funeral for Ashirifie*, and *JC Abbey, Ghana's Puppeteer*.

FRANCIO GUADELOUPE, a social and cultural anthropologist and development sociologist by training, is the president of the University of Sint Maarten (USM). Guadeloupe's principal areas of research have been on the manner in which popular understandings of national belonging, cultural diversity, religious identity, and mass media constructions of truth continue to be impacted by colonial racism and global capital. He has pursued these interests in his research and publications on social processes on the binational island of Saint Martin and Sint Maarten (St. Martin), Brazil, Aruba, Saba, Sint Eustatius, and the Netherlands. He is the author of *Chanting Down the New Jerusalem: Calypso, Christianity, and Capitalism in the Caribbean*. His articles have appeared in *Transforming Anthropology*, *Latin American and Caribbean Ethnic Studies*, *Social Analysis*, *Women's Studies International Forum*, and the *Journal for the Study of Religion*.

JOCELYNE GUILBAULT is Professor of Ethnomusicology at the University of California, Berkeley. Her work is concerned with power relations, global industrialization, labor practices, and work ethics in Caribbean popular musics. Stressing a multidisciplinary approach, she addresses these issues in the scholarly intersections of music, anthropology, cultural studies, and history. Her research in Saint Lucia, Martinique, Guadeloupe, Dominica, and Trinidad is reported in articles and in *Zouk: World Music in the West Indies*, *Governing Sound: The Cultural Politics of Trinidad's Carnival Musics*, and *Roy Cape: A Life on the Calypso and Soca Bandstand* (coauthored with Roy Cape).

JORDI HALFMAN is a cultural anthropologist who obtained both her bachelor's and master's degree in cultural anthropology from the University of Amsterdam in 2012 and 2013. In the fall of 2014 she started her PhD journey at that same university, a place she soon exchanged to do fieldwork on the island of Sint Maarten. On the island she draws together her interest in coexistence, equity, and creativity with her love for and experience in working with children and youth. Her current work aims at learning from the rich imaginations of children in relation to the complicated issues of (national) belonging.

SUSAN HAREWOOD is Associate Professor at the University of Washington–Bothell and the director of the Master's in Cultural Studies Program at UWB. Her research examines media and Caribbean popular culture as key sites at which the pursuit of justice is contested, constrained, and shaped. Her published work has appeared in a number of journals and edited collections and focuses on the roles that Caribbean popular music and popular culture play in facilitating and/or impeding community formation within the region.

PERCY HINTZEN is Professor in the Department of Global and Sociocultural Studies in the School of International and Public Affairs at Florida International University where he is the Director of the African and African Diaspora Studies Program. He is also Professor Emeritus at the University of California, Berkeley. He earned his Ph.D. in Comparative Political Sociology from Yale University. His research has focused on the political economy of the West Indies and Africa, and on black immigrants to the United States. His most recent published works have focused on issues related to regionalism, democracy, development, postcolonialism, and HIV/AIDS in the Caribbean.

TIMOTHY ROMMEN is Davidson Kennedy Professor in the College and Professor of Music and Africana Studies at the University of Pennsylvania. He specializes in the music of the Caribbean, with research interests that include folk and popular sacred music, popular music, critical theory, ethics, tourism, diaspora, and the intellectual history of ethnomusicology. He is the author of *"Mek Some Noise": Gospel Music and the Ethics of Style in Trinidad* and *Funky Nassau: Roots, Routes, and Representation in Bahamian Popular Music*. He is also coeditor, with Daniel Neely, of *Sun, Sea, and Sound: Music and Tourism in the Circum-Caribbean* (Oxford University Press, 2014) and editor of and contributing author to *Excursions in World Music* (Routledge, 2016).

Index

Jackson, Michael, 149
James, C. L. R., 122, 135
Jaworski, Adam, and Crispin Thurlow, 108
John, Telvin, 179–80
Jumbey Village, 48
Junkanoo Carnival, 75n31

Kaul, Adam R., 37n16
Keeling, Kara, and Josh Kun, 37n13
Keil, Charles, 36n6; and Steven Feld, 14
Kelley, Norman, 14
Kempadoo, Kamala, 191n5
Khan, Aisha, 25–26
Kincaid, Jamaica, 77, 103n1, 112
King, Carol A., 37n10, 37n11, 165. *See also* hospitality
King, Trevor, 169, 173–74, 179
Kingsbury, Paul, 109
kinship: between colonizer and colonized, 110–12; between tourists and colonizers, 111–12, 121
Kirshenblatt-Gimblett, Barbara, 38n26, 111
Krüger, Simone, and Ruxandra Trandafoiu, 37n15

labor, 2, 12, 201, 205; affective, 189, 196; concerns, 52; contractual, 98; division of, 22; force, 18; and happiness, 95; historical relationship of human, 13; of hospitality, 204; issues of, 5; of love, 197; market, 203; material and immaterial, 32, 39n31, 106n37, 197, 199; mechanical sounds of, 88; music, 10, 21; and musicians, 1, 162, 180; and the plantation, 87–88; politics, 31–33, 128; practices, 23; structures, 2, 82, 102, 201–2, 204; unions, 73n10; (un)noticed, 26, 132. *See also* gender politics
Lamen, Darien, 191n2
Landship, 128
Largey, Michael, 41–42
Lash, Scott, and John Urry, 38n25
Lashua, Brett, 15
Layne, Richard, 108, 127–29
Lee, Benjamin, and Edward LiPuma, 12, 36n7
Lefebvre, Henri, 4, 80–81, 104n11. *See also* rhythmanalysis

Leonce-Charles, Charlyn, 166, 178, 181
Lévi-Strauss, Claude, 77, 104n2
Lewin, Olive, 129
listening, histories of, 7
Löfgren, Orvar, 105n27
Lord Burgess. *See* Burgie, Irving
Lovelace, Earl, 9

MacCannell, Dean, 37n15, 77; and the tourist, 80, 82
Maitel, S., 33, 175
Malinowski, Bronisław, 89
Manuel, Peter, 42
Marx, Karl, and Friedrich Engels, 135, 149
McKittrick, Katherine, 139, 149
McPhee, Carlton, 54–55, 57
mediations and expectations, 24–26
Meier, Leslie, 73
Meintjes, Louise, 37n13
Meredith, Sharon, 133n1
Merleau-Ponty, Maurice, 138
methodology, 16–17, 35–36; and auto-ethnography, 4, 80
Miller, Rebecca, 42
Minca, Claudio, 27, 109, 126, 133n2
Mintz, Sidney, 154
modernity: contradictions of, 88
Moeran, Brian, 181
Mondesir, Curtis, 173, 184, 189
Mohammed, Patricia, 191n5; and Catherine Shepherd, 191n5
Moore, Robin, 42
Munro, Martin, 88, 104n11
musical style/genre: as niche sound market, 153
musicians (including singers): and affect, 5, 32; and all-inclusive hotels, 52; creative agency, 34; and entertainers union, 50, 52, 58, 75n27; hiring of, 169–74; history, 164; and labor politics, 31–33; material and immaterial labor, 32–33; and nation-states, 30; performance of hospitality, 184–88; professionalization, 46; and questions of authenticity, 31; as seasoned travelers, 30–31; state of precarity, 172; strategies, 162; and tourists, 130; and tracked accompaniment, 68–70; women, 169–70; as workers, 16, 31.

Smith, Mark, 117–18

Smythe, Dallas W.: and commodity audience, 35, 39n33, 129

Sprague, Jeb H., 195

Solomon, Maynard, 36n3

soundscape curation, 29–30

sound studies, 7

sound systems, 71

Sterne, Jonathan, 14–15, 80, 100, 104n11; and Emily Raine, 117–18

Stewart, Gordon "Butch," 163, 164, 191n4

Stolzoff, Norman C., 88

Strachan, Ian Gregory, 86

subjectivity: emplaced, 3, 104

Taylor, Peanuts, 45

Taylor, Timothy, 12

Thomas, Deborah, 101

tourism: advertising, 129; anti-imperial analysis of, 113; Bahamian history of, 43–53; and colonial thinking, 112; as critical starting point, 6; and disciplinary effects, 109; employment, 17–18; growth of, 25; and heritage, 116; history of, 2, 42; industry, 9, 10; and pedagogical project, 127, 129–31; studies, 1, 15; visual and material aspects of, 9; worker, 126. See also hospitality; tourist

tourist: activities, 125; and all-inclusive hotels, 16; audience, 41, 129; clientele, 168; as commodity audience, 129; consumption, 80; definition, 38n29, 77–78, 80, 103n1, 133n4, 150–51, 160n9, 167, 175; demand, 46; desire, 43; destination, 110, 112; encounters, 23, 41; events, 133n1; expectations, 22, 25, 182, 186; experience, 35, 56, 59, 65, 82, 162, 164, 173, 191n8, 194–96, 199–202, 204; gaze, 99, 104n8, 168–69; imagination, 45; as inauthentic subject, 2; industry, 25, 35, 47, 87, 109, 157, 163, 196–97, 201, 204–5; island, 109–10; and island music, 37n7;

marketing, 198; musical tastes, 188; as an opaque multiplicity, 151; other, 1, 26–27; packages, 48; perspective, 89–94; practices, 112; sites, 9, 12, 15, 25, 49; space, 29, 31, 107, 179–81, 190; studies, 15, 164; subjectivities, 3; territories and performances, 19; vacation, 161; wishes, 128; and workers, 17, 148. See also all-inclusive hotels; entertainment tradition, 186–88. See also authenticity

Trouillot, Michel-Rolph, 97, 203

Tsing, Anna: and the notion of frictions, 42–43, 65, 70, 72, 73n4

Tucker, Hazel, and Elizabeth Carnegie, 111

tuk music, 123, 128, 133n1

Urban, Greg, and Kyung-Nan Koh, 20

Uriely, Natan, and Yaniv Belhassen, 191n2

Urry, John, 104n8; and Jonas Larsen, 37n15, 104n8, 108, 116; and Scott Lash, 38n25; and Chris Rojek, 37n15; and Mimi Sheller, 104n6

Veal, Michael, 82

Veseth, Michael A., 10

Walcott, Derek, 133n1, 136

Waterton, Emma, and Steve Watson, 108

Williams, Alistair, 191n9, 192n19

Williams, Eric, 116, 193

Williams, Raymond, 186

Williams, Stephanie, 129

workers: managers and musicians, 164. See also entertainment; hotel management; musicians

Wynter, Sylvia, 135–37

Yelvington, Kevin A., Jason L. Simms, and Elizabeth Murray, 37n15